T0382985

"A thoughtful, thought-provoking read on what makes our jobs significant. This book won't give you all the answers, but it will help you ask the right questions."

—Adam Grant, #1 *New York Times*–bestselling author of *Hidden Potential* and *Think Again*, and host of the *WorkLife* podcast

"Whether you're at the beginning, middle, or nearing the end of your career, this book will help you navigate important questions about balance, purpose, and legacy. Michaelson and Tosti-Kharas masterfully weave personal narratives, philosophy, and science together to produce an invaluable guide to making more informed career choices."

—Katy Milkman, James G. Dinan Professor, the Wharton School, University of Pennsylvania, and author of *How to Change*

"The first question you hear when you meet someone is often 'what do you do for a living?' But people rarely follow that with 'why?' This book digs into this critical idea, using interesting and compelling anecdotes to contemplate what it means to do purposeful work. It challenges us not with answers but with questions we rarely take the time to consider. Why do we work? What purpose does the work you do serve? What role can your work play in creating the world you wish to see?"

—Shannon Schuyler, chief purpose and inclusion officer, PwC

"An exploration of work that will speak to your head, heart, and soul. As touching as it is essential."

—Dolly Chugh, professor, NYU Stern, and author of *The Person You Mean to Be* and *A More Just Future*

IS YOUR
WORK
WORTH IT?

IS YOUR

WORTH IT?

HOW TO THINK ABOUT MEANINGFUL WORK

Christopher Wong Michaelson

Jennifer Tosti-Kharas

PUBLICAFFAIRS

NEW YORK

PublicAffairs
Hachette Book Group
1290 Avenue of the Americas, New York, NY 10104
www.publicaffairsbooks.com
@Public_Affairs

Printed in the United States of America

First Edition: May 2024

Published by PublicAffairs, an imprint of Hachette Book Group, Inc. The PublicAffairs name and logo is a trademark of the Hachette Book Group.

The Hachette Speakers Bureau provides a wide range of authors for speaking events. To find out more, go to hachettespeakersbureau.com or email HachetteSpeakers@hbgusa.com.

PublicAffairs books may be purchased in bulk for business, educational, or promotional use. For more information, please contact your local bookseller or the Hachette Book Group Special Markets Department at special.markets@hbgusa.com.

The publisher is not responsible for websites (or their content) that are not owned by the publisher.

Print book interior design by Marie Mundaca

Library of Congress Cataloging-in-Publication Data
Names: Michaelson, Christopher Wong, author. | Tosti-Kharas, Jennifer, author.
Title: Is your work worth it? : how to think about meaningful work / Christopher Wong Michaelson, Jennifer Tosti-Kharas.
Description: First Edition. | New York, NY : PublicAffairs, 2024. | Includes bibliographical references and index.
Identifiers: LCCN 2023047488 | ISBN 9781541703407 (hardcover) | ISBN 9781541703421 (ebook)
Subjects: LCSH: Work—Philosophy. | Job satisfaction. | Meaninglessness (Philosophy)
Classification: LCC HD4904 .M514 2024 | DDC 331.01—dc23/eng/20231013
LC record available at https://lccn.loc.gov/2023047488

ISBNs: 9781541703407 (hardcover), 9781541703421 (eBook)

LSC-C

Printing 1, 2024

For those before us who worked without asking whether it was worth it so that we could.

CONTENTS

PREFACE

Tell me, what is it you plan to do
with your one wild and precious life?
                              —Mary Oliver, "The Summer Day"

IMAGINE THAT YOUR WORK IS SO WORTHY THAT YOU
will keep doing it—of your own accord—until the very end of
"your one wild and precious life." What would that work be? Is it
what you're doing right now? What you are planning to do one day?
How easy is it to imagine?

When David Robert Jones suffered a heart attack at the height
of his long and productive career, he slowed down at work. He
reduced the number of projects he committed to, traveled less, and
broke his habit of working late nights so he could spend more evenings with his family.

A few years later, he received a prestigious award from his
industry peers for lifetime achievement. He was pushing sixty years
old, and money was not an issue—most people would say this was
probably a good time to start thinking about retirement.

However, Jones was not most people. He once said, "If you feel
safe in the area that you're working in, you're not working in the
right area. Always go a little further into the water than you feel
you're capable of being in. Go a little bit out of your depth, and when

1

you don't feel that your feet are quite touching the bottom, you're just about in the right place to do something exciting."

During his career, the shape-shifting artist, who felt less anxious when he adopted a character, had played the role of an interstellar traveler who crash-lands on Earth. He had acted like "a lad insane" during a promiscuous and drug-addled period of his career. And he had personified a benevolent, alien rock star who succumbs to celebrity. And at age sixty-six, the number-one bestselling vinyl artist of the twenty-first century released a new record. The title on the album cover intentionally obscured a youthful photo of him from a previous album. Subsequently, he crossed off a bucket list item by writing a musical, based on the character of a man brought back to life so that—in the words of the actor who played him—"he may ready himself to die."

As a younger man, the creator of a metaphorical astronaut, who, it was speculated, was on a drug high, had intermingled his penchant for going on psychedelic benders with his professional artistry, as though the risks were part of the job. By the time he had matured, the prescription drugs he took were to fight cancer.

Still breaking new creative ground as he kept his diagnosis a secret from all but his closest friends and family, "pop's original chameleon" embarked on a jazz collaboration while undergoing treatment. The music video for the song "Lazarus" was shot in a film studio in what appears to be a hospital bed during the same week he learned his illness was terminal. He was determined to work until the very end.

Three months later, on his sixty-ninth birthday, David Bowie released *Blackstar*, the album on which "Lazarus" appears, to widespread critical acclaim. Only two days after that, the world would learn that the rock icon, epitome of cool, and antithesis of the working stiff had given up his place in this world, prompting an appreciation of his life and work and a shocking new reading of the opening lines of the song, "Look up here, I'm in heaven."

For the man who was not "content to be just a rock and roll star all my life," work was never a choice; it was a necessity. His work was who he was. As he once said, "Always remember that the reason that you initially started working was that there was something inside yourself that you felt that if you could manifest it in some way you would understand more about yourself and how you coexist with the rest of society."

INTRODUCTION

IS YOUR WORK WORTH IT?

Life changes fast.
Life changes in an instant.
You sit down to dinner and life as you know it ends.
　　　　—Joan Didion, *The Year of Magical Thinking*

A WORLD CHANGED

IT WAS A TUESDAY MORNING. A MAN, WEARING A WORSTED wool suit that was too warm for the weather, checked out of his downtown Washington hotel on a multicity business trip. At the same time, a woman with long red hair and still wearing her pajamas was waking up in her Upper East Side apartment after an all-nighter at the office. We didn't know each other yet. But we were both management consultants based in the New York City offices of competing firms, and both of us were wondering to ourselves: Is my work worth it?

We went through the motions, nurturing our careers, which we believed would take us on a general upward trajectory toward a vaguely outlined partner track.

We were privileged to have secure positions and promotions to aim for, so there was no urgency in our question. We treated it as if it was a luxury to ask rather than a necessity to answer. What if we did something else? There was no real harm in pondering the question, just as there was no genuine risk in not responding to it. We both figured we had time on our sides, that if we didn't figure it out today, there would always be tomorrow to consider whether our work gave back as much as it took away.

Everything changed that morning as we learned of the 9/11 terrorist attacks that claimed the lives of 2,977 innocent victims, most of them in the city where we lived. The *New York Times* published a series, "Portraits of Grief," that chronicled the victims' legacies in the months that followed. Along with many New Yorkers—and the world—we read them every week. Many of those who were lost that day had arrived early to their jobs with the same fundamental concerns about work and worth as ours. They too had careers to cultivate and lives outside of work to look after.

They included workers who had made calculated choices about their work lives and daily lives, such as Patricia A. Cody, a risk management executive who commuted from her home all the way from the Jersey shore because "she felt it was worth it to be near the water"; Angelo Amaranto, a security guard who when he began working nights at one of the twin towers said "it was worth it because it was a better building"; and Susan Bochino, who was so happy in her new job as an insurance client specialist that it was "well worth the sacrifice" of the disorienting feeling of the building swaying slightly from her 92nd floor office on a windy day.

Some of them had chosen jobs that they knew might be dangerous but worth the risk. For example, Peter Brennan was one of more than four hundred first responders, some of whom were still climbing up the building stairs to rescue others when the towers came crashing down. He had aspired to be a firefighter since childhood, volunteering from age sixteen and joining the Fire Department of New York as an adult. Even on the final day of his life, he was there by choice, leaving a vacation to take a shift for a colleague. After Brennan died, his wife suggested that his passion for his work was worth the sacrifice he made, imagining that he "died doing what he loved at probably the greatest fire he'd ever been to. I can see him on the truck being excited on the way."

However, most of them worked at jobs that ordinarily would not put their practitioners in considerable jeopardy. Michael H. Waye was a data center manager who was climbing the career ladder at Marsh & McLennan Companies, an insurance giant that lost more than three hundred employees and contractors that day. After his death, Waye's surviving spouse also reflected on whether the worthiness of his achievements and aspirations—he was moonlighting in an MBA program, working toward his dream of being a CEO someday—justified the long hours away from his wife and young son that they would never get back. She wondered, "All the success, he did all these things—for what? After all this, he's gone."

In the wake of the tragedy, working professionals reported being prompted by 9/11 to seek lower-stress positions, retire early to travel the world, or search for more meaningful work. Around the first anniversary of the attacks, there was a documented exodus of people leaving mundane jobs for work that they viewed as their calling or that contributed to society.

The events of 9/11 led many workers, including us, to ask whether work was worth it. Few had the means to switch jobs or stop working, but they may have wondered anyway what it would be like to be able to make a change or even to have the freedom to ask the question. What we didn't know then was that, nearly twenty years later, we would again be in a position to ask this question, perhaps with more empathy, intention, and urgency than before.

Within a year of 9/11, we were both pursuing different work. Christopher, who had earned his PhD in philosophy before his consulting career, took his first full-time faculty position. He taught corporate responsibility at the Wharton School of the University of

Pennsylvania, keeping a foot one day a week at his consulting firm for the real-world experience, for the better pay, and in case professorship didn't pan out. Jen, who had gotten her bachelor's degree at Wharton, was applying to PhD programs in organizational behavior, where she would go on to specialize in research on meaningful work and work as a calling. Our paths would converge a few years after 9/11 at a gathering of scholars who study meaning and purpose. We first became friends during a break in sessions on a group hike through the mountains near the conference venue, at which point we realized we had similar experience and dissimilar expertise, which led a few years later to our first research collaboration.

We have a combined forty years of experience in two different communities of what management scholar Laura Empson calls "insecure overachievers": occupations composed of highly educated, competitive, and ambitious professionals who are constantly working to prove themselves worthy of their organizational position and social status. One of those professions is management consulting, where we observed high-potential colleagues toiling and traveling incessantly to climb the ladder to partner, the most coveted reward of which was, ironically, early retirement. The other profession of insecure overachievers is the one we are in now, academia, where we have both successfully traveled the tenure track but still face the stereotypical pressure to "publish or perish."

Although we may have worked and studied at elite—and sometimes elitist—institutions, our perspectives on work are also the products of our modest origins and experiences. As a grad student, Christopher parlayed his unusually fast typing skills into temporary jobs around New York City—emulating his mother, who had learned from her father to cultivate useful clerical skills before he sent her from Brazil at age fourteen to the United States, where she studied to become a language teacher. Christopher's paternal grandfather was the night switchman at the telephone company, where he worried his entire working life that he would be fired for lying about his eighth-grade education. His last paycheck was less than his son's first paycheck as an attorney.

As a child growing up outside Scranton, Pennsylvania—which would infamously become the setting for the hit television series about worthless work, *The Office*—Jen couldn't hear enough about the jobs of the adults around her and the value of hard work. Her parents and grandparents held jobs ranging from blueberry sorter to department store clerk, from pharmacist to coal miner, and from teacher to artist. Jen's own initial forays into the world of paid employment involved working as a librarian, summer camp counselor, waitress, delivery person, and file clerk and phone answerer. We are aware of the irony that we have enjoyed the privilege of asking whether our work is worth it because our parents and their parents worked without ever questioning why. And we hope that our children and their children after us are inspired to pursue work worth doing that makes not only their own but also others' lives worth living.

A WORLD CHANGED, AGAIN

On March 12, 2020—the day after the World Health Organization (WHO) declared COVID-19 a pandemic and three days before the United States locked down—Christopher sent Jen an email outlining some recent thoughts about something he was working on that would eventually become part of this book. It was the type of email we send each other several times a week in normal times.

But these were not normal times. As the number of COVID-19 casualties reached unimaginable proportions, a new class of "essential workers" was designated on the front lines of health care. They included Celia Marcos, a Los Angeles nurse who contracted a fatal case of COVID-19 after giving emergency chest compressions to an infected patient, and Lorna Breen, a New York doctor who took her own life when she became overwhelmed by the conflicting challenges of caring for infected patients and protecting the providers she supervised. Health-care professionals were hailed as heroes during the first wave of infections, but after the nightly applause waned, they continued to work unheralded through subsequent surges to the point of exhaustion.

Other uncelebrated essential workers—such as bank tellers, delivery drivers, and meat-packers—were often coerced into showing up to work or risk losing their jobs. Agustin Rodriguez Martinez was "mopping the floors with a fever" before he became the first person to die in connection with a COVID-19 outbreak at a Sioux Falls pork processing plant, where employees were offered a "responsibility bonus" to finish their shifts even as the virus spread. In the end, those who fell ill missed more shifts—or worse—than the $500 was worth. Many of them were recent immigrants who were not fluent in English and could hardly afford not to work. One of the unfair ironies of work during the pandemic was that the amount of peril associated with one's work was often inversely proportional to one's pay. White-collar work was typically more amenable to remote working arrangements than manual labor.

Many people who were used to the humdrum of office life found themselves isolated at home, teleconferencing into meetings wearing collared shirts paired with pajama bottoms. Compared to those of frontline workers, the risks they took were modest. Zoom video-conferencing gaffes became a new category of reality humor, from the journalist who inadvertently exposed himself to colleagues to the lawyer who appeared in video court with a cat filter covering his face that he could not figure out how to turn off.

Though convenient, this new working normal came with inconveniences as well. Some started new jobs without ever having met a single coworker in person. As work life bled into home life, people found their initial appreciation for no commutes and lunch at home replaced by the realization that leisure had vanished as all available hours became potential work time, while children continued "school from home" seemingly indefinitely, and even the once-annoying office pop-in from a colleague seemed a treasured relic of the past.

Both 9/11 and COVID-19 irreversibly changed everything for victims and their close relations. Moreover, they reawakened us to the potential worthiness of life-saving work and of underappreciated work that we also cannot do without. Although both catastrophes led us existentially to consider *whether and why* our work is worth doing, COVID-19 led us also to wonder about *how and whether we work*. In 2001, 9/11 was a workplace tragedy because at that time it was still typical for many of us to commute to work in urban skyscrapers and to fly to business meetings where we could see others face-to-face. After COVID-19, we were forced to question the necessity of those workplace norms—and even the necessity of work itself.

LIFE WORTH LIVING

In an 1895 speech entitled "Is Life Worth Living?" philosopher and psychologist William James had argued that the answer to this question depends upon whether you are an optimist or a pessimist. Around a century later, the Conference Board and Gallup began surveying American workers about whether their work was worth doing, perennially finding during the prepandemic decades that roughly half of respondents were satisfied with their work and one-third were engaged at work. Even if you were a glass-half-full optimist, it was at best a lukewarm endorsement of the working life. Either way, the data confirmed a widespread problem: that work was perceived by many to not be worth the sacrifices it demanded and that it didn't offer purpose, much less a positive contribution to a life worth living.

The problem of work and worth was reinforced in the findings of an economic study that suggested many people were wasting what would be the most productive time of their lives doing work that was not worth living for. In markets around the world, happiness peaked before people started working, in their late teens and early twenties, and again in their sixties, after they retired. Contentment bottomed out in their forties, usually when workers were making the most money. This phenomenon was known as the U-bend for its shape on a graph. Google "U-bend" and you will be rewarded with plumbing imagery, the pipe that funnels wastewater—an appropriate metaphor for the working years—which too often disappears down the drain.

As children of parents whose generation stereotypically considered work to be the sacrifice they made for their families, and as working parents of children whose generation is said to seek meaning and purpose through work, we both have experience wondering about the worthiness of our own work, which we have, at turns, loved and loathed. When the pandemic hit, Jen's kids were in first and third grade, while Christopher's kids were already in middle school, high school, and college. Jen's husband's work in research and development at a government-contracted laboratory, much of which can only happen in-person and in a highly controlled environment, was quickly deemed essential. Christopher's wife was managing a nonprofit program that introduced senior citizens to high school students who taught them how to use technology, work that became more essential than ever but which she had to do from home.

Many of the stories in this book originated in timeless works of literature where, as Christopher's research at the intersection of the humanities and business explores, our unusual access into the minds of others reveals their beliefs and motivations about why they do what they do. Other stories emerged from the timely forces that, during the pandemic and after, were changing the world of work while we were writing. Still others came from interviews we conducted with real working professionals as part of our research plan. However, the original impetus for this book emerged well before the pandemic, from the epochal crisis of 9/11, which led us and many others to wonder whether work was worth it. According to the illusion of history, human beings always think we are living in singular times, and ironically, these times were no more singular than any others. As we lived and worked through 9/11 and COVID-19, we all thought the world had changed and was asking us to reassess the worthiness of our lives and to reconsider whether our work was worth it. Rather, the world of work was, is, and always will be asking us to ask this question. Sometimes, though, it takes a catastrophe for us to pay more attention.

WORK WORTH DOING

In the absence of a federal strategy to combat COVID-19, Governor Andrew Cuomo of New York coached a country from the pandemic's epicenter through its early days, only later to ruin his legacy, ironically, in a workplace sexual harassment scandal. Almost two decades before, a documentary about 9/11 aired in which Mario Cuomo—Andrew's father who had served three terms as governor of New York between the rise and fall of the twin towers—was asked what he had learned from that tragedy. Paraphrasing the philosopher Pierre Teilhard de Chardin, he said, "9/11 is not going to tell you *what to do* with your life. But it is going to tell you *to do* with your life."

Similarly, this book is not going to tell you *what to do* with your work. But it is going to tell you *to do* work that is worth it, whatever that may be. It is about the priority of work worth doing in a life worth living. As Studs Terkel once wrote, "Work is about a search for daily meaning as well as daily bread," but it has the possibility to become the legacy that we leave. The prospect that there might be such a thing as work that's worthy is ultimately hopeful. At the same time, unrealized hope for a better job, professional recognition, or a purposeful calling can also lead to heartbreak. Few lives are more heartbreaking than those that go to waste because they were spent working too much, being worked literally to death, working for the wrong reasons, or doing the wrong work because we never adequately considered what work was worth in relation to other priorities and aspirations in our lives.

Work can contribute to our self-worth, our net worth, and the worth we bring to the people around us. As long as we work, we will continue to wonder about whether it is worth it, to think that we deserve to be paid fairly for what our work is worth, to dream that there is more to a life worth living than the sacrifices that work demands of us, and to search for work that makes a worthwhile contribution to solving the problems of our age.

This book shares the stories of people—past, present, and future, real and fictional—grappling with the practical necessities of whether their work is worth it. These include a burned-out public interest lawyer who is "slowly becoming OK with" not knowing where her career is going, an army veteran living on a converted school bus that he plans to drive down the Pan-American Highway toward a life without work, and a graduating college student who confessed to being "utterly terrified thinking about how this is the first time in my life where I didn't really have a concrete knowledge of the next step I was going to take."

The book is also a series of questions that we might ask and evidence that may help you to answer whether your work is worth it. The questions are posed by starving artists who risk it all to perform; former heroes forced into a tedious workaday existence; and retired workaholics who advise us to "think hard about time" with our children and families that will never be recaptured. And this book applies the evidence and insights of classic and contemporary sages who have studied these phenomena. They include ancient thinkers who never had to lift a finger because they had servants and slaves working for them; the moral philosopher widely regarded to be the founder of modern capitalism; and contemporary social scientists and scholars who study work, artwork, overwork, and work as a calling.

We believe that this book is for anyone who works, regardless of age, occupation, or career ambition. It is also for those whose work holds the potential to affect scores of other workers, like those in positions of leadership, influence, and policymaking. We recognize the evident luxury of being able to ask the question of whether work is worth it and the privilege of being able to ask it ourselves. Too many people don't have the freedom to dream of work that might be worthy. We believe, however, that anyone should have the right to ask whether their work is worth it, and that anyone who is in the position to employ others has the responsibility to ask whether those jobs are worth it and, when those they employ call for worthier work, to provide it. Anyone who will work in the future, who is working now, or who has already retired from work can ask the question of whether their work will be, is, or was worth it.

If you are about to graduate from college, you may be asking, "Will it all be worth it?" You are on the prework precipice of the U-bend and may have been counseled to pursue your passions in a labor market that pays more for productivity than passion. You may feel torn between the romance of worthy work and the real need for net worth as you face the first momentous decisions about your career and possibly very real debt as well. If you are in early-to-mid career, you may be asking, "Is it worth it?" You may be sliding down the slippery slope of the U-bend or stuck trying to climb back up in jobs that sometimes feel—or make you feel—worthless. You may be searching for something more than the daily grind you already have. In a world in which employment changes frequently and some workers are preparing for planned obsolescence, your career decisions and transitions are constantly at the fore. If you are retired or preparing to retire, you may be wondering, "Was it all worth it—and what can I still do to make it all worth it?" You may be reflecting from the postwork peak at the end of the U-bend. You may be seeking to understand and assess your own life and legacy while deciding whether you are headed for retirement or an "encore career" in which there is still time to do something more worthwhile than you have already done.

The book is timely in the present moment, in which there is often too much work to do and a glorified "hustle culture" that makes people unsure what they would do if work went away due to automation, artificial intelligence, or retirement. Yet, its questions and stories are timeless. The questions the book explores are about universally important human experiences pertaining to the centrality of work to life—both literally, in terms of hours spent performing work and the various sacrifices work often entails, and mentally, especially in a world in which our work selves are inseparable from our self-worth.

This is the book we have been wanting to write our entire careers, the one we looked for during our own career transitions, that we wished our graduating students could read when they were looking for work, that we hoped to give to friends going through career crises, and that we wanted our parents to read when they retired. The question of whether work is worth it is not original to us, nor is it unique to our time, tragedies, or stages of technological advancement: it was asked by the first human beings to work. We have asked it our entire working lives, as likely you have too, and people will continue to ask this question long after the so-called end of work, when technology will supposedly do all the work for us—although we will, in all likelihood, continue working.

Thankfully, the early days of the pandemic eventually subsided: the kids went back to school, our in-person classes slowly resumed, and we were able to write again. This book contains what we—a philosopher and a psychologist—have learned from our own and others' research and experience about the reality, value, and meaning of work that's worthy, work that can make life worth living or consume us in the process.

PART I

Work

CHAPTER 1

WHAT IS WORK?

You know what work is—if you're
old enough to read this you know what
work is, although you may not do it.
Forget you.

—Philip Levine, "What Work Is"

THE HUMBLEST AND HIGHEST WORK

N 1968, WONG JUN-CHOW TRAVELED FROM HIS ADOPTED home in São Paulo to Minneapolis, where he stopped to visit his daughter and posed for a photograph with his ten-day-old grandson. He was en route to Los Angeles to sell a few semiprecious stones—aquamarine, tourmaline, and topaz—which he had acquired inexpensively in Brazil. The business purpose of his trip turned out not to be worth the trouble: he would return home weeks later with less money than his plane ticket had cost and his suitcases still heavy with unsold inventory. But as Wong held his grandson proudly for the camera, he told his daughter exactly what all stereotypical

Chinese grandfathers say about their stereotypical grandsons, that this boy was smart and might someday become a doctor.

Although the trip would be one of Wong's last failures as a businessman, that photo would be framed and hung on his grandson's bedroom wall and served as an inspiration for Christopher's career as a philosopher seeking to discover what work is worth doing in a life worth living. Wong had always insisted his children and grandchildren work hard at respectable careers, regaling them with stories from his past. It wasn't until after "Gong-Gong," his grandfather, had died that Christopher, as an adult, learned the truth behind his trip, that his grandfather had not traveled to America just to see him. Only then did Christopher reflect upon his grandfather's work—that his work life consisted of survival and successes followed by failures and that the man who more than anyone else had taught Christopher about finding work that was worth it was technically retired from what society considered to be work for most of Christopher's life. To the extent that what we consider to be work informs how much economic value it has, whether it is socially recognized, and how we feel about doing it, determining what is work is inseparable from what work is worth.

Born in 1907 to subsistence farmers in the Hunan countryside in central China, Wong walked away from home at age fifteen after his mother died and his father remarried, leaving his family one less mouth to feed. He went to Changsha, the provincial capital, to catch up on school so he could pursue a career in the military, the only path to social mobility for a peasant. While climbing to the rank of general in the Nationalist Army, he married the daughter of a senator and became wealthy while never finding permanent stability in a war-torn society. During those years, he fought four enemies—warlords, Japanese invaders, backstabbing colleagues, and the People's Liberation Army—before fleeing his homeland in 1949 when the communists declared victory. Only forty-two years old, he had reached the pinnacle of his career, but in the course of his professional journey, he also suffered personal tragedies. He lost his first two children to illness in infancy and his first wife during a failed medical procedure before his army lost the war, which led him also to lose his country, his work, his wealth, and his sense of self-worth.

After he remarried, he, his new wife, and six of their surviving children escaped to Hong Kong with a few trunks of possessions and plotted their next move. Taiwan was too risky; Australia was also deemed too close; and the wait for the United States was too long. They emigrated to the shores of Rio de Janeiro by sea and by plane, some of them arriving during Carnival with woolen knit formal clothing while the locals danced practically naked in the streets. As Wong ran out of valuables that he had taken with him from China to sell in his new country, he followed a friend's advice and moved his family to the more industrious city of São Paulo, where he misfired in business several times—as a laundry owner, a food cart operator, an importer of so-called Oriental decorative items, a silk farmer, and, of course, a gemstone broker.

Wong instilled in his children the Confucian value that the worthiest work is that which helps others. Although being in the army demanded from him, as a defender of the government, personal effort and sacrifice and long periods of separation from his family, it also conferred recognition and status. Medicine (two of his sons became physicians) and education (three of his daughters became teachers) were also high in the Confucian hierarchy. In contrast, selling semiprecious stones, which he considered a useless endeavor, humbled him. He was the consummate middleman with no real purpose other than to line his own pockets. In general, he considered business to be self-interested and placed it at the bottom of the hierarchy—although at least three of his children found considerable net worth in business, going on to enjoy far more economic success than he ever had. After his final humiliation as a businessman, his children promised to support him and his wife.

He did not earn another paycheck for the rest of his ninety-eight years, but he did not stop working. He was the patriarch of a large family. He stayed informed, watching and reading about current events and forming opinions, which he communicated with authority to his family and friends. He advised his children and grandchildren about their education, work, and relationships. He carried the young ones to the park on his shoulders. He wrote letters, in which he shared his wisdom. He exercised. He perfected his Chinese calligraphy. He cataloged for posterity the letters and photographs he had exchanged with his wives when he was away at war. He worried about the work ethic of the younger generations and what would become of them after he died. And he shared with his children and grandchildren the essential wisdom of his education and experience, exhorting them to work hard at the humblest work if you must, but aspire to the highest work if you can.

WORK AS PURPOSEFUL, EFFORTFUL, AND RECOGNIZED

When Marcel Duchamp submitted a tipped-over urinal to a Society of Independent Artists exhibit in 1917, he set off more than a century of debate among art aficionados. "Is that art?" they asked indignantly, the very question implying that it was not. One criterion historically associated with artwork was that it ought to be beautiful, which certainly did not apply to the practical porcelain receptacle, impractically positioned on its back. Another was that artwork ought to require skill to produce, but the only evidence of an artist's touch on the piece was the pseudonym "R. Mutt," scrawled carelessly next to the year in which it was presented for consideration. Furthermore, it was associated with human waste, not what the art world recognized as the highest art. Yet, there it was, a candidate for inclusion in a prestigious show that the organizers had agreed would be jury-free, leaving it to the artists themselves to decide what was art. Their covenant notwithstanding, Duchamp's peers narrowly voted to exclude the urinal from the Grand Central Palace exhibition, prompting him tempestuously to resign from the board of the organization.

Perhaps it had been his intent all along to invite controversy. It even remains unsettled whether Duchamp was the original creator or if he stole the credit from his fellow artist, Baroness Elsa von Freytag-Loringhoven. Whatever the provenance, it sealed its professed provocateur's reputation as a working artist who earned fame and fortune for placing "readymade" objects—which also included a hat rack, a snow shovel, and a vial of Parisian air that he brought with him to present in New York—in unconventional settings and claiming they were art. The original *Fountain*, as Duchamp playfully called the urinal, has been lost, but replicas are now on display—away from the washrooms—in some of the world's most revered art museums. *Fountain* has come to be recognized as one of the most influential works in the history of modern art, not for the beauty or the skill required to produce it but for the debate it incited about the essential characteristics necessary for something to achieve recognition as a work of art. Even while Duchamp's gallery of readymades often went unnoticed as art by museum visitors, it did its work, arousing debate about how far the term art could be stretched before it snapped.

Art and work have more in common than that they share the word artwork. Art remains a contested term among scholars. It encompasses a wide variety of modes—calligraphy, sculpture, performance art—and engages a variety of senses—visual, auditory, tactile. Works of art can be small, large, or unmeasurable. Art can defy easy categorization.

The range of possibilities included in the term work is even more diverse but harder to define. How could one word possibly do the work of characterizing a range of occupations that includes farmer, funeral home manager, financial analyst, social media influencer, surgeon, and silversmith? When we classify something as work, we imply it is worth doing, so to write about what makes work worthy, it helps to have a sense of what work is and is not.

Folk wisdom about work assumes we know what work is. All-time great 400-meter hurdler Edwin Moses attributes his success to the doctrine of "work before play," implying that the difference is self-evident and that work has a purpose that the play does not. Cosmetics magnate Estée Lauder famously counseled her sales staff that "I didn't get there by wishing for it or hoping for it, but by working for it," urging them to recognize that her success did not come without effort. Technology evangelist and author Guy Kawasaki argues, "It's called work for a reason," suggesting that work by its nature is not supposed to be enjoyable or desirable. These sentiments are echoed in the famous whitewashing scene from *The Adventures of Tom Sawyer*, in which the title character tricks the other neighborhood children into painting his aunt's fence for him by pretending the chore is so fun that he is doing it by choice. The narrator wryly concludes: "Work consists of whatever a body is obliged to do, and . . . play consists of whatever a body is not obliged to do."

While this fanciful conclusion can be taken to suggest that making your work worth it is just a matter of mind over matter, it mirrors a reality in which work that is primarily performed by our bodies is often undervalued in relation to work that is primarily performed by our minds. When work is about matter, it pertains to the physical exertion of manual labor. The etymology of the word labor has roots in the fourteenth century and refers to a burden. The laborers of early capitalism worked in factories that were dark, dangerous, and dull, focusing their attention on, as Adam Smith describes in *The Wealth of Nations*, "some one simple operation, and . . . making this operation the sole employment of his life." In Charles Dickens's novel *Hard Times*, the laborers worked in an "ugly citadel, where Nature was as strongly bricked out as killing airs and gases were bricked in." Similarly, in a meatpacking plant during the COVID-19 pandemic, laborers were sheltered from news of an outbreak in the tightly packed spaces where they slaughtered and cut meat and the virus spread like wildfire.

By contrast, ancient thinkers from Confucius to Aristotle who had the privilege to write about work left the dirty work to their servants and slaves while they extolled the work of the mind. The ancient Greek term for everyday toil was *a-scolia*, or the opposite of leisure, the word for which was *skole*, the root word for school. The purpose of labor was to make leisure possible, and the purpose of leisure was enlightenment. In this way, labor and leisure are different forms of work.

The Greek concept of *a-scolia*, which was held largely by intellectual elitists, suggests a hierarchy that holds mindful activity above manual labor, a viewpoint that continues to this day in conventional attitudes toward work. Labor is seen as subordinate to management. Laborers work with their hands while managers manipulate spreadsheets with their minds. We see this in what we now call *knowledge work*—which is usually done by people with advanced degrees or experience that qualifies them for management and is highly paid. This is separate from manual labor—which typically involves lower compensation and less control on the part of workers over their hours, methods, and employment security.

Of course, not everybody agrees that the life of the mind is better than manual labor. Throughout history, exceptions to this prioritization of head over hands have involved populist uprisings requiring all hands on deck. During communist revolutions in both China and the Soviet Union, for example, propaganda posters glorified industrial production, while elites and intellectuals were persecuted and "reeducated" in the countryside. In *Shop Class as Soul Craft*, a motorcycle mechanic with a PhD in political philosophy describes the triumphal satisfaction of getting a dormant engine to growl.

Aristotle says work is whatever needs to get done. Bengali poet Rabindranath Tagore counsels that work can be hard, becoming "easy only when desire has learned to discipline itself." Beloved singer-songwriter Dolly Parton recognizes in her song "9 to 5" that work is what happens between those hours, what society conventionally considers to be the workday. Social anthropologist James Suzman defines work as anything that involves purposefully expending energy or effort on a task to achieve a goal or end. His sweeping historical account begins with the "work" required of the first single-celled organisms to inhabit Earth to survive and reproduce, and it ends speculatively about how the first artificially intelligent robots will disrupt our world of work. Focusing his account of work on that which can be performed by human beings, economic sociologist Paul Ransome offers more contemporary criteria for work. He says work is "purposeful expedient activity; requires mental and/or physical exertion; is carried out in exchange for wages or salary; is a public activity; [and] is recognized as work for 'official purposes' such as taxation and insurance."

So, we take the collective wisdom of the ages and sages to coalesce around a few essentials about work, starting with the sentiment that whether or not we like to do it, someone has determined that it is worth doing. Moreover, we all have an idea of what work is even though our ideas may not all agree. Work may be a mindful privilege or a manual burden, or even a mindful burden and a manual privilege. Work is not the same as leisure or play. And though it may not always be clear what work is and is not, a worthwhile working definition (if you will) for our conversations about work is that it generally shares three formal characteristics: it is *purposeful*, *effortful*, and *recognized* by society as work—which often, though not always, means it is worth getting paid for. Our definition of work, however, doesn't always match up with the work opportunities presented to us.

WORK THAT IS PURPOSEFUL—OR PURPOSELESS

Purposeful activity is a means to an end. It has an end goal and a point, a use. So, purpose*ful* work is full of justification for why it matters, why the world is a better place because of that work and would be worse off without it. Purposeful work doesn't just involve the intrinsic satisfaction of the work itself; it also involves the sense that the work is making a difference in the world.

Modern capitalism is full of work that is unlovable but serves a purpose. Vacationers in certain parts of the Caribbean and Mexico have noticed the rise of ripply, red, fetid sargassum seaweed, proliferating as the waters warm due to climate change. The seaweed clogs the coastal waters, making them almost unswimmable, and litters the beaches. Needless to say, spendy beach resorts don't look kindly on having their pristine sandy beaches tarnished by ripply, red, fetid seaweed. So they employ people, typically male groundskeepers, to rake and shovel the seaweed out of sight. This work continues—from dawn to dusk, day after day, one batch of seaweed removed only to have more pour in by the waveful—to maintain an illusion. This work is as close to Sisyphean as one can imagine; yet the resorts clearly justify the existence of this job and the expense to maintain it, subsidized by vacationers glad not to have to look at the seaweed mess. In other words, this work has a purpose. We might think, "What's the point of *that*?" But every potentially maligned job—from telemarketer to evangelist to reality television star—has a purpose. We might quibble over whether every job has an equally worthwhile purpose, but that will come later in this book.

On the other hand, anthropologist David Graeber put a fine point on the issue of purposelessness by coining the term *bullshit jobs*: "a form of paid employment that is so completely pointless, unnecessary, or pernicious that even the employee cannot justify its existence even though, as part of the conditions of employment, the employee feels obliged to pretend that this is not the case." In other words, working a bullshit job compels the worker to act as if their work serves a larger purpose. Bullshit jobs have existed since the beginning of work, in the form of ministerial roles that pump up the egos of superiors whose primary function is to perpetuate the bureaucracy. In *The Pale King*, David Foster Wallace's novel about the ultimate bureaucracy, the US Internal Revenue Service, one examiner attributes his ability to survive in such a workplace to his "unusually high tolerance for pain."

Bullshit jobs are different from shit jobs, which "typically involve work that needs to be done and is clearly of benefit to society; it's just that the workers who do them are paid and treated badly." Whereas shit jobs are typically blue collar and paid by the hour, bullshit jobs are typically white collar and salaried, and yet the world is no better off with them than it would be without them. These jobs give the illusion of respectable worthiness, but an illusion all the same.

Just so it doesn't appear that we are staring down from our ivory towers in judgment on other people's purposeless work, we will admit that our own work can sometimes seem purposeless. When Jen was in graduate school, she happened upon an episode of the television series *30 Rock* in which the Alec Baldwin character sheepishly admits, "We may not be the best people." Tina Fey rationalizes in response, "But we're not the worst," after which they say in unison, "Graduate students are the worst." This seemed to speak to the universal truth of Jen's existence at the time. Her doctoral stipend was not enough to meet basic needs in most locations, let alone in New York City, and her work mostly consisted of trying in vain to finish a two-hundred-plus-page doctoral dissertation that maybe five people would read. The financial strain and existential malaise of many graduate programs have contributed to a recent epidemic of doctoral students leaving their programs without finishing. During her time at NYU, Jen's fellow graduate students started a push to unionize, a difficult effort that eventually succeeded—though not until after Jen was long gone.

And then there is Christopher's own career as a philosopher. He still remembers when as a graduate student he was at the head—or was it rather the foot?—of a tableful of intimidating academics who had gathered to decide whether the proposal he had submitted to them was sufficient for him to move forward with his doctoral dissertation. They were steeped in an ancient tradition of philosophical dialogue that originated on Athenian street corners, where wise Socrates would hold court debating the essential nature of knowledge and justice—work that was worthless to his wife and children, who practically starved. When Christopher irreverently proclaimed to the group of professional philosophers that he wanted his work to be more useful than that of, umm, *professional philosophers*, they were unbowed. Rhapsodizing to her colleagues over their shared profession, one of his advisers proudly proclaimed that it was "quite useless," as Oscar Wilde once said of art. "I can't believe I get paid to do this!" she went on, with Christopher's ironic agreement. After all, there has never been an emergency in which someone called out, "Quick, get a philosopher!" In his final dissertation,

Christopher declared philosophy to be, at the same time, the most and least important work in the world.

These stories speak to some elements that might make work *seem* to the individual worker to be purposeless. Sometimes work seems anachronistic, useful in a previous time, perhaps, but not in this time, such as the work of philosophers or human toll booth collectors. Sometimes work seems purposeless because it does not enable survival at even a basic level, such as the work of graduate students or retail workers earning less than a living wage. And sometimes work seems to serve no purpose to anyone other than oneself, like the navel-gazing of intellectuals or social media personalities. If you have ever wondered, "They actually pay someone to do that?" you are probably thinking of a job whose holder has at one point asked the very same question. Work that feels purposeless to the individual worker may still be purposeful work, even if that purpose is solely determined by forces more powerful than we are. But even if it serves a purpose, how sustainable is work that even the person performing it cannot honestly justify?

WORK THAT IS EFFORTFUL—OR EFFORTLESS

Effortful work demands physical and/or mental exertion to get done. In "To Be of Use," poet Marge Piercy expresses admiration for those who are willing to expend the effort to "strain in the mud and muck to do . . . what has to be done, again and again." While it is possible to engage in effortful activity that is not work—as anyone who "works out" as a hobby can tell you—it is not possible for work to be effortless.

That said, work can be immensely effortful without having an obvious use or purpose. Competitive eater Joey ("Jaws") Chestnut, the sixteen-time—and counting—winner of Nathan's Fourth of July Hot Dog Eating Contest, "never imagined it'd be my full-time gig." But to keep his place at the top of his field, he travels around the world while maintaining a rigorous and potentially dangerous training regimen to enable his body to set several records, including

28 pounds of poutine in ten minutes, 390 shrimp wontons in eight minutes, 121 Twinkies in six minutes, and 76 hot dogs in ten minutes, once winning the Nathan's contest while fending off an animal rights protester. Asked how he feels after a contest, he waxes philosophical about work: "I do feel like garbage afterwards, but so what? Most people feel like garbage after a long day of work."

The prospect of effortless work is often idealized. Society simultaneously embraces and bemoans reality TV stars like the Kardashians who get paid vast sums of money to be trailed by cameras, seemingly famous for no reason. As Dire Straits famously sang: "Money for nothin' and your chicks for free." The British royal family, perhaps the most famous heirs of a longstanding family business, is a stark reminder of how simply being born propels some people into a work role, complete with expectations and guidelines for behavior, as well as a corresponding salary and perks. This is not to suggest that it does not take a lot of effort to be famous, royal, or famously royal—as Harry and Meghan can attest—but from the outside, we might wonder if the level of effort justifies the associated rewards.

Of course, sometimes the people who are the most skilled at their jobs only appear to outsiders to perform their work effortlessly. The stress involved in having one's every move and mistake documented by cameras is difficult to imagine. Effort, particularly on creative endeavors, can be hard to quantify or discern. Many museum-goers have looked at a Jackson Pollock drip painting or one of Duchamp's *Fountain* replicas and thought, "If that's art, then I can do that." In response to critics who claimed that anyone could have suspended a shark in formaldehyde like he did, Damien Hirst, who reportedly sold *The Physical Impossibility of Death in the Mind of Someone Living* for somewhere between $8 and $12 million, replied, "But you didn't, did you?" Malcolm Gladwell wrote about the ten thousand hours required to gain mastery of a skill, effort that may be invisible to audiences when a musician or athlete seems to perform effortlessly. Work might appear effortless when the investment of resources—time, money, blood, sweat, and tears—required to do it does not appear to justify, or is vastly out-paced by, the rewards from doing the work.

Many a "get rich quick" scheme promises maximum payoff for minimum effort. Yet, as anyone who has fallen for such a scheme well knows, there is always a catch, always some sacrifice that makes things less quick and easy than they were purported to be. In search of effortless work, people have sold something of themselves for money—sperm, eggs, a kidney—in an attempt to monetize something their body has more of than they need. Although each of these goods often may be donated for humanitarian reasons, the fact that they can be sold opens up the potential for exploitation. Being an anonymous biological parent, whether sperm donor or surrogate mother, can impose unanticipated emotional labor on donor, parent, and child. Meanwhile, unregulated markets in organ trafficking can exploit donors desperate for money into suffering that is often not worth the financial rewards.

Further complicating the picture of work effort are changes in how, when, and where we work. The kind of work we do and the way we do it are evolving. Collectively, modern workers in the United States do less heavy lifting—literally, not metaphorically—than any other time in the last century. But while work that is done both indoors and while sitting down was once considered a luxury, new perils have arisen. As the dominant place of work has moved from farm to factory to office, work has gone from backbreaking in terms of actual physical labor to backbreaking as in injuries due to poor ergonomics. The maladies of cubicle-bound office workers include eye strain, carpal tunnel syndrome, and neck and shoulder stiffness. Repetitive stress injuries in the United States alone cost companies $20 billion per year in workers' compensation and $100 billion in lost productivity.

In recent decades, many of us have been more mobile in our careers than the so-called company men of the past. By choice or by necessity, gig workers in recent years have taken mobility to an extreme, sometimes moving between multiple gigs within the course of a single workday. During and after the 2020 coronavirus pandemic, many professions that did not require interaction with physical objects discovered the potential for remote work to be more productive than work in the office had been. The boundaries between work, play, leisure, and life are evermore blurring. Being untethered to a company as a gig worker may seem like a desirable life of being your own boss, making your own hours, and ultimately working less. But most research supports the opposite conclusion: that being a freelancer is often *more* effortful, as people now need to handle their own benefits, training and development, and marketing and sales—things that were once provided by their employer. Still, the pandemic brought about a reckoning in terms of flexible work hours and location for those who have the luxury to make these kinds of choices, which may result in work being more varied than standardized.

WORK THAT IS RECOGNIZED—OR UNRECOGNIZED

Some gig work is still fighting for legitimacy—whether it's informal recognition as work worthy of societal respect, or more formal recognition that would allow for employment benefits, like health care, social security, and paid time off. Purposefulness and effortfulness tend to be easier to identify and agree on in a way that recognition is not. Recognition seems to be in the eye of the beholder. What is recognized as work depends on individual judgment and is socially constructed.

The simple and sad truth is that much work that is necessary, difficult, and even demeaning goes unrecognized in our society. The people doing this work toil away at unrewarding endeavors for which there is unrelenting demand but which are not formally considered by society to be work. It is a recursive cycle of devaluation: an activity is not paid because it is not perceived as work, and it is not perceived as work because it is not paid.

Perhaps the most glaring example of unrecognized work is housework—the daily, deleterious, and endless tasks that need to be carried out to keep a home running and other human beings happy. Economic sociologist Ransome distinguishes between work, which is public, and housework, which is no less necessary but only privately worthwhile. The former is carried out in exchange for financial compensation, whereas the latter, though valuable, is neither paid nor taxed.

Although the term has fallen out of favor, *homemaker* used to be a common way for women to describe their occupation if they did not work for pay outside the home, as depicted in Maya Angelou's poem "Woman Work," which begins: "I've got the children to tend / The clothes to mend." Today, people speak about being stay-at-home parents. They populate online profiles with cheeky titles like, "CEO of the [Family Surname] Corporation." The purpose and effort involved with running a household can't be denied. Sociologist Arlie Hochschild coined the term the *second shift* to describe how, once women entered the workforce, they would often spend an eight-hour day at their paid jobs, only to have a second eight-hour day begin when they returned home to perform childcare and household chores. While Hochschild's book was originally published in 1989, housework remains largely the domain of women. Men today do more housework than in previous decades; yet women still spend over twice as many hours on housework, on average, even when they make as much or more money than a male partner. In some places, like Scandinavia, the balance is more even than in the United States, and in others, like India, less so. In same-sex couples, where the balance of household work among partners is generally more equal than among straight couples, once kids enter the picture, the parent who does more childcare also does disproportionately more housework. Part of the reason society does not tend to recognize tasks like housework and childcare as work is precisely because they are feminized.

While housework is a type of unrecognized work that is unpaid, there is another that is paid under the table. Just under 5 percent of the US workforce consists of undocumented workers who perform services from work on factory floors and in restaurant kitchens to domestic labor. This work is essential to the functioning of society but lacks the protections and stability of recognized work. Of course, there is also work that, while recognized as work in general, is nevertheless *under*recognized by society. Workers can be literally invisible, such as the delivery drivers who are only seen by security cameras leaving packages on the steps when homeowners are away; figuratively invisible, like the bathroom attendants who endure the most intimate smells and sounds of people who will not deign to look them in the eye; or conveniently invisible, such as sex workers whose work is hidden. How can the people who do invisible work experience the rewards of work when what they do is never recorded or acknowledged?

All of this means that what work gets counted as work depends greatly on who exactly is doing the counting. Those in positions of power often are in the role of decider, while those in the most vulnerable positions must simply forge ahead regardless. At least three important forces—historical, cultural, and economic—determine what work is recognized in a given time and place and with a certain set of shared values. How do these forces guide your employer's attitude toward your work and how much they are willing to reward you? If you are privileged enough to occupy a position of power, how do these forces affect what you consider to be work worth doing and what you are willing to pay others for their work?

HISTORY AND WHAT WE RECOGNIZE AS WORK

A world in which people called bullshit on their jobs, in which they could get rich and famous for being rich and famous, and in which men participated equally in household chores would have been unrecognizable to Wong Jun-Chow. Because recognition is largely subjective and socially constructed, it is not surprising that what we recognize as work today looks quite different from what people in centuries and even decades past would have considered work.

Typically, these shifts over time have to do with technological advancements or changes in how we understand the world. We read news online instead of relying on the town crier. We no longer need a person to reset the bowling pins after each frame because a machine can do the work. Street lamps are lit by electricity, not by a lamplighter's hand. More recently, offshoring has moved much of America's manufacturing capacity overseas, taking countless jobs with it. People no longer work at a Blockbuster video rental store, except at the one surviving location for nostalgia seekers in Bend, Oregon. As we look to the future, we wonder what work will look like and what current jobs might someday be automated—from truck drivers to baristas to radiologists, as we discuss in a later chapter.

Western scholars of work have tended to describe the evolution of attitudes toward work as a historical progression from, in the words of philosopher Joanne Ciulla, "curse to calling." In her book *The Working Life*, Ciulla traces the view of work as a curse to ancient Greece, where the gods made humans "toil out of spite." Athenian democracy was only democratic for landowning men, who perceived manual labor to be beneath their business of governing and contemplation. Over time, as political democracy advanced and citizenship enlarged, more people had to rely on their own effort to earn a living. Centuries later, political economist Max Weber observed a shift in production toward Protestant countries that embraced the principles of capitalism. In particular, he credited Calvinism with connecting honest work both with the worldly necessity of fulfilling material needs and the spiritual purpose of becoming better human beings, using our occupational skills to make a worthwhile contribution.

Of course, the point in history when we work does not alone determine whether our purposeful and effortful activity is recognized as work or whether it is a curse or a calling. It does, however, influence the cultural attitudes toward work and the economic system that determines the rewards of work. The good news is that, unlike ancient laborers, we may be fortunate to live in a period in history when more of us are empowered by technology and democracy to pursue work as something more than a curse. The bad news is that some of the same historical curses that afflicted workers in the past continue to be all too present today. The fear, of course, is that our failure to learn from the past may doom us to repeat it.

CULTURE AND WHAT WE RECOGNIZE AS WORK

The cultural traditions that Wong inherited prescribed that women worked within the home while men worked outside, but his lived reality was quite a bit more complicated than that. When he fell in love in Shanghai with his first wife, she was—against the norms of the time and place—in school, preparing for a career in telegraphy, before renouncing it to raise their children. His second wife was also in school planning to work when they met but went on to take charge of a growing household of her stepchildren and her own children. Unable to afford to school their eight surviving children, Wong and his second wife sent some of them away for high school and college, where they all—five girls and three boys—trained for careers outside the home. The girls opted for education and business, while the boys went into medicine and business. As in most families, work in the Wong family was a product of its cultural inheritance, time in history, and economic opportunity.

Culture—which may take the form of national, regional, ethnic, and religious differences in norms and attitudes—can profoundly influence what society recognizes as work. In subsistence societies, work involved performing whatever tasks most needed doing on any particular day by whoever was available and capable of doing them. Typically, as markets advance economically, work is increasingly accompanied by job titles, clearly set roles and responsibilities, and necessary credentials, like the level of education needed to perform the work. And often, the rewards are dictated upfront, like payment and benefits.

A quick world tour of these advanced markets reveals sometimes arbitrary differences in what national governments recognize as work. In the United States and India, skincare specialists are a recognized occupation and have a bright outlook in terms of their occupational forecast. Meanwhile, "skincare specialist," or the equivalent, does not even appear on the European Union's International Standard Classification of Occupations. Comparing the US, EU, and Indian classifications reveals additional disparities. India recognizes beekeepers and basket weavers as occupations; the EU only recognizes beekeepers, and neither are recognized by the United States. The EU includes watchmaker and fellmonger—we had to look that one up; they remove hair from hide in the process of making leather—neither of which is recognized by the United States. For its part, India lists "pelt dressers, tanners, and fellmongers" as a main occupational category, under which subspecialties like "flayer" and "flesher, hand" reside.

Norms around whether it is acceptable for women to work outside the home, at what age people pursue full-time work versus full-time education, and when and whether to take retirement are all culturally dictated. For example, China currently mandates retirement at age fifty for women working in blue-collar occupations, fifty-five for women in white-collar jobs, and sixty for all men. Contrast China with the United States, where, although the voluntary retirement age is between age sixty-six and sixty-seven depending on year of birth, financial concerns prevent many people from retiring when they would like to, and a culture of overwork pervades to the point where people may not ever retire, by choice or necessity.

So much of what we expect for our work—including when, where, how much, and ultimately what work is—is culturally determined. Yet, work is not wholly determined by culture. This means that, while in general Americans are unlikely to consider a career as a fellmonger, undoubtedly artisanal leather crafters perform the work of one. Cultures can shift rapidly, whether in the face of a global pandemic that necessitated remote work and flexible hours or via longer-term societal shifts, resulting in family leave rather than maternity leave. We both shape and are shaped by our cultures, which means there is an opportunity for individuals to influence their cultures, however slowly.

ECONOMIC FORCES AND WHAT WE RECOGNIZE AS WORK

After he retired, many sunny mornings Wong would walk to Parque Ibirapuera for *taijiquan* exercises—an ancient Chinese martial art—and stop on the way back at the market for bread and oranges. Following a nap, he would spend afternoons performing the ancient art of calligraphy—one of the three perfections of the elite Chinese ranks to which he had spent years earning and later losing admission. For him, demonstrating the discipline to make the last character as uniform as the first was work worth doing. His calligraphy now hangs on the walls of the homes of his eight children and twenty grandchildren—a signifier of perhaps his greatest success, raising a family of eight immigrant children to flourish where he had not. But was it work?

It was a purposeful endeavor to copy the characters in the Great Harmony, a Confucian depiction of the utopian society that he espoused. It was effortful, demanding intense concentration and patience and requiring him to start over for an errant splash of ink or water. It was recognized by the few people who were in a position to appreciate it. He thought it was worthy. Did it matter that calligraphy was not counted by the Brazilian tax authorities as work? There are people who are designated to decide what art is: those who appraise, evaluate, and consume objects of art. But who is on the jury that decides what work is?

The economic market determines not only whether an activity is recognized as work, but also how much it is worth. The relationship between the economic worth and societal worth of work is fraught with complexity: Is a job's salary indicative of its worth to society? As we explore further in a later chapter, it is often the opposite. The buying power of well-compensated occupations like investment banking makes them endlessly attractive to business school graduates, regardless of the persistent questions about the value they add. After the Great Recession, which led millions of average homeowners into foreclosure and bankruptcy, Lloyd Blankfein, then CEO of one of the world's wealthiest investment banks, had the audacity to half-joke that Goldman Sachs—which profited handsomely off the failures of some financial institutions—was "doing God's work."

The conventional association of pay with work can lead to some other gray areas: the amateur musician who spends thirty hours a week writing and recording music but also has a so-called real job; the difference between college student research and teaching assistants who are not recognized as workers and graduate students who are recognized, but with a stipend nowhere near a living wage; the stay-at-home parent gauging how much part-time work tips them into working parent territory; and of course the realization that cleaning our own toilets and painting our own walls is not considered work but paying someone to do it for us is.

So the mighty economic system, along with history and culture, determines what society recognizes as work. What is perceived as purposeful, effortful, and worthy of recognition is typically decided by pay. Which means, ironically, that arguably the most purposeful, effortful, and worthy of recognition work of all—raising the next generation—often goes unrecognized.

WORK IS WHAT?

Wong Jun-Chow did not live lavishly in his old age. His children split the bill for the rent on his tenth-floor apartment on Rua Marcos Lopes in a nondescript neighborhood in São Paulo, where he lived for decades. His unit had two small bedrooms and two small bathrooms, plus the maid's quarters behind the kitchen. That may seem luxurious by some standards but was a reminder of how history, culture, and economics influenced work: having a maid was a conventional middle-class privilege at one time in Brazil, the last country in the Western Hemisphere to outlaw slavery.

The office space in the back of the apartment with a round window like a porthole was too dark for him to work, so he usually spread out his brushes, ink, and rice paper or silk—depending upon the importance of the project—on his circular kitchen table after lunch. It had been decided for him by his children that he deserved to retire from work. After all, he had worked hard since he was a boy to build the military career that he lost. The fact that he failed to take any money away from his business ventures did not diminish the amount of effort he put into them. After a few decades of disharmony and distress, Wong Jun-Chow could return his full attention to his life's work of his growing familial utopia.

The first time Wong and his grandson, Christopher, met, the grandfather had traveled to the United States for work. The last time they saw each other, Christopher had traveled to Brazil for work and spent an afternoon with his grandfather. By then, the older man was widowed again. He had trouble seeing and no longer did calligraphy. Although his body appeared strong and his mind was still sharp enough to command his grandson to keep working hard and to commend him on being a new father, he retreated to the couch after lunch and sat silently with his eyes closed, a position he assumed for most of his final three years. He said much less than he used to say about his own work or the work of others, but in those long silences, was he wondering about what made it all worth it? What purpose would all the effort that he put into raising the next generation in the final fifty-odd years of his life add up to, and was it worth the recognition he had received for all the work he had done in the first forty-two? Might his greatest work have been fulfilling a purpose that is often not recognized as work at all, the effort of raising his family?

Even if we cannot agree on an answer to what work is, we need to ask the question. What we classify as work is inherently laden with our historical, cultural, and economic values, potentially leading us toward work that is worth doing or to challenge received notions of work and worth. What will be your life's greatest work? At its most worthy, work gives us a reason to wake up, to exercise our unique talents, to contribute to something that is bigger than ourselves. The effort we put into the virtue of hard work can be satisfying, build stamina, and prepare us for greater work ahead. In a perfect market, the recognition we get would equal the contribution we made, but even in our imperfect market, the rewards we receive can stoke our egos or build our bank accounts. However, just as the conventional characteristics of art can be thrown into chaos by a urinal, the specter of useless, effortless, and unrecognized work gives us reason to question what work really is and whether it is worth pursuing it when a few others seem to get away without working and many more others seem to work so hard for so little in return.

CHAPTER 2

WHY DO YOU WORK?

"This may shock you, Bean, but not everyone works exclusively for the money."

"Of course they do. That's why they call it work. If we got paid just to sit around and look cute, they'd call it something else entirely."

—Eleanor Brown, *The Weird Sisters*

WORK WORTH DYING FOR?

WHEN PRESIDENT GEORGE W. BUSH ADDRESSED THE American public on the evening of September 11, 2001, he said that the American way of life had come under attack. He reassured the country that the government was "open for business," that the country's "financial institutions remain[ed] strong," and said that the next day, "the American economy will be open for business, as well."

With his words, the president acknowledged that the terrorists had not only murdered human beings but had also sought to destroy potent symbols of American economic strength—the twin towers of the World Trade Center—and military might—the Pentagon. Declaring that its money-making machine would not stop working was a quintessentially American act of defiance and maybe one of the reasons why the anniversary of 9/11 is not (yet) a holiday from work. Self-determination is integral to the American dream that supposedly enables anyone with the resolve, whether they were born in the United States or came to pursue the promise of a better life, to make it here. Whether or not that dream becomes a reality is a more complicated matter, but the pursuit of that dream often begins with working hard to make money.

Poignantly and tragically, most of the victims of the 9/11 terrorist attacks were doing just that. Many in New York City had arrived early to their jobs at or near the twin towers that Tuesday morning and were looking forward to whatever came after putting in a hard day's work, whether seeing their families, relaxing with friends, or moonlighting at another job. As the paper of record for the city most directly impacted by the 9/11 tragedy—although its impact was felt around the world—the *New York Times* began a section devoted to "Portraits of Grief" that memorialized the victims. The style of the portraits was less a traditional obituary and more what was described by reporters as an impressionistic sketch, illustrating the victims' lives by emphasizing some of the things that brought meaning to them, based on interviews with loved ones. This approach was novel at the time but would become the conventional journalistic format for mass casualties going forward. The portraits were published in batches over the course of the months following the attacks, allowing readers to mourn the lives lost and perhaps contemplate their own lives, and were ultimately compiled into a book. A few reporters on the project saw the work as so worthy that they wrote more than one hundred portraits, while some others could only cope emotionally with writing a few.

Among the 2,977 innocent victims, most were people working in the twin towers or the Pentagon, first responders, passengers on airplanes, or people on their way to meetings. Most of them would never reasonably expect death to be a risk of their going to work—and it wouldn't have been such a risk, had the terrorists not chosen this particular target. To account for their place of work—often one and the same with their place of death—these portraits typically provided a factual account of where the victim had worked and what they did for a living. But they also sometimes told stories, ranging from practical to profound, about *why* they worked in the eyes of the close relations who survived them.

As two scholars who study why people do their work, we thought the portraits might provide a unique insight into this question. For people to reflect on their lost loved ones, many of whom died while performing their work, it seemed like at least some would account for what role that work played within their lives as a whole. Was it a paycheck, a source of status, or a source of fulfillment? Of course, the portraits are unable to tell us how the victims themselves would have answered these questions, but they reveal how their work was viewed by those who knew them well. These include the spouse who did double duty at home given their partner's long working day and lengthy commute, the parent who hoped for something more for their lost child than the work they did, and the coworker who noticed the energy the victim unfailingly brought to even the most mundane work every day. Because the people being interviewed were considering a complete life, albeit one that was tragically cut short, the things they mentioned that gave that life meaning really mattered. It is a kind of *ultimate meaning*—with the word *ultimate* implying both final and consequential. As noted by Janice Hume, a professor of journalism who studies obituaries, the "Portraits of Grief" are reflections of our cultural values at an important point in history, a turning point at the start of a new millennium. They signify not only what makes a given person's life worth living, or their work worth doing, but also ask us to think about what *ought to* make *anyone's* work worth doing and life worth living. We wanted to understand more about the work of those who were lost that day. We thought that one way we could honor their memories was to learn from their stories as a starting point for answering the question "Why work?"—not only how we wish to answer it for ourselves but also what society regards as worthy reasons to work.

Although those stories emerged from an epochal tragedy at a particular point in time, the lives that were lost arguably represented the diversity of the modern working world. Unlike traditional obituaries that might favor the rich and famous, the portraits celebrated every life lost on equal footing. Victims came from more than ninety countries and represented a variety of races, religions, ethnicities, and economic classes. They were young and old with an average age in their late thirties, included new immigrants and lifelong New Yorkers, and performed a variety of work. In our analysis, the most common occupations of the victims were financiers and first responders but also extended to many other work types and social statuses and reasons for working.

Of course, every story and every life is uniquely worthy unto itself, but as researchers, we looked for patterns. Among them, we encountered people who were working primarily for money. However, working for money is rarely an end in itself but rather a means to other worthwhile ends. Those ends include caring for others. Jonathan Connors, the senior vice president of an investment bank, "loved to make money, wear Armani, dance the Lindy, [and] dine at Nobu." But the rest of his story reveals that he was not just working for money alone but rather to support his wife who was living with a progressive illness. Material symbols of success, like the purchase of a home, were sometimes as much a part of these people's stories as they are central to the American dream. Working to finance his home purchase was a source of status for Daniel Afflitto, a bond broker who "loved to show off his large new house." But it was much more than a sign of wealth, the "place where everyone went, to take a swim, watch a game, and hang out on the patio." Buying a home might have provided financial security for Martin Giovinazzo, a maintenance worker and young father of three. His widow lamented after his death, "I've always daydreamed of having a house where the children can have their own rooms. Now I'll never have it."

Some victims of the attacks were new immigrants working hard to support their families toward the worthwhile end of a better life for the next generation. Inna Basina had fled from religious persecution in Russia, working days and studying nights so she could become an accountant. Her husband recalled, "Our son is the first thing in our lives. Everything for America was for family and son, not because she liked accounting." Meanwhile, Godwin Ajala was still trying to earn enough to pay for his wife and three children to join him in the United States. He had been a lawyer in his native Nigeria—the photograph of him that was published in the *New York Times* shows him in his *peruke*, the white curly wig that barristers sometimes still wear there—although to make ends meet while studying for the bar exam in his new country, he was working at the World Trade Center as a security guard.

Other victims worked to fund their passions away from work, including two administrative assistants who worked for the same insurance company. Eugene Clark's portrait said that he "loved his life away from the office," his partner observing that he "danced like Tina Turner." Carrie Progen's passion was art, and though illustrating children's books did not generate enough money to constitute a living, an exhibition of her work was produced after she died. As we will see throughout these pages, the arts are often a source of meaning in people's lives, but one that may not provide enough stable income to live on. That is one reason to explain why Elizabeth Gregg got her MBA in finance and was working at a securities firm in the twin towers after earning a doctorate in medieval studies from Yale.

Sometimes, people saw working for money as a short-term means to eventually making their passions their full-time work one day. Juan Cisneros planned to "work as a bond trader until he could pay off his college loans and put away money for his parents. Then . . . go to graduate school and become [a] professo[r]." Brooke Jackman followed her father and brother into bond trading but had "decided there were more important things in life than making money," said her brother. Her goal was to get a master's in social work. Alan Linton Jr. also wanted to help people but sought to do so from Wall Street. His goal was to become a philanthropist because he believed that "if people accumulated great wealth and didn't give it away, they were failures."

A few were working hard to accumulate enough wealth toward retirement. Peggy Alario "was always the first one in the commuter lot and the last one out" so that she and her husband could retire at the same time. Trading firm executive vice president James R. Paul, at fifty-eight years old, "was working very hard, six days a week, to make enough money to retire early," his wife said. Yang Der Lee, sixty-three, delivered meat, fish, and vegetables to Windows on the World, a restaurant at the top of the North Tower. Although he earned only ten dollars an hour, which went to his family, charities, and his Buddhist temple, his children had convinced him to retire in two years at age sixty-five. John D'Allara was only forty-seven years old, but that was old enough in the emergency services office of the New York Police Department (NYPD) for him to go back to being a physical education teacher. "'He loved the Police Department,' said his brother, Dan. 'But he was counting his paychecks to retirement.'"

Individually, these stories attest to the endless variety of worthwhile values motivating working for money that are about more than money alone. Collectively, however, these portraits lay bare that for many people the question "Why do I work?" has a simple answer: we work to provide a decent standard of living for ourselves and possibly our families. In our societal structure, this typically means working to provide money for basic human needs like shelter, food, and clothing, although the 9/11 victims' stories also show that what we need and believe we need can vary greatly depending upon our life experiences. Of course, there are myriad other reasons to work, among them to alleviate boredom, feel useful, be part of a community, and find personal meaning. But compared to providing for our families' needs and saving enough for when we may no longer be able to work, these may seem trivial. We work, perhaps most often, because we can't afford *not* to work. Consider the ends toward which you may be making money. One question you may ask yourself is whether you are making enough to realize those ends. But another question worth asking is whether the ends you may be working toward are worth the work you are doing.

Why we work is also deeply culturally embedded. In America, the answer to "Why do you work?" is decidedly *not* along the lines of a casual "Why not?" Rather, work is essential, a societal given. We assume that people of working age and adequate fitness will work. Often, the first thing we ask, upon meeting someone new and after learning their name, is "What do you do?" Jen's colleague, Julie Levinson, likes to push back on this notion, answering, "About what?" What we do is thought to be synonymous with who we are. To *not* work is so counter to the American societal norm that it is often seen as a sign of failure, waste, or being a bum, as we discuss in a later chapter.

Although improving our standard of living is also fundamentally American, the quest to improve our standard of living can be a vicious cycle of its own for many of us, an endless quest to "keep up with the Joneses." Even millionaires feel they need at least twice as much money than they have to achieve optimal happiness. Psychologists refer to a phenomenon they term the *hedonic treadmill*: our tendency to return to a baseline level of happiness, regardless of how many positive things happen to us. In a famous 1978 study, researchers reported that even those who won the lottery were not happier years later than those who had not won, which may explain why the majority of lottery winners continue to work. Although we may believe that *if only* we had that promotion, vacation, or Ferrari, we would be demonstrably happier, research shows that it would most likely be a short-term high. As we will talk about more in the next chapter, we are very bad at predicting our happiness levels in general. We know that money doesn't buy happiness and often the opposite—as the rapper the Notorious B.I.G. famously said: "It's like the more money we come across, the more problems we see."

There has been a lot written about Millennials and Generation Z, being the *purpose generations* who care more about meaning and making a difference and less about money when it comes to their work compared to prior generations, to the point where they would purportedly leave a job if it didn't provide a sense of purpose. Perhaps the cataclysms that these generations have experienced—from 9/11 to the Great Recession and pandemic—are among the reasons for their prioritization of meaning. However, longitudinal data collected over almost eighty years reveal that young people today value making money from work as much as any generation, and perhaps even more so.

When we ask ourselves whether the work we are doing is worth doing, it helps to have a sense of why we work in the first place. What are we hoping to achieve, from making ends meet to personal fulfillment and everything in between? Let's look at the different motivations people have for working and the rewards work provides. Do you see your own work experience in any of them? And another question: What would your close friends and family say about your motivations for work? Would they align with your own views?

FOR THE LOVE OF MONEY?

If the basic answer to why we work is to earn money, then it should naturally follow that the way to get people to work harder would be to pay them more. Yet, the stories of 9/11 victims as well as theories of human motivation challenge this notion. To understand why we work, we need to understand why we do anything. Psychologists have spent over a century trying to understand the motivation to work. What have they learned?

One of the first theories of motivation most people learn is Abraham Maslow's (in)famous hierarchy of needs, often depicted in the form of a pyramid. The pyramid purports to represent a strict ranking, in which basic needs like food and shelter must be met before higher-order needs, like love and relationships, become relevant. Highest on the pyramid is self-actualization, or feeling a sense of meaning, purpose, and personal fulfillment. Interpreted literally, this means that those who struggle to make ends meet are not in a position to seek fulfillment or even camaraderie from work. The implication that only socioeconomic elites can aspire to self-actualization is thoroughly at odds with portraits that captured what made 9/11 victims' work meaningful and their lives worth living across socioeconomic categories.

Moreover, recent research has cast doubt upon much of what we think we know about Maslow's work, including most scandalously the assertion that Maslow never presented his theory in the form of a pyramid at all! While this might sound like—and is—something that concerns a relatively small group of professors, ourselves included, it matters for how we all understand the main takeaways of the theory for our own lives. Rather than a hierarchy of needs, precluding deep purpose if one does not feel love and belongingness, Maslow himself acknowledged that most activities satisfy multiple needs at once, which means that it is rare for a given need to be completely satisfied, period, let alone before advancing to the next-highest need. He also believed that people differ in their own personal needs hierarchy, such that some are more motivated by, say, love and belongingness than by self-esteem. Indeed, we know that people often strive to make meaning of their situations, even in very dire or humble circumstances. We are such purpose seekers that meaning has been described by psychiatrist Viktor Frankl as "the primary motivational force in [hu]man[ity]." To assume that people who work primarily to pay the rent do not seek meaning could be used to justify offering them only meaningless jobs.

Psychologist and motivation expert Frederick Herzberg, a contemporary of Maslow's, is perhaps best known for his so-called two-factor theory of work motivation. The factors refer to rewards people can get from working and can be separated into those that are *extrinsic* to or outside the work itself, like pay, benefits, relationships with bosses and peers, and working conditions, and those *intrinsic* to or an inherent part of the work itself, like advancement, achievement, recognition, and the reward of the work itself. Herzberg's true insight was that extrinsic factors were related to levels of employee dissatisfaction while intrinsic factors were related to satisfaction. So the opposite of job dissatisfaction is not job satisfaction. When employees didn't have good wages, working conditions, or supervision, they say they were dissatisfied with the work; however, improving any of those things didn't truly make them satisfied or motivated, just less dissatisfied. Anyone who has had a paltry raise on an already paltry salary can likely relate to this feeling. The truly motivating forces came not from fixing the extrinsic factors but doubling down on the intrinsic factors: showing employees why their work was decent, even good, why and how it mattered, that their efforts were recognized, and that their work could be a venue for growth. Herzberg called this *job enrichment,* essentially adding motivator factors to jobs. Building on Herzberg's early work, economists and psychologists have explored the relationship between the two types of motivation.

Many of us have at one point or another fantasized about quitting our jobs and pursuing as work something we love doing as a hobby. If something is so enjoyable, our reasoning goes, why not make it our work so we can spend hours every day doing it. Windows on the World beverage manager Stephen Adams "could not figure out what he wanted to do professionally" until he turned one of his hobbies into his work, graduating from the French Culinary Institute and studying to become a sommelier. Although his new position "was the first time he had a job where he was appreciated and happy," it is not always the case that an avocation can be easily turned into meaningful paid employment.

Have you ever, for example, painted a room in your home or baked and decorated a cake and thought, "This is great. I love this. I could imagine doing this for a living. It would be wonderful, a combination of meditative and productive work that would probably never get old." If so, you are likely falling victim to the illusion that a hobby can readily be turned into an intrinsically motivating career, and that everyone who has a satisfying hobby should seek to make it their day job. Certainly, people do make the jump from their hobby of bread baking to being a professional baker, like Ken Forkish, the owner of the famed Portland, Oregon, bakery Ken's Artisan

Bakery. Ken quit a corporate sales job after two decades to pursue his vision of opening a French-style bakery in the United States. He describes "escaping the corporate womb" and says that "small business has so much more heart than big business." But he is upfront about the challenges faced on the way—including neighbors protesting his backyard wood-fired oven because "flour dust can be very explosive." Ultimately, he did find success pursuing what he loves to do, but the difference between baking, painting, or doing any other hobby when, where, and how we wish to producing on schedule, within a budget, and to a customer's satisfaction is indeed quite large.

Researchers in both economics and psychology have grappled with the issue of how money and love relate to motivation. In 1970, public policy professor Richard Titmuss famously compared the US policy at the time of paying donors to give blood with the UK's reliance on volunteers. Titmuss argued the introduction of payment to an activity that is already deeply altruistic and intended to help others could backfire, even leading people to reduce their blood donation. This finding has been described as one of the most important anomalies in the study of economics, and the theory goes that when extrinsic rewards are introduced, they override and therefore diminish the intrinsic enjoyment of doing the task itself. When it comes to jobs, being offered pay-for-performance and bonus payments was found to reduce motivation relative to fixed pay. There is even the notion that monetary rewards can be too large and therefore seen as an attempt to control workers.

At this point, it is reasonable to wonder whether this all amounts to an argument that employers should hire people who are intrinsically motivated and pay them peanuts. And, indeed, people are often told they should accept lower pay for work that is fulfilling and benefits society. So what prevents people who are intrinsically motivated from being exploited for the crime of being so devoted to their work? It comes down to fairness. We are extremely sensitive to whether we are treated equitably, as anyone who has a sibling well knows. We see this not just in adults but also in infants, and we see it as well in primates. Psychologist J. Stacy Adams developed an equity theory of motivation that speaks to these effects. Picture a classic balance scale with a central base from which hang two plates that are level with each other when the weight is equally distributed between them. On one plate we weigh what we get *from* a job, like money, benefits, stability, enjoyment, and so on. Note that both intrinsic and extrinsic rewards count here; any reward from the work counts. On the other plate we weigh what we *give* to our job, including time, energy, effort, and our ability to put up with whatever the work requires. All equal, we should feel that what we get justifies what we give. The scale should be balanced. Interestingly, people who worry they get too much tend to increase their work effort to balance the scale and justify their rewards.

A key part of equity theory is that this scale is not balanced in a vacuum where we only consider ourselves. Rather, we "calibrate" the scale, so to speak, by comparing our own situation to that of others whom we perceive to be similar to us. Maybe we are satisfied with our own jobs until we meet someone from a similar company, with similar years of experience, who gets paid more, or is entitled to more vacation, or has more flexible work hours or location. There have been movements to increase transparency in job offers through company reviews on websites like Glassdoor, which would facilitate such comparisons across industries. In our own field, we have noticed graduating PhD students who are looking for academic jobs crowdsourcing an anonymous Google Spreadsheet where people post the details of their job search, including invitations to interview as well as the terms of the ultimate job offer. We admit to having participated in these spreadsheets ourselves—and in the process have driven ourselves crazy checking them while in the heat of a job search.

Indeed, during a job search and when we first accept a job are key times to negotiate for the terms we want and feel are equitable. When we first sign an employment contract, we likely already have certain expectations about the job's rewards and costs, whether gleaned from the interview process or through our own research, which the contract simply codifies. A psychological contract also exists concerning what employees believe they owe their employers and their employers owe them. This contract is periodically updated as we go on to work in our jobs, no longer newcomers. Perceiving a psychological contract breach is not an uncommon experience, especially as we no longer expect lifetime employment with a single company. Yet, the consequences of a breach are serious, including workers withdrawing, retaliating, and leaving their jobs. Again, we are never far from the basic compulsion to compare our own situation to others' to see if we have gotten a raw deal.

So, we've learned that money matters to a point—we want to be compensated fairly. But it does not improve our motivation to work. Too much money, or too much pressure on money, can backfire, and we'll lose our will to work, especially if it's work we already love. What seems to matter most of all is that our jobs are enriched, meaning healthy, fair, and essentially good. But, of course, when it comes to why we work, there is more nuance to be explored. We don't all work for the same reasons—one person might be in it for the money while another is in it for the love.

WHY DO WE WORK?

Jen's own version of "escaping the corporate womb" occurred when she left her career as a well-paid but overworked management consultant to embark on a new journey—that of an underpaid and overworked graduate student. Her path to academia, as career stories often tend to be, was somewhat random and prone to luck and happenstance.

The academic seed was planted when, as a business major in college, Jen became a teaching assistant for a class that taught teamwork, leadership, and communication—all cornerstones of an organizational behavior curriculum at the college level. It was uncommon for undergraduate students to be teaching assistants, but since this class was a requirement of all first-year students, meaning large sections and lots of them, upper-class students could apply for the position. Part of Jen's responsibilities as a TA involved leading weekly recitation sessions, where she met with a small group of students to help reinforce the course concepts and answer any questions they had about the material. It was a *very* introductory taste of teaching at the college level: all classroom work and student interaction, with no syllabus preparation, curriculum tweaking, grading, or any of the other things college professors might complain about. Perhaps unsurprisingly, given this, Jen relished the whole deal: getting to work closely with the course professors, and see how they ran the class, getting to be in charge of the classroom that one time per week, and, of course, getting paid.

She started to imagine being a business school professor herself one day. The question was: How? If she wanted to be a management professor, there appeared to be two routes: either have an illustrious career in a management-related field, but at twenty-five years of age that seemed like too long to wait, or get a PhD, not a small investment, given that most programs take five years to complete. Jen started researching business school doctoral programs in earnest.

It seems important to clarify here that admission to a PhD program in management is not like in other disciplines in the humanities or sciences. There really is no one "typical" management doctoral student; work experience is valued in addition to research experience, and ultimately this means that programs essentially place a calculated bet on which applicants might ultimately be successful. Jen will fully admit that the ambiguity in the admissions process likely worked to her advantage. She had a consulting pedigree, in which she had done research as part of industry reports and internal whitepapers. She had teaching experience in a related field and, probably most importantly, had maintained a connection with her professors from college, including those for whom she served as a teaching assistant, who could write her letters of recommendation.

But the reality was, as she prepared to start at NYU, she had no concrete idea what doing academic research entailed. No one in her family had a PhD in any subject. She tried reading academic journal articles in her field, and they seemed interesting but light-years away from something she could ever write. She truly had no idea what she wanted to study and maybe eventually write her dissertation about. It was a "fake it 'til you make it" situation if there ever was one. When Jen came into NYU, an initial task was to identify a faculty member to work with as a research assistant, and she homed in immediately on Amy Wrzesniewski, a tenure-track professor fairly new to the school and scholar of something alluringly described as "the meaning of work." Amy would go on to become Jen's research adviser and eventually dissertation chair, to whom Jen referred, affectionately and not jokingly, as her "Mr. Miyagi," after the famous mentor in *The Karate Kid* who encouraged Daniel-San to "wax on, wax off." One of the biggest legacies of working with Amy was adopting her view of how people relate to their work, in other words: What does work *mean* to the person doing it?

Amy had recently published a paper about how people described their relationships to their work. She and her coauthors developed several measures that allowed people to rate how much they identified with their work as a *job* or a means to an end, a *career* or a means to advancement within a status hierarchy, or a *calling*—a meaningful end in itself. They gave people in a variety of occupations a survey that asked them to assess themselves on these dimensions, as well as a variety of other measures designed to assess their overall well-being. The paper found that people were easily able to sort themselves into one of these three categories, which they termed *work orientations*. People were fairly evenly distributed across the three work orientations regardless of their occupation, underscoring the subjective nature of work orientation: two people in the same occupation could view their work very differently.

Jen still vividly remembers learning about these findings. She can picture herself sitting in Amy's office with its view of Greenwich Village. It was like a veil had been lifted, one that Jen had never known existed, revealing the inner lives of working people. Once she saw the three categories, she couldn't unsee them. Indeed, even though it might be obvious that there are other orientations toward work that do not neatly fit into one of these three classifications, the explanatory power of this typology has been enormously influential in subsequent academic scholarship about work and in management practice. Jen started talking to friends to diagnose: Did they have a job, career, or calling orientation? What about their bosses? Coworkers? Siblings? Other friends they knew? Jen's then boyfriend (now husband) Dave had a classic calling orientation: a materials engineer who was nothing short of obsessed with taking things apart to see how they worked and had been since he was a young child. Get Dave talking about the fabrication of micro- and nano-scale electronics in a cleanroom environment, and you'll be sorry you asked (but he won't!). Jen's roommate at the time worked in customer relationship management for an IT start-up. She self-identified as a job orientation with an aspiration to a career orientation. Another close friend was an elementary schoolteacher in Washington Heights through the Teach for America program, clearly a calling orientation.

And what about Jen herself? Her work in consulting felt like it should have been a career at its best but felt more like a job in reality. Earlier positions, like restaurant and administrative work, were more clearly jobs. It was too early to know if research was a calling, but teaching certainly could be. Both her grandmother and mother were teachers; perhaps it was in her blood. Jen also observed that when professors around her talked about their research, they professed to have callings, but acted like they were career driven, seeking ever-higher status markers of a successful academic career: the next publication, the next award, and so on.

When we look back at Wrzesniewski's work, we find that most of the benefits—for employees and employers—seemingly accrued to the calling-oriented alone. They reported significantly higher satisfaction with work and life compared to the job- and career-oriented and missed fewer days of work. However, their overall physical health and their satisfaction with their health was not significantly different. Although the authors never make the explicit suggestion that people should be calling oriented, the implication seems clear, and certainly started picking up steam in the popular zeitgeist, where "Do what you love" approached something like a mandate, especially for people with the luxury of choice.

For now, it may be helpful to consider the nuances of each work orientation in turn as you think about your own work. Which of the work orientations seems to best describe your own relationship to your work? Have you experienced any or all of them in your career before? Work orientations won't tell you what you ought to do and be, but they can help you consider what your work means to you, whether that is what you want it to mean, and if it is delivering the rewards—money, advancement, satisfaction—you are aiming for. And even if you fall within one category now, it is possible that your work orientation could change over the course of your career, as either your work role changes or as you change.

For those with *job orientations*, work is instrumental and a means to an end rather than an end in itself. Ideally, this means work can allow people to live their fullest lives outside of work, which we sometimes observed in the "Portraits of Grief." Accountant and single mother Janice Brown worked to provide for her family, whose "weekends were a hullabaloo of children . . . off to the zoo, the skating rink, or the movies." By contrast, Christopher Cramer, a tax specialist at a financial firm, was only 317 more days of "commuter hell" away from taking a buyout at age thirty-five after eleven years in a job that his fiancée said had already "turned him gray." One of the definitional aspects of a job orientation is that if the people doing it were financially secure, they would not choose to continue to work or to do the work they were doing. Work may not be central to their identity, nor do they necessarily believe it helps the world. When Wrzesniewski and her collaborators created the work orientation measure, job and calling anchored opposite ends of the same dimension, meaning a job orientation is an anticalling orientation and vice versa.

Many people upon first entering the workforce view their work as job oriented, where work provides spending money and maybe a glimpse of the adult working world but not much else. However, the high school kids who take these positions quickly notice that there are adults working alongside them for not much more than minimum wage. Jen's husband Dave's first job at age fourteen was janitorial work at the local Dunkin' Donuts—cleaning the floors, taking out the trash, washing dishes. At the time, Dunkin' had a famous commercial that featured a cheerful yet weary mustachioed man repeating his catchphrase over and over: "Time to make the donuts." Like the fabled mail carrier, the donut-maker was shown leaving his house for work in daytime and at night, in rain and in snow. In one clear nod to quantum physics, the man opens the door to leave for work only to encounter himself returning home *from* work. Despite, or perhaps because of, this famed commercial, Dave was surprised to recognize the middle-aged man whose job it was to come in at all hours of the day to "make the donuts." Indeed, about 1.1 million adults work for minimum wage or less, according to the US Bureau of Labor Statistics, and more than half are older than twenty-five. Barbara Ehrenreich famously documented the difficulty of living on minimum wage in her book *Nickel and Dimed,* in which to earn enough money for rent, food, and basic necessities, one minimum wage job is not enough. In other words, many prototypical jobs may ironically be those that pay the least.

Feeling that work is not central to life, or to one's identity, and that someone might even choose not to work if they could afford it is—as we have mentioned—not in line with the typical American ideology that who we are is what we do. So, perhaps it is not surprising that in American cultures, callings are prized while jobs are not. However, there has been a recent rise in a job-oriented approach to work that seems distinctly American, meaning young, entrepreneurial, and promising riches. In this view, work is absolutely a means to enable one's life outside of it. The assumption here is well in line with the ancient Greek assertion that work can stand in the way of people achieving their highest purpose, and that lei-sure is where we develop ourselves most fully. Yet, there is a mod-ern spin. Devotees of this approach to work use the term *life hack* to describe the various ways they minimize the time they spend on a number of daily tasks—from eating to cleaning to, yes, working—to maximize their available time for leisure.

One of the most famous advocates of this modern job orienta-tion is writer and entrepreneur Tim Ferriss, whose plan involves spending no more than four hours per week—not four days, four *hours*—on each of a number of important tasks, from preparing food to learning new things to physical fitness to, you guessed it, working. His book *The 4-Hour Workweek* shares strategies that purportedly allow the reader to make more money while working much, much, much less. We will talk more about this in the next chapter, about when and how much to work, but in short, the idea is to minimize the work you absolutely need to do yourself, out-source the rest, and view your resulting life as a series of vaca-tions in which you will escape and have fun, in Ferriss's words, and fully live. This view is appealing, particularly to a person who, for whatever reason, is able to travel whenever they want and organize work into the recommended short work bursts. Ferriss himself is an avatar of this person: entrepreneurial and success-ful, yet carefree and living his best life outside of work. In some ways, this view is a refreshing alternative to the so-called hustle culture popular among a certain class of entrepreneurially minded go-getters. However, this approach does not seem well suited for someone who has, for example, dependent care responsibilities. Ferriss is unmarried and has no children. This lifestyle is also not for someone who craves the predictable routine of having a tradi-tional job with all of the trappings, like an office and coworkers and set working hours and scheduled vacations. We also can't help but notice that Ferriss does appear to be hustling quite a lot of late with a veritable media empire of books, speaking engagements, and a podcast—not the hallmarks of someone truly trying to make the minimum amount of money to enable a meaningful, albeit less glamorous out-of-work lifestyle. More to the point, it seems like a rarified version of a job orientation, that does not truly represent the many people who work primarily for money and who are decidedly not working four versus forty hours per week.

Career orientation sits in the middle of the job and calling typology, which accurately reflects its in-between status. Compared to job orientations, careers indicate a certain privilege of having somewhere to aspire to, a ladder to climb. They bring to mind a professional workforce of white-collar workers in offices. When we use the term *careerist*, a notion comes to mind of a sharp-elbowed striver, so set on reaching the next rung that they don't care who they knock off or what is sacrificed along the way. Yet, career orientations, similar to jobs, have the potential to be viewed by society as lesser than callings. The prototypical career orientation may be the competitive and conniving white-collar professional portrayed in films like *Wall Street* (with the famous tagline, "Greed is good"), *Glengarry Glen Ross* ("Always be closing"), and *The Wolf of Wall Street* ("I've been a poor man and I've been a rich man, and I choose rich every fucking time").

One of the problems with careers is that, as they say, it can be lonely at the top. Yet, far from feeling isolated in their ascension, those who climb the career ladder might find meaning in success. The career stories that were remembered with admiration in the "Portraits of Grief" were not just about success for its own sake but also about why it mattered to achieve. For example, electricity broker Lesley Anne Thomas "took a big bite out of New York," her husband said. "She was proud of making it in a man's world." Herman Sandler, one of the namesakes of investment bank Sandler O'Neill & Partners, "looked like Daddy Warbucks" and helped grow his firm "from seven guys in a makeshift office to some 170 employees occupying the 104th floor of 2 World Trade Center." Moreover, the job versus career distinction is less about having an actual potential for advancement than the person's perception that this is what work is about for them. Indeed, the "Portraits of Grief" contained several stories of administrative assistants who likely saw their work as more than just a job, such as Linda Mair Grayling, who literally and figuratively climbed the career ladder to a high floor with a view from the World Trade Center that "she so adored."

With the advent of mid-twentieth-century corporate office culture, the primary form of achieving career success was through upward mobility, often literally, as people ascended to higher, corner offices with nicer furniture, better views, and more capable secretaries. Clerks working in the 1850s, progenitors of today's office workers, endured toiling in tedious, dull, and unpredictable positions in part because they saw them as a path, perhaps the only path, to becoming managers themselves. The conformity not only of the office but of the predictable, linear career path that accompanied it stood starkly in contrast to the American notion of individualism, exceptionalism, and freedom. Yet, almost two centuries later, it is difficult to deny the staying power of status markers like job titles, salaries, and bonuses, and the material perks these provide. Corporate America today, as then, provides no shortage of ladders to be climbed or golden rings to be reached for.

However, just as not everyone sees themselves working for the same company for the duration of their work lives, so too have career goals shifted away from the organizational domain. With the rise of knowledge work in the 1990s came an acknowledgment that some people value recognition within their occupational peer groups over recognition by their organizational bosses. While the quest for vertical advancement might be reduced for these people, the desire to build one's reputation and gain in status remains. So advancement within an occupational hierarchy may not look much like a hierarchy at all.

The *calling orientation* has leaped into another stratosphere compared to the other two based on attention from both researchers and the business and popular press. It may not be surprising that in our 9/11 research, many calling stories were found in the portraits of heroic first responders, such as firefighter Dennis Mojica, whose work "was his dream, it was his life, it was his first love," according to his fiancée. However, we were also intrigued by the prevalence of calling stories in the portraits of financiers such as Joshua Reiss who was said to have been "practically born a savvy dealer," and James Munhall, who died in a workplace where he was "surrounded by close friends." These sentiments were sadly but understandably common and may even be taken to suggest that if one must die at work, it is better to die for something one is passionate about doing with people one loves. In our 9/11 research, we found that callings were disproportionately represented both among financiers and in the portraits as a whole, reflecting a broader cultural trend.

Exalting calling is so significant in our culture that we will devote most of a later chapter to it. It has such cultural sticking value that a study of managers found that they believed calling-oriented employees worked harder, performed better, and were more committed to the organization than those with job or career orientations—and therefore deserved to be paid more and promoted faster. The managers perceived a so-called halo effect around the calling oriented—but that halo was misplaced, as the employees in question did not in fact differ on these dimensions. The "Portraits of Grief" offer a unique perspective into this fallacy.

WORK WORTH LIVING FOR

When we, Christopher and Jen, first read the "Portraits of Grief" shortly after the 9/11 attacks, we read them seeking to understand more about our fellow human beings, whose lives had been taken too early. Yes, they were factual accounts of how the victims had lived, why they worked, and what made their lives each uniquely worthwhile. But they also seemed to be telling us how we *ought to* live, why we *ought to* work, and what makes life universally worth living—what philosophers call *normative* questions. This led us to embark on a research project in which we considered these stories sometimes to be idealized depictions of how close relations wished for their loved ones to have worked—much as obituaries often emphasize the positives to show us how we ought to live. Ironically, the tasks we were required to perform to study the portraits as objects of academic research—plugging letters and numbers into a spreadsheet and reducing each portrait to a series of codes— sometimes felt dehumanizing, not only to us but to the people we were reading about. Plus, as people who work primarily in the field of management, we were not used to having to take breaks from research to cry.

Upon re-reading many of the portraits, we couldn't help but see those work orientations—job, career, and calling. However, while work orientation was clear in some of the portraits, we found that work seemed "incidental" in nearly two-thirds of the portraits. More often, they mentioned where the victim worked as a matter of journalistic protocol to explain why they were at an attack site that day but focused on other domains of the victim's life away from work. Carol Flyzik's portrait was primarily about her journey to familial acceptance when she moved in with her girlfriend. Although she died on a business trip while on American Airlines Flight 11, work was so incidental to her narrative that her stepdaughter was "unsure exactly what her stepmother did."

While most people who study the meaning of work would stop short of recommending that employees should find their callings and employers should hire those who have callings, there is an undeniable cultural zeitgeist that romanticizes callings while viewing jobs as "just" a job. However, when we analyzed the portraits, the results very much challenged a hierarchy with callings at the top and jobs at the bottom. For example, after his death while working at the Fine & Schapiro deli in the World Trade Center, Juan Ortega Campos's portrait, excerpted here, appeared in the *New York Times*:

> In Wall Street's swirl of power and money, he was just a delivery boy, a young man with a heavy Spanish accent who carried meals up to the suits working in the World Trade Center. But back home in Jonacatepec in central Mexico, Juan Ortega Campos was the very picture of success, a hard working adventurer who lived in America, called his family every day, and sent back money to build a dream.

Campos's portrait depicts a clear job orientation in which he worked for money, and it even suggests that "the suits" in more lucrative professions may have looked down, literally and figuratively, upon the delivery boy. But Campos was a hero in the eyes of his family. Callings, rather than jobs, are supposed to be in the service of helping others or the world; yet, as Campos's portrait illustrates, many jobs serve similar ultimate ends. In this view, a job could potentially be as heroic as the highest calling. This kind of observation led us to consider that the meaningfulness of our work may not just be how we feel about it but how our close relations perceive it and its effect on them. What is the ultimate end of your work? During a difficult work day when you're doing a job you may not love, how often do you stop and reflect on why and for whom you do it?

Few if any jobs are rewarding all the time. Most contain necessary evils that need to be performed along with more enjoyable elements. But to endure work that might be a slog for little recognition or reward—such as ferrying meals throughout skyscrapers—is a difficult path for anyone. However much time he spent interacting with his family back in Mexico, Campos probably logged far more hours schlepping breakfast and lunch orders to the suits in the towers. Knowing that his work served a noble ultimate end certainly might have helped, but did his daily toil feel truly fulfilling to him? Perhaps not; we have no way of knowing for sure. Heroic jobs might be as noble as the highest calling, yet the experience of them often pales in comparison. (And for those on the receiving end of such service, it helps to acknowledge that the person ferrying your bagel or preparing your coffee is a fellow human with a family and goals.)

There were also plenty of instances of career orientation on display, including climbing ever higher within one's organizational ranks to burnish one's own personal status, ambition, and pride. Yet, there were other clear career orientations that were put to the use of helping pave a similar path for others by, for example, breaking glass ceilings and racial barriers. They included JoAnn Heltibridle, who wanted to prove to her family that a woman could "be somebody," and Daryl L. McKinney, whose mother thought he did well for himself after a difficult childhood "coming out of the South Bronx, an African-American man." There was also Carlton Bartels, who rose through the ranks of utility trading to be a partner at Cantor Fitzgerald, where he specialized in commodity markets "to encourage the reduction of greenhouse gases." These portraits demonstrate again that a calling orientation does not appear to be the only work orientation that involves serving others. As you may be rising through your career, how else might you also be making the world better through your work?

Essentially, what we noticed in coding the portraits was that each work orientation had the potential to be self-oriented or other-oriented in the eyes of others. The reasons the subjects of the portraits were said to work ranged from self-realization, usually in the form of achieving a work goal or identity that is personally meaningful or consistent with personal values and goals, to service to others, whether specific people or society at large. Our aim was not to judge any individual's reasons for working but to understand them and why those various reasons for working were regarded as worthwhile. We spend so much time dealing with the daily challenges of our work or focusing on climbing the ladders of our careers that we may not have time to reflect upon how we might have worked and lived differently when it is all over. The portraits are both a tragic sign that the longevity of our work and lives is beyond our control but also a poignant reminder to consider today how we may be remembered tomorrow. How would you wish for those who knew you best and loved you most to look back on what made your work worth doing and your life worth living?

Adding a normative perspective to work orientations led us not so much to unsee the job-career-calling typology—which we still believed to be a powerful lens through which to answer, "Why do you work?"—but rather to see the work orientations with new eyes. This insight led us to realize that not all jobs, careers, and callings are created equal. Superimposing a hierarchy upon these orientations, as we so often do in society, does a disservice to the work that people, like many 9/11 victims, do. None of the three work orientations are inherently "wrong" answers to the question, "Why do you work?" We learned that those who designate their work as a job or career can find it just as worthwhile as someone who is pursuing a calling. And that measuring the worth of work is not nearly as straightforward as some may think.

Thinking about work in the context of 9/11 already has the potential to make us want to seek deeper meaning, as many people did in the wake of that tragedy. Thinking about our own mortality unavoidably brings up not just why we work in the day-to-day, but the ultimate meaning of our work within the scope of our lives. The "Portraits of Grief" also remind us that—although pondering how we will think about our work upon our deathbeds is an unappealing cliché—how we think about our work in relation to others informs how they see the meaning of our work, which matters as much in the day-to-day present as it does in the final analysis of our lives. Our close relations, whether spouses, friends, children, bosses, or coworkers, are often deeply invested in our work and have their own narratives about whether that work will be perceived to be worth the sacrifices we make to do that work, including spending time away from them and getting resources to give back to them. If you're wondering how they view your work in the broader context of your life, it may be worth asking them now.

Our analysis also demonstrated that the social hierarchy of job-career-calling can be impractical and elitist. Of course, our work, whether primarily for money, advancement, or fulfillment, can nonetheless serve a variety of ultimate ends. Any of these can be morally justifiable, so while we should think consciously about why we work, we should be careful not to privilege one over the other. In other words, any of the work orientations provides a worthy reason to work. Yet, each has its own considerations. If you are working primarily for money, consider whether you are being paid fairly relative to others and whether the day-to-day grind justifies whatever the money enables. If working for advancement, what is the ultimate end goal of your achievement: your own personal status, paving the way for others, or advancing other ideals for the betterment of society? Our insights suggest that, rather than focusing attention on improving our self-worth through either moving up the hierarchy or finding a calling, we could instead move along a work orientation continuum and consider what our work brings to others, not just to ourselves.

CHAPTER 3

WHEN—AND HOW MUCH—
SHOULD YOU WORK?

Can't this wait 'til I'm old? Can't I live while I'm young?
—Phish, "Chalk Dust Torture"

CAN'T THIS WAIT 'TIL I'M OLD?

IN HER BESTSELLING MEMOIR *BECOMING*, MICHELLE Obama describes her unlikely path from growing up on the South Side of Chicago to life in the White House. She meets Barack, her future husband and the United States' first Black president, in her first job out of law school at a storied Chicago law firm. For anyone who has had a workplace romance, elements of Michelle and Barack's story may seem familiar. The future First Couple, eager to be taken seriously early in their careers, hides their budding relationship from their coworkers. They are soon busted, both by her assistant, who gives a knowing smile every time Barack walks by, and by one of the firm's most senior partners, whom they encounter

while waiting for popcorn on their very first date to see Spike Lee's
Do the Right Thing.

Michelle describes how the early days of their courtship were
defined by their shared work in "Big Law":

> The bulk of our time, of course, was spent at work, in the plush
> stillness of the Sidley & Austin offices, where every morning
> I shook off any dreaminess and zipped myself back into my
> junior-associate existence, returning dutifully to my stack
> of documents and the demands of corporate clients I'd never
> once meet. Barack, meanwhile, worked on his own documents
> in a shared office down the hall, increasingly fawned over by
> partners who found him impressive.

Michelle and Barack's story is one of ambition and ascendance,
both moving from humble beginnings to Ivy League schools—
to Harvard Law School, and then to coveted jobs at a prestigious
firm—all leading to the ultimate achievement. Their story reflects
the attainment of the American dream, a reward supposedly worth
their hard work and drive to succeed. Working, constantly and
hard, was a rite of passage for junior associates with their eyes on
making partner—or beyond. Michelle reflects, "I was a lawyer and
lawyers worked. We worked all the time. We were only as good as
the hours we billed. There was no choice."

A foil for Michelle's corporate diligence is her roommate from
Princeton and close friend, Suzanne Alele. Michelle describes
Suzanne—who was born in Nigeria and raised in Jamaica and
Maryland—as "unhooked from any single cultural identity." She
is a free spirit. In college, Suzanne partied on weekends while
Michelle studied in the library. Suzanne "measure[s] the value of
her days purely by whether they were pleasurable or not," a stark
contrast with Michelle when their paths diverge after graduation.
Rather than pursue her MBA at another Ivy League school, Suzanne
chooses to attend a state school, which Michelle assumes would be

less stressful (although we note, based on our own experience, that students at state schools work just as hard).

Suzanne later leaves a job at the Federal Reserve to travel the world with her mother, with no set plan apart from living life to the fullest. Michelle laments, "While I wore patent leather pumps and sat through long, dull conference room meetings at Sidley, Suzanne and her mother were trying not to spill curry on their sundresses in Cambodia and dancing at dawn on the grand walkways of the Taj Mahal." The story turns tragic: upon their return from these travels, both Suzanne and her mother will be diagnosed with aggressive forms of cancer. Suzanne dies of lymphoma at age twenty-six, just a few weeks from the passing of Michelle's father. Struggling to process this double loss, Michelle reflects that, although Suzanne did not prioritize happiness over her career *because of* her cancer, "I was suddenly glad for all the times she ignored my advice. I was glad that she hadn't overworked herself to get some fancy business school degree. . . . Suzanne had lived in ways that I had not."

Even if you are not acutely aware that our time on Earth is limited, you face a choice about how to spend your waking hours. You can choose to measure your days in terms of productivity, like Michelle, or pleasure, like Suzanne. Sometimes it may seem there is no choice: circumstance and necessity dictate that you either work or don't. Yet, in a world obsessed with working more and more, it's important to consider the question, "When—and how much—should you work?"

For the average person, it's a short question with a simple answer—many people live a daily reality in which there is not enough time in a single day to earn a living and live a life. Our time is divided into demands by supervisors and subordinates, parents and children, wants and needs, with scarce opportunity to imagine what other possibilities there might be. And when we earn an hourly wage, time is literally money. But a more contemplative version of the question concerns how we use our limited time on the planet in a way that is worthwhile. How much work is too much?

Is it better to work now or later? Many of us follow a traditional career path of working while we are younger to save up for retirement when we are older, though as Suzanne's story makes clear, there is never any guarantee that this investment will pay off. There is a finite number of hours in a lifetime. Finding the answer as to whether to work for tomorrow or live for today requires thinking about the real trade-offs that may be necessary in choosing one or the other.

CAN'T I LIVE WHILE I'M YOUNG?

A graduating business school senior once asked Christopher for advice about how to talk with his mother about his future. He had a plan to start out as a hedge fund analyst, become a billionaire by forty, and then retire into philanthropy and amateur golf, and she was raining on his parade.

Christopher decided to ask him a few questions: What if you don't make it to forty? This didn't make much of an impact. Few twenty-two-year-olds can imagine their own premature death. What if you don't make your first billion that fast? Also ineffective. Many people are vulnerable to the overconfidence bias. He simply could not envision a future in which he did not become a billionaire by forty. If you have children by then, will you hesitate to give away their inheritance? This question made minor progress, although children were still too far off for him to concretely imagine. Won't you get bored playing golf all the time? Perhaps the most preposterous suggestion of all!

Jen, for her part, would regularly poll her undergraduate students on the age at which they expected to retire. For every response of "never" or one hundred years, there were students who gave estimates in the thirties and forties. For those who are unable to prioritize life over work while they're actually young, early retirement may seem like the next best option: hard work in our early years can only be rewarded with time to enjoy while we're still reasonably young. Right?

That certainly is the hope, dream, and implicit promise of the FIRE movement, an acronym for Financial Independence, Retire Early. "Independence" here means independence from paid work. The goal is to save much, much more than most people (the target savings rate is around 70 percent, more than seven times that of the average American) and spend much, much less, so that one can live indefinitely off so-called passive income—including things like interest from investments and revenue from renting out a room, a car, or other property. The movement gained popularity following a 2018 *New York Times* article, but has origins in a book published in 1992, *Your Money or Your Life*, whose title makes the trade-off explicit. One of the authors, Vicki Robin, said she initially wrote the book not to encourage people to quit their jobs, but to urge them to consume and spend less to promote environmental sustainability. But it really caught on as a movement among Millennials in the 2010s, Robin said, because "the worker in this economy has very little sense of control over their existence. People are expendable. You're a young person and you look ahead and you say, 'What's there for me?'" People are looking for a financial justification to be free from their jobs, which are increasingly demanding more and providing less, especially as the cost of living soars in cities across the globe. The book was reissued in 2018 to embrace this bend, complete with a foreword from noted FIRE blogger, Mr. Money Mustache.

Laura Sonday is a management professor at UNC Chapel Hill's Kenan-Flagler Business School who wrote her dissertation on the FIRE movement. In her interviews, she heard stories that were largely consistent with Robin's interpretation. People described their former jobs as overly controlling of their time, even though many of them liked the work itself and found it meaningful. The goal was not to stop working completely but to only work when, where, and how they wanted. Financial independence allowed treasured freedom. One said, "A good life is [being] active and engaged on your own terms, and being able to say no to things that you don't really want to do. . . . [Wealth] provides a little freedom to say no." By figuring out how much money they truly need to live—a nod to the reduced consumption that was Robin's original goal—they can "choose the price of how much it costs for your freedom," as another member noted.

A strong sense of community sustains the FIRE movement. Sonday notes the prevalence of online forums, such as a Reddit forum dedicated to financial independence, which grew from 550,000 subscribers when she was writing in 2019 to over 2 million in 2023. On the forum people share their stories—replete with statistics like number of household dependents, breakdown of personal assets, and spend rates—as a source of inspiration or a basis to seek advice. Many have questions about the logistics of making early retirement work for them, yet few appear to have regrets, with the prevailing sentiment being that any FIRE fate is preferable to a full-time working life. Sonday notes that those who appear to succeed at FIRE tend to have a college degree and more disposable income. Yet, FIRE is not the exclusive territory of the well-off; about one-third of her dissertation sample described themselves as growing up lower class or lower middle class.

What makes the FIRE movement so provocative is that it stands in such stark contrast to the model of a working life that has been dominant for decades. Mid-twentieth-century corporate office culture dictated that people started working around the time they graduated either high school or college and kept it up until approximately when government retirement benefits kicked in (currently sixty-six to sixty-seven years in the United States, depending on birth year). Taking aside the question of what one would do with so much free time in their relative youth—or in other words, what does it mean to *not* work, which we will address in a future chapter—we are faced with part of this chapter's central question: When (in our lives) should we work?

Philosopher Joanne Ciulla turns to Aesop's famous fables for an answer. She notes the particular significance of this interpretation of Aesop's work because the ancient storyteller was allegedly a former slave who bought his freedom. In "The Ant and the Grasshopper," the grasshopper sings all summer, enjoying each day to the fullest, while the ant works all summer, storing up enough food for the winter, prioritizing security over fun. In Aesop's tale, the grasshopper is held up as a cautionary tale about the unforeseen consequences of the choices we make, as he is on the brink of starving after the weather turns cold and has to beg the ant to share.

Rationally, prioritizing personal enjoyment and leisure when we are young, which is to say in the now rather than the uncertain future, makes sense. These are the years when we are likely to be at peak health and without the many entanglements that often accompany age: mortgages, insurance policies, dependents. We can potentially take a risk and, being young and unencumbered, still bounce back from a failure. Yet failing to launch, as the phenomenon is sometimes called, in our early twenties is so far from the cultural norm that it requires being comfortable being out of step with one's peers. Princeton's graduating class likely yielded more Michelles than Suzannes, a phenomenon not limited to the Ivy League. It also requires embracing the grasshopper-ian uncertainty about what the future will hold and whether security will take priority as life decisions are made, such as having kids, investing in a community, providing or receiving eldercare, or facing unexpected health problems.

One can also make a rational case for protecting our later years of life, should we be lucky enough to reach them, from the toils of work. The trade-off, of course, is yet another acronym: FOMO, or fear of missing out, while others are having fun, seeing the world, and generally living their best lives. That these lives can now be lived all the more publicly with the advent of social media only makes FIRE culture even more visually salient. The ant-like Michelle imagining Suzanne grasshopper-gallivanting around the world was envy inducing enough without seeing daily posts detailing her adventures in living color.

YOUTH IS WASTED ON THE YOUNG

Thinking about when we should work requires considering our lives as a whole, with the understanding that we can't possibly know what our futures will look like. Taking into account the grasshopper analogy, time spent in leisure today has the ability to rob our happiness in the future, a prospect that is unsettling. Easier to work today to ensure a better tomorrow, especially if "everyone else is doing it." FOMO can operate in the other direction as well. But what if the very decision to work or not to work causes unhappiness or regret later on?

It is obvious that we can't predict our actual futures, but research shows we are equally bad at predicting how we are likely to *feel* in the future in light of the choices we make now. Psychological studies on affective forecasting consider our predictions of how happy we will be if something good happens, like getting a promotion, or how upset we will be if something bad happens, like getting passed over for that same promotion. Such future predictions drive our decision-making in the present, whether deciding which car to buy, whether to adopt a pet, or whether to change jobs. All else equal, we generally aim to enhance happiness and reduce anger, sadness, and regret. We make choices we believe will serve those emotional ends.

As it turns out, this emotional calculus is predictably flawed. Studies show that we can usually correctly predict the valence of our emotions, meaning that getting a promotion will make us happy and not getting a promotion will make us upset and angry. But we—consistently and across all types of people and situations—overestimate how strong our emotions will be and how long they will last. So we might, for example, imagine ourselves being so devastated by not getting that promotion that we cannot recover from it, whereas in reality, we may be upset but not devastated and bounce back fairly quickly. Similarly, quitting a job that has been bringing us down will likely make us feel better, but not to the extent or for as long as we hope. Remember that our level of happiness can shift in the short term, up or down, but tends to return to roughly its previous level. This observation is both glass half-empty and half-full: we are unlikely to dramatically ruin our own lives, but we are equally unlikely to dramatically improve them. We can always act to significantly shift or prioritize our happiness or minimize our upset, and in fact this motivates us whether we realize it or not. The bad news for Christopher's former student is that whatever he was hoping to gain (or lose) through a decision would likely not work out quite as he planned. The good news is that he would probably have time to adapt to circumstances and to his evolving priorities, to make mistakes and change course if needed.

Another way we tend to misread our future emotions is by oversimplifying them. We often focus on experiencing one dominant emotion rather than the more common mixed emotions. Very few things that happen to us are in the end purely positive or purely negative. We get an incredible job opportunity (positive) that means we will have to move our family (negative) or stop working with our current, amazing boss and coworkers (negative). This means our overall experience will be less positive than we might have imagined had we not considered the potential negatives.

We are especially bad at predicting our emotions accurately when we are contemplating the distant versus near future. The further away, the more inaccurate we become. In particular, young people, who have so much life ahead of them, may have a harder time accurately picturing the future and making choices in their own best interest. This means contemplating in our twenties how we will feel in our forties, the same age Christopher's student was pondering retirement, is not a fair question—to say nothing of how we will feel in our mid-sixties as we approach the age when retirement benefits kick in. When we imagine how happy we will feel in the future (whether near or distant) to be free of work, unencumbered, and doing as we please, we run the risk of not fully considering the downsides: whether we will miss having a means for interacting with others, a way to pass the time that is not dependent on our choice, or a sense of identity, purpose, and feeling that we are doing something worthwhile. By contrast, we may feel perpetually one step away from feeling fulfilled in our current jobs. We just need "X" to happen, whether X is getting a promotion, closing a deal, or finishing a problematic project. Again, reality will probably pale in comparison: we won't feel as good or for as long as we imagine, and any positive emotions will be offset by unexpected negative ones. It's a shame; it would be so much easier to know with accuracy what is the right decision for us, now and in the future, and navigate life (and work) accordingly. But part of the mystery of life is in the unknown, for better and for worse. This means we can't know, and can't predict, but still have to get comfortable making decisions now that likely affect our future selves.

We also aren't accurate in how we perceive our lives in retrospect. Time dulls past wounds, plus our own literal survival might be proof of success. From the vantage point of our completed careers, the difficult times might be recast as having been "worth it all along," when in the moment when they were playing out, we would have spoken about things very differently. This makes it difficult for older generations to advise younger ones: it is impossible to advise our children (or similarly aged coworkers) at the peak of their own juggling of work and family based on how we actually juggled our own work and family. Talking to others in different career stages can provide empathy and compassion but does not substitute for lived experience. It may be a balm to know that no one has it completely figured out: not those who come after us in life, nor those who came before. We are all muddling through, trying to answer the big questions as best we can in a given moment.

SEASONS OF LIFE

Gail Sheehy's own brush with death led her to ask the big questions. A journalist, she was on assignment in Ireland for a story about women during the Troubles, when she found herself in the middle of the infamous Bloody Sunday massacre. Sheehy had been interviewing a young man from the relative safety of a balcony—they had retreated there after a Catholic civil rights march had been tear-gassed—when "a bullet blew his face off." The act was shocking, traumatic, and irreversible; Sheehy knew at once not only that his life was over but also that everything in her life had changed.

She returned to New York but found herself unable to write—even to file the Ireland story—her temper short and impulses raw. Sheehy ended a romantic relationship, fired her assistant, and reflected: "As spring came, I hardly knew myself. The rootlessness that had been such a joy in my early thirties . . . all at once didn't work anymore." She goes on:

> Ireland could be explained simply: real bullets had threatened my life from the outside. It was an observable event. My fears were appropriate. Now the destructive force was inside me. I was my own event. I could not escape it. Something alien, horrible, unspeakable but undeniable, had begun to inhabit me. My own death.

Sheehy was, in essence, having a midlife crisis. These most commonly occur in the decade between her then age, thirty-five, and forty-five. Being a writer who was suddenly repelled from her former work, Sheehy set out to better understand midlife crises, only to realize that "there were crises all along, or rather, points of turning." Her attempt to chronicle the many crises and turning points of life resulted in *Passages*, published in 1976. The book spent three years on the *New York Times*'s bestseller list. It would be named one of the top ten books that most influenced people's lives according to a 1991 US Library of Congress reader survey.

In *Passages*, Sheehy ambitiously aims to chart "the adult condition," the period of time between when adolescence ends and gerontology picks up, which receives comparatively less media attention than its bookend eras and also happens to contain most people's prime working years. She seeks to identify the stages within this broad swath of life and detail the predictable crises that accompany them. The book is broad, with a special focus on relationships, primarily with spouses and children, but also covers work and career. Recognizing the enormity of the task, and the impossibility of accurately capturing life in a way that applies to most people, Sheehy interviewed 115 middle-class Americans, citing evidence that the middle-class mentality often stands in for a more generalizable culture at large.

The "Trying Twenties" are where *Passages*'s adult condition begins, shortly after we "pull up roots" from both our childhood and parents. In this period, we seek to establish ourselves as independent, torn between a desire for stability, upon which to build our futures, and exploration, to learn more about the world and ourselves. A critical ingredient in our decision-making in our twenties is what we see others around us doing, including peers and in the culture writ large, which serve as guideposts for our behavior. With regard to work, we simultaneously face the challenge of trying to establish ourselves in a career and the still vital possibility that any future dream remains attainable. Our dreams have not (yet) been dashed.

In her chapter "Catch-30," Sheehy writes about the restlessness that sets in during the thirties, often manifesting in a deep desire for change, whether in one's home life or career. Often this is the decade where families are established or deepened: children born, home mortgages procured, "real" careers embarked upon. There is often a sense of wanting to expand and of, as Sheehy writes, "an absolute requirement to be more self-concerned." There is also a distinct tension between career and family—usually but not always borne by one spouse disproportionately, typically the female spouse. This is a tumultuous time for couples, earning the Catch-22 comparison.

Most of what Sheehy writes about work and career features in the next stage, from the mid-thirties to the mid-to-late forties, or the "Deadline Decade." This is the decade often marked by midlife crisis: "In the middle of the thirties, we come upon a crossroads. We have reached the halfway mark. Yet even as we are reaching our prime, we begin to see there is a place where it finishes. Time starts to squeeze." Feeling the pressure of a last chance, most people will accelerate their careers or families. Some will seek change, embarking on either a new career or a family before it's too late.

Passages presents the fifties as a time of mellowness, warmth, and acceptance and a "no more bullshit" attitude, the calm after the preceding decade's storm. Reading this in the 1976 edition, today, all we could think was that this seems at least ten years too early. Decades later, in her 1995 book *New Passages*, Sheehy acknowledged the irony that, writing her first book at age thirty-five following her own midlife crisis, she "couldn't imagine life beyond 50, and I certainly couldn't bring myself to consider it as a time of special possibility or potential." She adjusts the timeline in *New Passages*, describing the years after fifty as a "second adulthood" in which a person in good health could potentially live another thirty to forty years, enough time for a new or deepened career.

The notion of dividing human life into stages, each with an attendant ideal activity, is not a new one. A monologue from Shakespeare's *As You Like It* outlines seven stages, from helpless infant "mewling and puking in the nurse's arms," to young schoolboy and adolescent lover, to brave and impetuous young adult soldier who then settles down to pursue middle-aged justice "full of wise saws," before becoming a feeble old man "with spectacles on nose and pouch on side," and finally entering a second childhood before death. Philosopher Robert Nozick was struck by the realization that the older person whose approval and recognition he had sought as a child turned out to be the adult he would become.

Of course, no one theory can map the predictable stages of lives that vary so much in circumstance, privilege, and pure luck. The natural rhythms of life are dictated by several patterns: maturing into our mental and physical primes, childbearing and rearing years for some, caring for aging parents (and sometimes both at once for the so-called sandwich generation we both are in), our own physical limitations as we age. Many of the markers of success and the American dream, like homeownership, carry with them a sort of limit on freedom, as mortgage payments must be met and how far is an acceptable commute weighed. Each of these has an impact for when we work, including, of course, laws stating how early we can start working and enticements like government-sponsored retirement—to say nothing of mandates in communist countries where people are required both to work and to retire at a certain age.

Career progression is partly also a function of the norms for a given line of work. Lengthy training programs, as in medicine or academia, and certifications, as in law or building trades, provide barriers to easily entering these occupations in midlife. Such career changes may be improbable but not impossible, as Kristine Enea's story reveals. Disenchanted with her work as a freelance attorney and having just run for office (unsuccessfully) and donated a kidney (successfully, to a previously unknown recipient), Kristine was looking for her next career move. She took a strong interest inventory assessment—like a vocational questionnaire a guidance counselor might administer—that proclaimed her best-fitting careers: attorney, architect, or surgeon. The first one no longer appealed, but the last one caught her attention. Kristine started the necessary coursework to apply for medical school, to test the waters. When she took biology, she remembers, "Like Dorothy in Oz, everything was in color. Everything in my brain turned on." She started med school at age fifty-three, alongside a cohort of people in their twenties and early thirties. When we spoke, Kristine was a few credits from completing her medical degree.

She credits her successful midcareer change to a few things. First, she describes herself as "comfortable with being unconventional," having grown up in the proudly nonconformist Bay Area. Second, she joined a group for, in her words, "old premeds" that provided support. At this point, Kristine says, "I gave myself permission to just keep doing this until I don't like it anymore, permission to quit at any time." Third, importantly, Kristine had a financial cushion: stock options from her first employer, plus she owned valuable, always appreciating real estate in San Francisco and San Jose. As predicted, Kristine's favorite part of med school was the surgery rotation. She loves that it's curative and cutting-edge and is attracted to the research potential. Should she pursue this specialty, which requires a five-year residency, she will be sixty-three in her first position as a surgeon. Kristine is in good health and looks younger than her age, but she still worries about the physical toll of the profession. Like many people in their fifties, her eyesight is changing, and she now needs reading glasses. This, coupled with the prospect of spending ten-hour days on her feet to perform surgery, is daunting but not a deal-breaker, as there are longtime surgeons still working well past the years when many retire.

Which decade are you in now? Do you find that Sheehy's life stages seem relevant to you? What will be your next turning point? Are you seeking to embrace the next passage or to delay it? Kristine's story may be inspiring in that it seems to defy the logical progression of passages that can constrain us. It reminds us that it's likely never too late to make a career change, even for professions that seem out of reach, but it also suggests that the capacity to make such a change depends on building in the financial and physical flexibility to afford it. Her story is real, in both the advantages and disadvantages she experiences compared to her decades-younger counterparts. When we find our passion later in life, is it better late than never or too little too late?

COUNTING UP AND COUNTING DOWN

Is FIRE right for you? It positions early retirement as a goal, which can make sense if you can pull it off and you're the sort of person who does not think that you can ever love your work as much as you will love not working. Maybe your calling is outside of the workplace and cannot be easily pursued given the constraints of the typical workweek. However, FIRE only accelerates the pace of the conventional logic captured in the original *Passages*, in which our "second adulthood" is likeliest to lead toward retirement, only sooner. Essayist and novelist Geoff Dyer recalls the mind-set in the world of "unpleasant and unrewarding work" that his relatives inhabited when he was a child, in which early retirement "was a form of promotion, practically an ambition." In such a world, the economic deck is stacked against our ambition to retire. Our earning power is typically inversely related to experience, so just at the point at which we may face a perfect storm of economic burdens—paying off education loans, seeking a home, starting a family—we are advised by financial planners also to be saving for children's college educations and our own retirements. Those who are lucky enough to live on less than what they earn are supposed to put the rest away in an IRA so that in some distant future they can have a retirement party where they are given coffee mugs and other swag with sayings like "Life begins when work ends."

The logic of *New Passages* may be more aligned with the Confucian aphorism: "We have two lives; the second begins when we realize we only have one." Dyer says that, among those who have the good fortune of finding work that is pleasant and rewarding, retirement may be "unheard of." Philosopher Robert Nozick published *The Examined Life* in 1989, after his mother died and his father fell ill, leading him to wonder when it would be his turn. Even as he recognized that life changes as we age, he rebelled against the kind of thinking and labels with which the original *Passages* is replete, that divides life into midpoints that imply an endpoint. He writes:

> I adjust boundaries accordingly to create new midpoints. "Not yet halfway through *life*"—that served until the late thirties or the age of forty; "halfway after college to the very end" gets me approximately to now. I next need to find still another midpoint not to be much beyond, and I hope to continue making these adjustments at least until old age, which too for a while I will be no more than halfway through. All this is so that I will be able to think there is as much ahead as behind, as much of something good.

Nozick wrote those words when he was barely fifty years old. He would die at just sixty-three—hardly old age and still less than halfway through more worthwhile projects, arguably still in his prime as an academic thinker and writer. However, in many professions, sixty-three is approaching if not past conventional retirement age. In consulting firms like those where we used to work, the mandatory retirement alarm for partners begins ringing in their fifties. Indeed, as we write this, some of Christopher's former peers are figuring out their second acts. Some, following Sheehy's *New Passages* path, have begun new careers as CEOs and board members. Others manage to attain what Christopher's former student dreamed of and prepare for a second life of leisure. A retired partner told us that the firm did a lot to prepare partners for retirement, mostly around financial planning. Part of this involved dividing up the postretirement years into three phases, adorably titled the go-go, slow-go, and no-go years, based on the assumption of health and activity level declining over time.

As much as we may not want to leave the world of work when we still have much to give, we also don't want to overstay our welcome. There are probably two primary reasons that firms like our former workplaces push out partners at (what seems to us to be) such an early age. One is to make room for new partners without unduly diluting the value of the remaining partners' shares. Often, a retiring partner may be accustomed to bringing in twice as much or more than a newer partner, but the firm may earn higher margins on the newer partner's lower compensation. In general, encouraging retirement serves to provide space for other, younger workers to contribute and reap the rewards. Another reason is that most experienced professionals reach a point at which their performance declines. For female gymnasts, that age may be as early as sixteen years old, after which biological changes and injuries make aerial acrobatics increasingly difficult and dangerous, unless you're Simone Biles and still winning national championships at the ripe old age of twenty-six. For a National Football League running back, studies suggest the tipping point is around twenty-nine, due to the wear and tear required for a relatively small player to bust through defensive lines composed of relative giants. The autobiographical book in which writer Geoff Dyer considers retirements and endings is called *The Last Days of Roger Federer*, referring to the men's tennis great who retired at the same age (forty) and in the same year (2022) as women's GOAT Serena Williams. Federer was finally felled by a bum knee; Williams won her last major tournament while pregnant with her first child and fell tantalizingly short of adding to her major total a few times before hanging it up just before she announced she was pregnant with her second child. (In case you're wondering, Kim Clijsters is the only woman to date to win more major tournaments after her first child than before.)

Although accountants and management consultants are probably still in their prime in their fifties, the way that the Big Four accounting firms appear to work their partners, it would be understandable if some of them were tired by that point. Christopher knew one partner who died of a heart attack within months of retirement and another who suffered a collapsed lung in his retirement year, and the way that people reacted suggested that they were shocked and saddened though not, unfortunately, surprised. The downside of the mandatory retirement policy is that there is hardly any gray hair in the room when important decisions might benefit from the wisdom of age or experience. There may be exceptions in the bylaws for senior leadership, but those are intentionally limited. A mandatory retirement age is only possible in firms that are partnerships because of the way federal age discrimination laws are written. According to law scholar Saul Levmore, there are relatively few other professions that permit mandatory retirement ages. They include judges in some states (age seventy in New Hampshire), commercial airline pilots (sixty-five), and public safety officers (varies by jurisdiction), presumably because the risk posed by a "past their prime" worker in these professions is perceived to outweigh the risk of age-related injustice.

When Shakespeare's King Lear retires at age eighty, he decides to give away the kingdom to his three daughters. His foolish choice to reward the two daughters who flatter him and to disinherit the sincere daughter proves disastrous. He eventually goes mad, not from age but in reaction to his insincere daughters' betrayal. Despite their youth, they prove to be inferior monarchs to their elderly father. Philosopher Martha Nussbaum discerns that modern productions of the play are "obsessively concerned with aging." She notes that Shakespeare's original Lear was played by Richard Burbage at all of age thirty-nine, and for centuries the role was perceived to require too much memory and endurance for an older actor. Of late, however, she observes playing Lear in one's mature years has become a badge of honor, with actors like Lawrence Olivier assuming the role at age seventy-six and Glenda Jackson at eighty.

The mind-set of working toward retirement involves counting down—and counting out those who may never have the financial means to retire. Financial planning algorithms count down to tell us if and when we are able to retire, but if our goal is to work so that we can cease working, what if we never, like Nozick, make it to retirement age? The 9/11 "Portraits of Grief" perhaps overrepresent the prevalence of people who were "counting the days" toward retirement, possibly because of the journalistic poignancy of stories about people whose lives were suddenly taken from them just when they were ready to live. However, they remind us that we will not know the date toward which we will be counting down until it arrives. The mind-set of being "not yet halfway" involves counting up toward a target that is ever-changing. It enables us to continue imagining new ambitions, new roles, and even the possibility of new careers.

WORKIN' 9 TO 5?

The question of *how much* to work is probably moot for someone whose every available waking hour is spent trying to make ends meet. As Barbara Ehrenreich notes in *Nickel and Dimed*, a classic of undercover journalism, for those trying to live on a minimum wage salary, two and even three jobs are barely enough to meet one's basic needs. A 2022 report estimated that 7.5 million Americans, or 5 percent of the workforce, are working more than two jobs, and the US Census reports that 11.7 percent of Americans (almost 37 million people) live below the poverty line. Here, the question is not how much should I work, but will I ever be able to afford to *not* work? This is an increasingly real question for the between 20 and 36 percent of people who feel like they will never be able to retire and the nearly half who said they are unable to save for retirement.

Many jobs state as a term of employment when and where the work needs to occur, especially if it needs to take place in person. Restaurants, retailers, and any office that serves the public rely on their schedules to ensure constant coverage and adequate service. Hospitals, construction sites, laboratories, and factory floors require the careful coordination of who does what and when. These schedules are typically ironclad and difficult for employees to change, even if they are sick or unable to work. Meanwhile, employers are typically free to change workers' schedules at will, especially for vulnerable workers like those in minimum-wage or part-time jobs. Members of Congress have proposed legislation that would regulate worker hours, requiring at least two weeks' notice for a schedule change and limiting retaliation against employees who ask for regular hours. However, the bill has yet to come up for a vote.

The lived reality of these schedules is grim. The Schedules That Work Act was inspired by Maria Fernandez, who died at age thirty-two from inhaling gasoline and exhaust fumes while napping in her car in between round-the-clock shifts at three different Dunkin' Donuts locations. Warehouses for retail giant Amazon have been the site of several on-the-job deaths. In one notorious incident, sixty-one-year-old Rick Jacobs died from cardiac arrest shortly before his shift ended. A makeshift barrier was erected around his body, and distraught employees were instructed to return to work. One employee, wishing to remain anonymous for fear of corporate retribution, commented, "No one should have been told to work alongside a dead body, particularly after witnessing it." Sadly, this was not the only instance where Amazon insisted that the work continue after a coworker died on the job. As in the warehouses, delivery drivers' every movement is surveilled by the company. Workers are pushed past the point of personal autonomy, with insufficient time for bathroom breaks.

The question of how much and when to work is answered *for* these workers and is not what they would choose. Most workers, however, are in this position, unable to choose when to stop working or to cut back on hours. For knowledge workers, who have almost complete control over when and where they work as well as what to work on at a given time, this question essentially amounts to how their days are spent. The obvious answer is that we should work for as many hours as it takes to complete the work at an acceptable level of quality and no more. Yet, in many industries standards are unspecified and outputs are subjective. Perhaps overachievers or those insecure about appearing lazy set the pace. These workers may have an unclear mandate but operate in a norm of overwork. A fellow graduate student trying to be helpful explained to Jen: "We get to work whatever sixty hours a week we want." Research on the relationship between overachieving and happiness is scarce; however, there is some indication that those who invested a great deal of time and effort in their work reported being happier than those who invested a more moderate amount.

What many people picture when they enter the working world is working nine to five (cue Dolly Parton), from Monday through Friday. These hours are considered such a default that they are highlighted in many daily planners, including the calendar function in Microsoft Outlook. What we consider to be typical work hours can be traced back from work's move from farm to factory to office. Farming followed the seasons, and the physical outdoor work was dependent on sunlight and weather conditions. Nature set the schedule, and the farmer worked in accordance or suffered the consequences. As in the biblical verse on which the Pete Seeger–Byrds song was based, there was "a time to every purpose under Heaven . . . a time to reap, a time to sow."

As work moved indoors, a twenty-four-hour cycle of production could in theory be maintained on the factory floor. Yet, turn-of-the-twentieth-century American mills originally had one day off per week—Sunday, the Christian sabbath—and then added a half day on Saturday. The first two-day weekend came in 1908 and became standard during the Great Depression. As man was considered integral to the machine he operated, the goal was to make him perform with machine-like efficiency and consistency. Time was closely monitored and production maximized. So-called scientific management aimed to quantify how quickly a task could be reliably performed as a standard for all to achieve. Time in fact was money. One of the most memorable scenes in the satirical 1936 Charlie Chaplin film *Modern Times* involves the demonstration of a feeding machine aimed to increase productivity by automating the employee lunch break. The pitch went: "Don't stop for lunch: be ahead of your competitor. The Billows Feeding Machine will eliminate the lunch hour, increase your production, and decrease your overhead." Chaplin unwittingly demonstrates all the ways the machine could go wrong—at one point he eats a hex nut from the machine that is pushed into his mouth, at another a hot bowl of soup is dumped down his front—to the delight of the audience and horror of his manager.

Along with the advent of office culture came the standard schedule that became a default for all kinds of work, regardless of whether the work truly necessitated the schedule. The office worker might have enjoyed relative autonomy compared to their factory counterpart, but the clock still ruled. Although all kinds of factors have changed that might have affected worker productivity over the decades—technology, advances in standards of living and physical health—the forty-hour workweek has remained a baffling constant. We covet the weekend as a time to unwind, but save for a number of holidays per year that could be counted on one hand, few days in the United States are truly free from work for most people. Other countries work longer weeks—Tanzania and Mauritania both top out at fifty-four-hour weeks, according to a 2023 report by the International Labour Organization—while some work far less. This is particularly notable among economically developed nations that might compare to the United States' thirty-seven hours per week, like the United Kingdom (thirty-three hours) and Australia (thirty-two hours).

There have been experiments with shorter weeks. In 1930, Kellogg's, the breakfast cereal company best known for Corn Flakes, traded three eight-hour days for four six-hour days with an attendant pay cut. The change, coming as it did during the Great Depression, increased jobs available for people. Importantly, workers responded well to the change, reporting more time to invest in their communities and leisure time. After World War II, the eight-hour day returned, although a small group of mostly women fought to keep the shortened workdays in their schedule until 1985.

More recently, companies and academics have asked what happens when employees are given four-day workweeks. Sociologist Juliet Schor published *The Overworked American* in 1991, documenting American workers' increased work hours and decreased leisure time, even as productivity standards rose. She hoped to find companies willing to experiment with reduced work hours, but in the 1990s, there were no takers. There had been standalone experiments with four-day workweeks, so-called summer Friday half-days and other novel configurations over the years, but always confined to a specific company. An unexpected upside of the COVID-19 pandemic was that companies, desperate to keep employees during the Great Resignation and recognizing that flexible schedules could work, were finally game to try a more widespread experiment with a four-day workweek. Schor, along with colleagues from Ireland and England, ran a broad pilot study in partnership with 4 Day Week Global (4DWG), a nonprofit community dedicated to making four-day weeks standard. Their report, published in 2022, followed over nine hundred employees at thirty-three companies, primarily in the United States and Ireland, who followed the "100-80-100" rule laid out by 4DWG's cofounders. Employees receive 100 percent pay while working 80 percent of their hours—thirty-two hours over four days—and delivering 100 percent of their standard workload.

The results were unequivocal: employers and employees alike reported that the trial was a success. Productivity and performance were high. Revenue rose, as did hiring, and absenteeism and resignations declined. Employees reported better performance and reduced stress, burnout, fatigue, and work-family conflict, as well as improved physical and mental health and positive emotions. They spent their newfound leisure time—most companies had Friday as the day off, allowing for a three-day weekend—in ways that were more meaningful to them, such as hobbies and self-care. There was a small, but notable, environmental impact as well, as carbon emissions from commuting declined. No company intended to go back to a forty-hour week, and it's a good thing: 70 percent of employees reported that they would need a 10 to 50 percent pay increase to return to the five-day week, with 13 percent reporting they wouldn't go back for any amount. As Charlotte Lockhart, one of the 4DWG founders, reported in *Time*, "We knew the results were going to be good. The only thing that surprised us is that they were *so* good." 4DWG is planning quarterly pilots in the coming years, hoping to add to the roster of companies adopting the shorter workweek.

The pandemic was indeed a watershed moment for employee flexibility in terms of when and where they worked. Almost overnight, people who never thought they would work from home, outside the watchful eye of supervisors and coworkers, suddenly found remote work to be their reality. A 2022 study by the McKinsey consulting firm found that the vast majority of workers (58 percent) are able to work remotely on at least a part-time schedule (35 percent can do so full-time). Workers deeply value being able to work remotely: 87 percent of workers offered a remote work schedule take it, for an average of three days per week at home. For those looking to change jobs, a remote schedule was the third-most important criterion in their decision, after better pay or hours and better career opportunities.

What do you value about your current work situation? What do you wish was different? And what do you prefer: predictable hours or flexible hours? Flexible location or a clear boundary between work and nonwork? Working toward a timed goal or a productivity objective? Interestingly, despite this desire for remote work, it is not at all clear that it is better for us. As our understanding of affective forecasting might predict, many people focus on the upsides of remote work—like not having to undertake lengthy commutes, being able to better focus without office distractions, and putting in a load of laundry in between meetings—but they neglect to consider the downsides. Studies found that during the pandemic most people worked more, not less, when they began working at home. This included longer workdays, more work on evenings and weekends, and less separation of work and home; rather than "working from home," our homes became our work.

EVERY DAY I'M HUSTLIN'

How much work is too much work? In the United States, working has historically been almost a moral imperative. The way we measure our worth by time spent at work could be a vestige of the Protestant work ethic, which viewed work as a direct service to God—so how better to serve him than by constantly working? Hard work is glorified in many of our most beloved stories, often feeding into the "rags to riches" narrative archetype, where success occurs not by dumb luck but on the backs of someone working day and night to make it happen.

This was the case for Alexander Hamilton, whose rise from "bastard, orphan" to "$10 founding father" is chronicled in both Lin-Manuel Miranda's breakout musical *Hamilton* as well as the biography by Ron Chernow that inspired it. In one song, titled "Take a Break," Hamilton's wife Eliza begs him to put his work aside to "go upstate" with the family. It's a plea not unfamiliar to any spouse (historically, as in Hamilton's time, this would have been a wife) imploring their partner to stop working already and spend time together. Eliza and Alexander each appeal to Eliza's sister Angelica, in for a visit from London, to help their respective causes:

Eliza: Angelica, tell this man, John Adams spends the summer with his family.
Alexander: Angelica, tell my wife, John Adams doesn't have a real job anyway.

Much truth here is said in jest: the only people who can afford to take a vacation are those whose contributions are trivial, whose jobs aren't real. Of course, in Hamilton's case, this work is justified by the formation of a new nation that needs people to lead it, no matter the personal cost. Hamilton later sings that he "can't stop 'til I get this plan through Congress." This is a not unfamiliar argument to those of us who have ever had to justify our long hours away from the family as both urgent and important. Another number in the musical, "Non-Stop," again refers to how hard Hamilton works, as in, "The man is non-stop." We learn that James Madison, John Jay, and Hamilton together were commissioned to write a series of essays to support the emergent US Constitution. The target was about eight essays per author, or twenty-five total. The *Federalist Papers*, completed within six months, in fact contained eighty-five essays, of which Jay contributed five, Madison twenty-nine, and Hamilton the remaining fifty-one. The song's refrain, from Hamilton's friends, family, and fellow countrymen alike, goes:

> How do you write like tomorrow won't arrive?
> How do you write like you need it to survive?
> How do you write every second you're alive?

Of course, the irony is that Hamilton's life *would* be tragically cut short; tomorrow, in fact, wouldn't arrive. That he spent his limited time hard at work helping to found the new nation was more virtuous, perhaps, than had he spent the summer with his family upstate. The net effect of the many mentions of Hamilton's work ethic, in both *Hamiltons*, is the sense that it alone is what enabled Hamilton's prominent role in the revolution—and in turn the country's success as a young nation.

Including founding a nation, some jobs by their very nature require round-the-clock, intense periods of work. Military deployments, journalists embedded in war, emergency responders, and foreign aid workers all have little choice but full commitment, with work and life necessarily consumed by their occupations. Other jobs have predictable seasonal ebbs and flows in their workloads:

accountants at tax season, performing arts schedules, summer camps, retailers during the holiday rush.

What kind of commitment does your work require? Is it imposed by the demands of the work itself or by a manager who demands your presence in the workplace whether or not there is real work to be done? In many lines of work, it may seem like the only choice is to work, work hard, and work all the time, not because the work demands it, per se, but because it is the cultural norm. How much work is too much? In our consulting days, we noted the regular use of overly grandiose phrases like "putting out fires" and scheduling a "come to Jesus" meeting to amplify the importance of what were essentially typical office-based tasks. When Jen was in college, the two occupations most prized upon graduation were management consulting and investment banking. A friend who had secured an internship in the latter said that a common complaint among the incoming full-time analysts was that the salary, which sounded impressive at first, was later revealed on a per-hour basis to be barely more than minimum wage. Part of this was a culture commonly referred to as face time, where lowly analysts were required to be in the office even when they didn't have actual work to do. As this friend explained, even though there isn't a lot of work from nine to six, you are still expected to be there. You can never leave work earlier than a managing director or vice president. Then, when they go home, the real work begins, as they email you constantly throughout the night with tasks to complete. Sure, the firm bought dinner and paid for a car service home, but the trade-off was regular ninety- to one-hundred-hour workweeks. Now that we are business school professors, we find that little has changed—these occupations remain in high demand.

All along Jen's career, she witnessed evidence of overwork. In college, friends would brag about how little sleep they got and how many hours they spent in the library studying for exams. At Accenture, a colleague powered through many late nights to deliver an important presentation, widely considered a success. But on her drive home that night, she reported having to pull her car over to the side of the highway: her hands were shaking so badly she could barely grip the wheel. A fellow graduate school classmate described working to the point that he hallucinated bugs crawling across his desk. At Jen's first faculty job, a fellow professor, who was on the tenure track with an infant at home, tried to leave for work in the morning, only to realize that in her sleep-deprived state she had driven into the still-closed garage door. What is particularly noteworthy about these stories is that, with only the last one as an exception, they were not shared as cautionary tales but rather as points of pride, evidence of how hard people were working and how resilient they were, so dedicated to work that they could endure such extreme reactions.

In the last decade, a so-called hustle culture has taken hold among young, upwardly mobile, would-be start-up founders, where hard work is seen as a surefire ingredient to success. Social media is replete with taglines like "Hustle harder," "Rise and grind," and "Don't stop when you're tired, stop when you're done." The latter statement was carved into a watermelon rind at a WeWork coworking location to inspire its clientele; any of these slogans might be painted on the office walls. Millennials were the target market for Soylent, a meal replacement smoothie that takes away the need to think about feeding oneself so that, among other things, one can remain engaged at work. (The name is a tongue-in-cheek reference to the 1973 movie *Soylent Green*, set in a dystopian 2022 in which dying oceans threaten the primary source of food and a gruesome new source is found.)

Essentially, hustle culture glorifies removing all barriers to working, like food, sleep, and human interaction, that isn't related to either work or posting about work on social media. It likely comes as no surprise that the concept of hustling among would-be Zuckerbergs and Musks is a cultural reappropriation of the Dutch word *husselen*, which means "to shake or toss," and later evolved to indicate hurrying and begging. The term was often applied to illegal attempts to get ahead—like sex work, cheating, or stealing—and in unfortunate negatively stereotyped references to Black youth conducting such acts. This chapter's subtitle takes its name from a lyric from the song "Hustlin'" by rapper Rick Ross, an explicit homage to drug dealing. Another lyric from the same song: "We never steal cars, but we deal hard." As in the Soylent reference, these comparisons indicate a winking irony among those using the term today, of being in on the joke while not confronting outright the more distasteful racial connotations.

The appeal of hard work may be in part an antidote to being perceived as lazy, uncommitted, or otherwise unworthy. Work quantity, in the form of observable work hours, substitutes for work quality. We work harder, if not smarter, but hope that line blurs. If we are always seen working, we cannot reasonably be accused of doing less than a stellar job. Anne Marie Slaughter, in her provocative 2012 essay in the *Atlantic*, "Why Women Still Can't Have It All," candidly discusses how difficult it was to maintain her high-powered government job and her family responsibilities. Slaughter coins the term *time macho* to indicate a competition over who can work more as an indicator of our value and commitment to our jobs. She describes a "ferociously competitive" budget director in the Reagan administration, who purportedly left the office with his suit coat strewn over his desk chair and the light on to give the impression that he was always at work. A modern-day equivalent might be setting one's text notifications so we can respond at all hours of the day (or night) or answering emails while on vacation. Slaughter rightly asks whether this culture is sustainable, not only for women or working parents, but also for anyone who wants a life outside the office.

There may be a more sinister side at play here as well, as working hard buffers us from the harsher realities of our life outside of work. As Ellen Ruppel Shell describes in *The Job*, being constantly busy signals to others that our free time is scarce, and what is scarce takes on an inherent importance. Having work as a default activity means we don't need to be fully present, making decisions in our lives outside of work. It means never having to confront the question: If we weren't working, what would we do with our free time? Work can provide an escape from the grind of family life, dependent-care responsibilities, house maintenance, and relationships with relatives we would rather avoid. The 2009 film *Up in the Air* presents work as escapism at its most poetic. George Clooney plays a consultant who spends "322 days on the road, which means I had to spend 43 miserable days at home." The film was an adaptation of a novel of the same title by Walter Kirn, who allegedly was inspired by a real-life passenger he met on an airline who maintained a storage unit instead of a home address and was on a first-name basis with the flight crew. That working hard appears virtuous—again, the opposite is unthinkable to most Americans, lazy being the ultimate insult—only provides cover to those who wish to hide behind it. We are just not culturally attuned to the notion of working *less*.

But perhaps we should be encouraging people to work less. There are several very real downsides of all this work. It's not clear that putting in more hours results in better quality work. Neuroscientists report that we don't hit our cognitive stride first thing in the morning (even after coffee), but rather several hours before we typically go to sleep, meaning the average workday likely doesn't capitalize on our peak productivity. Research also reports that five hours is about the maximum length of time that we can maintain focus on a task. And, of course, at best we're talking about attention spans that are increasingly subject to electronic distractions. Research has found that when we switch tasks, we are not able to focus completely on the new task due to what has been termed attention residue, a cognitive residue—like grease on our hands after eating pizza—that clings to the former task. Work may demand that we multitask or task switch, but that doesn't mean we can do it effectively.

In addition to a lack of benefits, overwork also carries real costs. Burnout has been reported in anywhere between 30 and 75 percent of the population, depending on the job (physicians tend to be particularly high on this list). Burnout typically consists of three dimensions: exhaustion, cynicism, and feelings of ineffectiveness.

The book *The End of Burnout* ponders whether statistics about burnout underreport the phenomenon because few measures consider all three dimensions. There is also a clinical condition known as workaholism, an internal urge to work beyond what is reasonably expected, to have persistent thoughts about work, even when not working, and to continue working despite negative impacts on other areas of life, like marriage and health. Workaholism, best thought of as an addiction to work, is distinct from merely working long hours, though workaholics do tend to work more than others. A review of research on workaholism finds that it is related to negative outcomes for the individual worker and their families. Workaholics are not better performers; they are less satisfied with their work and more stressed at work.

Think for a minute about your work. How often do you find yourself spending time you would rather not spend, maybe time when you should technically be away from work, doing work—even just responding to that one email or text? What would realistically happen if you didn't respond so quickly? How much are you contributing to a culture of overwork? Thinking about your ideal work life, are you a workaholic, someone who just happens to be a hard worker, or rather the kind of person who aspires to put in the least effort for the greatest return? Before you take a job or make a change, it can be helpful to find out both who you are and what your future position or profession demands. Will it work with your current lifestyle and the expectations of others who depend upon you? Will the workaholics around you impose pressure upon you to become one of them?

WORKING WITHOUT REGRET

There has been a small but growing and optimistic backlash against the culture of always being at work. Within our networks, people have begun including lines on their email signatures that say things like, "I recognize that my working hours may differ from yours. Please do not feel you need to reply outside your normal working hours." They increasingly make clear the precise days and times they are *not* at work—as in, no Fridays during the summer, no weekdays past 5 p.m. Out-of-office replies celebrate vacations, breaks, or other time away from work—not that employees should have to account for every second they are not at work. Managers, especially, send a strong signal when they use such disclaimers. We personally have counseled others—even each other—to work less, whether or not they have listened to us.

We hope organizations will take heed as well. Workforce mobilization events such as the Great Resignation give workers some added leverage to ask for things like regular and unchanging schedules, flexible workplaces or hours, or reasonable breaks. Organizational policies could, for example, make employee attendance at events outside normal work hours optional, or offer adequate compensation if employees are expected to attend. Rather than be seen as essential or, worst of all, celebrated, face-time culture could be discouraged. Regular conversations should happen between employees and their managers to assess whether the scope of work is appropriate, whether the tasks on which employees spend their time are the most essential. Imagine a manager asking not "Why aren't you here today?" but "Why are you here?"

We should probably disclose at this point that we are writing this book from the luxury of the single best perk of our academic jobs: a sabbatical. Far from an escape from work, these sabbaticals allow us to focus on ambitious projects that we might otherwise be unable to take on. To earn one, we have to put in several years of work at our schools and propose a worthy project. Our sabbaticals have shown us what we can accomplish without the typical disruptions—parts of our work that are necessary and (usually) enjoyable but are writing disruptions nonetheless—like teaching classes and serving on administrative committees.

Sabbaticals have become popular lately among professional firms in their attempt to win the war for talent. Silicon Valley companies offer them, as do our former consulting firms. Importantly, people actually take these sabbaticals, viewing them as a valuable opportunity to get space from their work and pursue other interests. Ideally, rather than needing to choose between taking a break *or* working, regularly spaced sabbaticals allow people to do both. A recent study investigated the impact of sabbaticals on people's careers. For some, this was the break from work needed to make a dramatic career change postsabbatical. For the majority of participants, however, they either returned to their previous jobs with greater confidence and desire for work-life balance or sought to find jobs in their field that better aligned with their goals. If more companies incorporated sabbaticals into their career tracks, it might lessen the desire for people to view work as an all-or-nothing: either retiring early *or* continuing the grind.

We also hope that policymakers will take action to regulate when and how much we work. The Schedules That Work Act would make a tangible difference in the lives of workers, preventing so-called deaths of despair from overwork, like Maria Fernandez's. Regulations could reduce instances of Amazon employees dying on the job—and their surviving coworkers having to work like nothing happened. National governments, like those in Iceland and Denmark, have taken action to reduce working hours. Like the 4DWG, the results of these experiments have been extremely promising. It is, admittedly, hard to imagine such experiments being sanctioned by elected officials in the United States, so committed are we to individual freedoms, including the freedom to work all the time. Perhaps companies like those in the 4DWG pilot program will have to lead the way, making it more socially acceptable to spend more time in leisure than at work.

The first chapter after the introduction to Robert Nozick's book *The Examined Life* is about dying. He performs a thought experiment in which he contemplates the possibility of a formula to determine "how unwilling someone is to die" as a way of determining how much their life is still worth living. When life is worth living, we wish for more time to live it, something that became viscerally clear when Christopher's stepfather died while Christopher was working on this chapter and his mother kept wishing for the impossible gift of more time together. Nozick observes that some deaths are considered to be "untimely," as when the person who died was not ready or their close relations were not—something we encountered often in our research on the 9/11 attacks that took the lives of many younger people as well as the pandemic research that particularly stole the final years of many older people. He suggests that any death is untimely when "much still was possible that went unfulfilled." This leads to a formula for regret as "the ratio of the important things he [or she] has left undone . . . to the important things he [or she] has done" and a formula for life satisfaction as the inverse—what one has done over what one left undone.

In that context, perhaps the death of Suzanne Alele, Michelle Obama's friend, though too early and tragic, was not untimely in so far as she lived a life she would not have to regret. And perhaps Michelle has been comparatively fortuitous to live longer because it has taken her longer to achieve life satisfaction. Their contrasting life passages suggest that, as with the phenomena of counting down toward retirement, we cannot know how much time we have left to influence those ratios. Since the future remains unknown and we are notoriously bad at accurately predicting much of anything about our future selves, we all would do better to *work meaningfully today instead of working for tomorrow.* While walking around asking, "How would I live differently if I knew today were my last day to live?" is not a functional hypothetical, it is no coincidence that when faced with events that threaten our mortality, many of us make different choices. What would it mean to reframe the way you think about when and how much to work so that you are aiming to do work worth doing rather than no work at all?

PART II

Worth

CHAPTER 4

SHOULD YOU WORK FOR LOVE OR MONEY?

*[The CEO's] time was no more valuable than my time,
his life no more important than anyone else's life—
except, by the terms governing the ecosystem, it was.*
                              —Anna Wiener, *Uncanny Valley*

THE PRICE OF WORK

IN "THE NECKLACE," A CLASSIC TALE BY FRENCH
storyteller Guy de Maupassant, Mathilde Loisel laments the "mistake of destiny" that sentences her, a woman of uncommon beauty, to the life of a commoner: "She had no dowry, no expectations, no means of being known, understood, loved, wedded by any rich and distinguished man. . . . She was as unhappy as though she had really fallen from her proper station." After the "little clerk" to whom "she let herself be married" improbably secures an invitation to a palace ball, she panics that she has nothing worthy to wear: "There's

nothing more humiliating than to look poor among other women who are rich." For the occasion, she purchases the most expensive gown she has ever owned and then prevails upon Mme. Forestier, an affluent childhood friend, to lend her "a superb necklace of diamonds" at the sight of which "her heart began to beat with an immoderate desire."

Mme. Loisel's taste of the life of her dreams is temporary. The price of one evening of profligacy becomes a decade of misery when she discovers after the dance, to her horror, that she has lost the necklace. Her determination to return it without disclosing her carelessness awakens in her a "heroism." Her husband cashes in his meager inheritance, and they borrow the rest to replace the necklace. To pay back their debts, they renounce all the accouterments of their middle-class life, experiencing "the horrible existence of the needy." While her husband works evenings, she learns "heavy housework . . . and the odious cares of the kitchen." Thirty-six thousand francs and ten years of labor later, the narrator observes that "Mme. Loisel looked old now." On a walk one day she passes Mme. Forestier, still young, who at first fails to recognize her. Spoiler alert: When Mme. Loisel recounts the ordeal she endured to buy the replacement, the other woman, "strongly moved," grasps her friend's work-worn hands and exclaims, "Oh my poor Mathilde! Why, my necklace was paste. It was worth at most five hundred francs!"

The story is typical of de Maupassant in its keen depiction of class divides and cruel ironies. He presents the circumstances—the want for more money to ascend beyond one's place in the social order, a woman's struggle for self-determination in a patriarchal society, the pricelessness of a necklace to a person of modest means that is essentially junk to a person of wealth, the greediness of moneylenders, the way hard labor ages a person—without judgment, as facts of nature. The pervasiveness of money in the tale is noteworthy. Among other things, it determines the station into which Mme. Loisel is born, the caste into which she marries, her material dependence upon a man, and the social and economic distance between her and her rich friend. Money is the cause of her temporary rise into affluent company and her permanent fall into poverty. The Loisels' desperation for money is the source of moneylenders' opportunity to charge usurious rates that compound the interest and the borrowers' indebtedness. The meager value of an hour of M. Loisel's labor compared to the market value of expensive diamonds imposes unrecoverable costs upon their lives. All for a necklace!

Literary critics classify de Maupassant as a naturalist, regarding human life with curious though omniscient detachment. His characters cannot step out of their immediate circumstances to observe their lives from a safe distance and so lack the wherewithal to wonder whether things could have been otherwise. Beset by the necessity of working for money, Mme. Loisel never has the luxury to ask: How much money will make me happy? Why are diamonds so expensive? Why is some work worth so much less than other work? Why is my own work worthless? Is the price I pay to work worth the value I receive in return? But if you are reading this book, perhaps you are at least lucky enough to be able to ask yourself such questions.

HOW MUCH MONEY WILL MAKE YOU HAPPY?

They say that money can't buy happiness, but it can buy many of the things that seem to make us happy. It bought the dress that Mme. Loisel wore to the palace ball; it could have paid for a diamond necklace so she did not have to borrow one; and more money might have absolved the Loisels of ten years of hard work. Importantly, money could have provided a kind of shortcut to the type of life Mme. Loisel wished to live, as though her life were one constant palace ball. Mme. Loisel was happy while her illusion of wealth lasted: "She danced wildly, with passion, drunk on pleasure, forgetting everything in the triumph of her beauty, in the glory of her success, in a sort of cloud of happiness." Had she been born with more money, Mme. Loisel would have lived a different life entirely than that of a commoner.

"*Esse est percipi* (To be is to be perceived)," wrote Bishop George Berkeley, the eighteenth-century British empiricist. His mantra of philosophical idealism seems to have been appropriated by any number of contemporary pretenders who hope, like Mme. Loisel, that the perception of their wealth will confer worth on their lives—"fake it 'til you make it," in today's parlance. These include Anna Sorokin, the working-class con artist who gained entry into the upper echelons of New York society by introducing herself as wealthy heiress and art dealer Anna Delvey; Billy McFarland, organizer of the Fyre Festival, a luxury Bahamian music gala that was promoted by the rich and famous until it became known as "the greatest party that never happened"; Elizabeth Holmes, the founder and CEO of the purported health technology company Theranos, whose breakthrough invention attracted more than $700 million in venture capital from investors who failed to verify that it actually worked; and the ironically named Sam Bankman-Fried, the cryptocurrency magnate whose multibillion-dollar net worth suffered the largest drop ever recorded on the Bloomberg Billionaires Index when the trading and research firms he founded collapsed into bankruptcy.

To confuse wealth with worth is to conflate pleasure with happiness. When we contend that money can't buy happiness, what we are really saying is that the kind of pleasure that money can buy is not the kind of happiness to which we ought to aspire. Economists characterize needs as things we would not be able to live without and wants as desires that we *can* live without. Western philosophers distinguish between hedonic pleasure, the pursuit of self-interested, fleeting gratification, and eudaimonic well-being, which is more enduring and grounded in the pursuit of virtue and value. It's eudaimonic well-being, rather than hedonic pleasure, that matters most for emotional and physical health. Philosophers in the Confucian tradition similarly counsel that the good life is not the one in which all of our desires are fulfilled but rather one in which our prudential desires—such as having a good education and respectful children—are satisfied. The trick, which is easier said than done, is to determine the difference between wants and needs and pleasures and virtues and to determine how much money we truly need to support our well-being.

Figuring this out is important to us individually but also to society collectively. It is no surprise that living at the very lowest end of the economic spectrum is extremely bad for our health. People living in poverty report lower well-being and higher rates of cancer. On average, people living in wealthier nations tend to experience higher well-being than those living in poorer ones, and increases in national wealth tend to be accompanied by increases in happiness. However, this does not mean that we need to be superrich in order to be superhappy. Rather, according to widely reported and hotly debated research by Nobel Prize–winning psychologist and economist Daniel Kahnemann and his colleague Angus Deaton, the amount of money we need to be happy is somewhere in between extreme poverty and extreme wealth. They claimed in 2010 that emotional well-being does not rise beyond $75,000, though they were asking people to evaluate their well-being retrospectively. A 2021 study does not find such a leveling-off effect when participants rate their well-being as it happens. In fact, for all but an unhappy 20 percent of respondents, happiness grew until about $200,000. Despite these differences, researchers generally agree that the impact of money on happiness diminishes as wealth rises. Further, those who struggle and strive to attain more wealth and money tend to be less happy and experience lower eudaimonic well-being.

According to Valerie Tiberius, a philosopher who draws on the work of contemporary social psychology in her book *The Reflective Life*, the right kind of life is one in which we are "living wisely within our limits." This can be challenging to achieve amid a culture of conspicuous consumption in which visible, material wealth is often an indicator of status. As this relates to the question of knowing how much money we need to be happy, there may not be a definitive, one-size-fits-all amount, though for many of us it will be above the poverty line and may not be more than the line at which happiness tends to level off. Perhaps the answer to the question is not about how much but rather about how we decide. Mme. Loisel's mistake may have been the same mistake that many of us make when we decide how much money we need to support the lifestyle we want— the same mistake that researchers make when they search for an economic threshold for happiness. Instead of choosing the work we need to support the lifestyle we want, what if we looked at it the other way around—that is, by choosing the lifestyle we can afford within the limits imposed by the work we aspire to do?

HOW DO WE PUT A PRICE ON DIAMONDS?

Unfortunately for Mme. Loisel and for most of us, the price of work, happiness, and the capacity of the former to pay for the latter are not completely within our hands. Rather, they are determined by the market forces largely beyond our control that are referred to as the "invisible hand." That famous phrase, which ironically appears by that name a total of only one time in Adam Smith's gigantic economic treatise *An Inquiry into the Nature and Causes of the Wealth of Nations*, refers to how price and production self-regulate when each market actor pursues their rational self-interest.

As a graduate student, Christopher learned about the invisible hand while studying what makes some diamonds more expensive than others. He undertook his research in the Diamond District, a stretch of nondescript storefront shops and warehouse counters on 47th Street in Manhattan that were just the tip of the iceberg of perhaps the world's largest shopping center for diamonds. But he had not come to this neighborhood intending to study economic theory. Rather, while living off temp jobs, irregular teaching gigs at local colleges, and education loans, he went there to contemplate the most expensive purchase he had ever considered: an engagement ring for his future wife's hand.

Much as Smith had explained that "it is not from the benevolence of the butcher, the brewer, or the baker that we expect our dinner, but from their regard to their own interest," the diamond merchants cared little about Christopher's meager means and marital dreams. Rather, they all adhered to a standardized, wholesale price sheet, which appears to be a perfectly rational economic pricing model in which cost escalates with scarcity, a classic supply and demand system regulated by the invisible hand.

Except that the diamond market is far from rational. The purchase of a diamond engagement ring is often a perfectly irrational transaction on the part of a buyer smitten with love. Just a few steps away from the Diamond District, seemingly comparable objects sometimes sold for twice as much in the heavily guarded flagship stores of Tiffany & Co. and Harry Winston. Christopher nearly fell for more than one ring at Tiffany's before he stepped back to wonder whether he loved the ring itself or was just infatuated with the heady experience of being helped by a well-dressed sales associate in a historic showroom that he had seen in an Audrey Hepburn film. Ultimately, the most unromantic part of the ring-buying process was deciding which of two diamonds with nearly identical certificates from the Gemological Institute of America he should buy: the less expensive one from a hole-in-the-wall on 47th Street that came with a suspicious offer to send an empty box to Christopher's grandmother in a state without sales tax, or the high-priced one that was to be wrapped in the store's signature robin's egg blue box, the real cost of which accounted for only the tiniest fraction of the total markup. When buyers act irrationally, sellers take advantage.

Evidently, Smith never had the romantic privilege of buying an engagement ring or selflessly scoring tickets to take his wife to a palace ball. As Katrine Marcal, the author of *Who Cooked Adam Smith's Dinner?*, notes, Smith never married and lived with his mother. But contemporary economists have come to appreciate how emotion and other irrational forces can put the buyer of a diamond at a disadvantage, who aspires to a material representation of happiness priced much higher than what his labor can afford. Diamonds demonstrate that the coincidence between money and worth in the market system is a consequence of rational market norms (the invisible hand) and irrational human behaviors—customs and conventions, along with the behavior of sellers, that influence the preferences of buyers. Our irrational behavior can lead us into the Loisels' lifetime of regret or reaffirm one of the critical claims of Christopher's academic research, that some of the most important things in life are priceless, even though we put price tags on them anyway. Similarly, we should be wary of assuming that how someone's labor is valued in the market is a true or fair indicator of that labor's worth. If the market for physical goods like diamonds can be so easily swayed by emotion, imagine the disparity in the market for human labor.

HOW DO WE PUT A PRICE ON WORK?

Kathleen Gluck knew at age four that she wanted to one day become a partner: the prestige, the recognition of her own hard work, the knowledge that there was a career pinnacle to be reached and she had made it. She recounts now, in her mid-forties, that "the goal was to be my father"—himself a successful partner in a New York City law firm. Her first paid employment came when, at sixteen, she became a law clerk at a firm specializing in immigration law. She applied after seeing an ad on the bulletin board at her high school, but—the world of NYC law firms being what it is—her employers knew her dad. By the end of that year, Kathleen was helping to fill out immigration forms, preparing visa interviews, and going to court, essentially working as a paralegal and compensated accordingly. She reflects, "Whereas some other young women my age were dreaming of things like their wedding, I was thinking more about my admission to the bar." In college, she threw herself into everything from chemical engineering to Gothic architecture because, in the words of the titular *Auntie Mame* from the 1950s film, "Life is a banquet and most of us are simply starving," reveling in the arts and sciences while applying to law school. Yet, three weeks before graduation, she had a realization that would forever alter her life and carefully considered career plans: she did not want to go to law school. She scrambled to find a job instead, capitalizing on her ability and preference to "figure stuff out." She withdrew from law school—a decision that her father brings up to this day—and went to work.

Upon the suggestion of a friend, Kathleen applied for and got a position at Arthur Andersen, one of the then Big Five accounting firms (now Big Four, following Arthur Andersen's collapse in 2002). The service that originally put these firms on the map was financial statement auditing, which involved making sure the world's largest multinational corporations were fairly stating the relative value of their assets, liabilities, and anything that might be prone to manipulation by managers seeking to burnish their stock price. As we would all discover when a series of accounting scandals accompanied a slide into economic recession around the turn of the century, auditing was "a cornerstone of confidence in the world's financial systems." Although the average worker's heart might not flutter at the thought of balance sheets and tax forms, supporting the integrity of these systems gave Kathleen and other accountants who did this kind of work a purpose worth working for. This system, where money is used to represent the value of everything, also has the effect of conflating wealth and worth.

Kathleen's arrival at Arthur Andersen unfortunately coincided with the firm's demise, caught up in the Enron accounting scandal. But her career in accounting had been born. She climbed the corporate ladder at one of Andersen's erstwhile competitors, earning an MBA to advance from senior associate to manager. At one point she left the firm to move to Chicago for her husband's career, only to return, as a director, without any noticeable disruption to her upward progress. Fortunately for Kathleen, her childhood dream of attaining partner status remained possible within this new profession. These firms were structured as partnerships, meaning that the people she worked for not only managed her work but also owned her workplace—shares in the firm that included an equity stake in the furniture, the intellectual capital, and even the staff who put in the largest share of the working hours. Within these organizations the singular metric of success from which everything else flowed was revenue per partner. It determined partners' share values, how earnings were divided among business units, how much money trickled down for staff salaries, and how much "human capital"—as staff were sometimes called in a system in which everything was monetized—was worth.

The Wealth of Nations opens with a brief report on Smith's observations of a pin-making factory that had a surprising amount in common with these firms. He explains that making a pin requires an astonishing eighteen steps that can be carried out much more efficiently on an assembly line, in which "one man draws out the wire, another straights it, a third cuts it, a fourth points it, a fifth grinds it at the top for receiving the head," and so on. He conjectures that an unskilled laborer working alone might be challenged to fashion more than one pin in an entire day, whereas he counts that a factory of ten men—each trained in performing two or three distinct operations—can produce more than forty-eight thousand of them in a day, or nearly five thousand per person per day. Smith's principal concern in *The Wealth of Nations* was to understand the production potential of division of labor capitalism, but along the way, it also explained the division of capital among those who labor and how some people get so much richer than others.

More than two hundred years after Smith's observations of the pin factory, accounting firms made their money deploying what they called a leverage model, which was essentially a microcosm of division of labor capitalism. In these "white collar sweatshops," as Jill Andresky Fraser has called these firms, the capitalists were the partners, whose investment fueled the enterprise, much as the owner of the pin manufacturer in *The Wealth of Nations* puts up the financial capital to build and run the factory. The staff were the laborers, each specializing in some form of technology coding, spreadsheet computation, or data analysis, the same way the manual laborers in the pin factory were each responsible for a different stage of the production process. Of course, the workplace conditions at an accounting firm are vastly improved over a pin factory in the late 1700s, but the economics of the two workplaces were fundamentally the same. Billing rates gradually increased with experience, creating the incentive to leverage the work down to the lowest skill level and involving as little partner supervision as possible.

Staff performance was measured indirectly as utilization, or the percentage of time that was billed to paying clients, meaning time in these firms was literally money. To an accountant, the productivity of a human being is calculated in the same way as that of a machine: how often it is used. Taking a machine offline for repairs is the same as vacation, sick days, and jury duty. The pressure to maintain utilization was such that many staff worked well over three thousand hours each year and were better off excelling at performing the same skill over and over again than at developing a wide range of expertise through professional training. That takes time. The hard work and travel took years from people's lives and was seen as a justification for why people were paid well. But those who grew tired of the relentless pace and expectations sometimes felt shackled to their jobs by "golden handcuffs" after they had grown accustomed to lifestyles that they could not afford if they were to leave. The more they repeated the tasks required to do their jobs, the better they were at them, and the better they were, the more bored they became, and the more bored they became, the more important money was to keep them motivated, and the more they were motivated by money, the more attractive partnership was supposed to be.

Even Adam Smith recognized that the pin-making could not go on forever. Toward the end of *The Wealth of Nations*, he recognizes that repetitive labor destroys us: "The man whose whole life is spent in performing a few simple operations . . . has no occasion to exert his understanding, or to exercise his invention. . . . He naturally loses, therefore, the habit of such exertion, and generally becomes as stupid and ignorant as it is possible for a human creature to become." Unlike poor Mme. Loisel and the pin factory workers, the typical Big Four accountant is lucky to have the ability to leave when it seems as though the price they are paid to work is no longer worth the value they receive in return.

But Kathleen was different, finding fascination with each new accounting equation. By her late thirties, she had made it: she was admitted to the partnership. She felt chosen, noting that "you yourself do not 'make partner,' the partners make you." Kathleen, a polymath who in our interview effortlessly tossed off references to the New Testament, *Harry Potter*, and *Auntie Mame*, loved the camaraderie of being a Big Four partner, which she likens to "finding your Hogwarts house." These were her people, and it feels good to be recognized by your people. At the same time, Kathleen acutely felt the darker side of the leverage model emerge: she had reached her lifelong goal only to find that in many ways the pressure to perform and commensurate opportunity for self-doubt had never been stronger. She was in the club, but felt she had to prove herself constantly to justify remaining there. As Kathleen reflects, "The central myth that drives that culture is that individual partner revenue is a measure of personal value and worth." Reconciling this myth with her own belief in her value would eventually challenge everything she had worked for in her career.

WHY DOES SOME WORK PAY SO MUCH MORE THAN OTHER WORK?

It is enticing to think that, because accounting and consulting are selective professions, requiring a college degree to get the job and often a graduate degree to advance, that they deserve the high salaries they earn. Stay at the firm a couple of decades, and you can live in a huge place in Manhattan, own multiple cars, and summer in the Hamptons.

In most organizations, a chasm exists between the salary of the highest- and lowest-paid worker and that chasm is only growing, a phenomenon *Fast Company* magazine referred to as "greedflation" in a 2022 article. This difference was 399-to-1 in 2021, on average, compared to 59-to-1 in 1989. In 2021, McDonald's CEO earned 2,251 times the average employee salary, and—lest we think workers have to be lower paid for these ratios to be so high—Expedia's CEO reportedly earned 2,897 times the average employee salary of around $100,000. To promote compensation equity, ice-cream maker Ben & Jerry's originally capped CEO Ben Cohen's salary at five times what its lowest-paid employee made, but when Cohen retired, the company could not find a qualified replacement unless it gradually increased that ratio and then sold out, literally and perhaps figuratively, to global conglomerate Unilever. The average top compensation for a CEO in this country is $15.6 million, enormous by any measure. We are perhaps so used to hearing about CEOs, in addition to professional actors, athletes, and the occasional lifestyle influencer, making staggering amounts of money that we are immune to it. But a similar scale of highest-to-lowest salaries exists in these professions too. The average salary in the National Football League was $2.7 million in 2022, but the top quarterbacks earned about seventeen times that. Similarly, big-name actors starring in television series—like Kevin Costner, Helen Mirren, and Mahershala Ali—are in the "Million-Dollar Club," earning salaries of $1 million *per television episode* while the newcomer stars of first-season series make one-tenth that amount—granted, that is still a lot. And this doesn't include the additional millions from advertising and promotional deals, allowing the rich to get richer. Economist Robert Frank calls this a "winner-take-all market," in which a few top performers receive a very large share of the available rewards, leaving a relatively smaller share to be divided among the rest. Their earning is justified not by proportionally better performance but by the sheer fact that they have "made it" to a position of prominence. Are those at the top *worthy* of earning so much more than their peers? And what are the chances any one of us will make it to that rarified position?

We are so accustomed to the notion that jobs are not compensated based on how much they benefit society that we don't question it. In a 2021 study, people in over 450 occupations were asked if they thought their work made the world a better place. The study then looked at salaries, and those who self-identified as having meaningful work earned less; in general, the more meaningful the job, the lower the salary was. Of course, there are outliers, those whose jobs are both beneficial to society and highly compensated, like surgeons and anesthesiologists. But clergy members, the number-one most meaningful job reported in this study, earned an average salary of $46,600. Also on the top ten list for meaningful jobs were kindergarten teachers, rehabilitation counselors, and directors of religious education, none of whom made over $40,000 per year on average.

Why do we often pay the least to jobs that are the most important from a societal viewpoint? On the one hand, some of the work that most benefits society does so because it benefits its neediest members who cannot afford to pay for services. This is why pro bono work at a law firm is typically done for good (or at least for good PR), not for the client's ability to pay, and it's offset by the higher fees paid by wealthier clients. But there may be another piece to it. Studies show that those who choose to work in jobs in the nonprofit sector tend to have more intrinsic motivation for the job, and the more they do the work for its own sake, the less concerned they are with increasing their pay. Jen has seen this in her own research, finding that, across all different types of work, people who believe the work is more meaningful will put in additional effort. They do this regardless of whether they stand to be compensated more.

In a market economy, for better and for worse, the going wage is often the wage at which someone agrees to be paid to do the job. And in markets—whether occupational or geographic—where jobs are few or the only jobs are poorly paid, low wages can persist. Academia has experienced a similar situation with the salaries of adjunct professors, many of whom are forced to take on multiple classes at multiple schools per semester, which in the aggregate may barely amount to a living wage, with no benefits or job security. As one school official callously remarked, "We can offer it [such low wages and no benefits] because people will accept it." Just as it seems shortsighted to believe that market outcomes must exist because they are fair, believing that wages accurately reflect a job's true worth masks the reality lived by those holding jobs who are underpaid relative to their worth. Instead of there being a financial incentive to make a career out of, say, managing financial accounts or selling insurance, what would society look like if the higher paid jobs were those of social workers or home health aides?

WHY IS "WOMEN'S WORK" WORTH LESS?

The Loisels undertake their decade-long ordeal, in which they adjust to a new lifestyle to pay for the lost necklace, together: "They dismissed their maid; they changed their lodgings; they rented a garret under the roof." However, Mme. Loisel does not earn a penny of their debt back. Instead, she does all the housework that they used to pay a maid to do. In accounting terminology, her work appears on the balance sheet in the phantasmic form of the absence of debits rather than the presence of credits. Her husband makes money from a second job. He cashes in his inheritance from his father. He signs the promissory notes. Economically, Mme. Loisel does nothing.

Times and gender roles have changed since "The Necklace" was published in 1884, but not as much as we might suppose. Kathleen Gluck made partner by age thirty-seven, but she was an exception. Her former firm has parity across all levels of its global workforce, 49 percent of whom are women, but only 23 percent of its partners are women, which is typical in the industry. Imagine being a female employee who never interacted with a female partner. It makes it more difficult to imagine yourself ever being in that position. Role modeling inspires women to see themselves as leaders and have confidence in their own performance. Clearly, something is happening at these firms between women's entry and their ascendence in the ranks, disrupted especially by the competing goals of professional advancement and personal fulfillment in the form of starting a family.

Similarly, in our academic profession, the greatest pressure to perform typically occurs around the age at which many people also wish to have young children. The realities of academic pressure to "publish or perish" leads some women to postpone raising a family until after they have received tenure. During the COVID-19 pandemic, women's productivity declined while men's increased, and women with children declined leadership positions at three times the rate of women without children, consequences that could reverberate over time. This is due, in part, to the societal expectations of how each gender should occupy themselves during lockdown. Around the world, when schools and day cares closed, the responsibility to perform a disproportionate share of unpaid childcare fell to women, even though they may have also continued with paid employment. In the United States, female participation in the workforce declined more than male participation, especially among women without a college degree and women of color. Particularly disturbing was that, amid the economic and employment stress of the pandemic, in some countries attitudes about domestic violence—which is more often perpetrated by men against women—became more permissive.

Although women in Mme. Loisel's social world may have had neither economic status nor the wherewithal to hunt and gather outside the home, women today continue to have less economic power than men. The gender pay gap—in the United States in 2020, women were paid on average eighty-four cents for each dollar that men were paid—has been widely reported, but its causes and consequences are complex and persistent. Studies reveal that the wage gap is not caused by differences in men's education, experience, or abilities compared to women's. One factor involves stubborn occupational stereotypes about the gender suitability of work that places more men in higher-paying fields involving science and mathematics. Motherhood, caregiving, and the associated disruptions in career and reduction in work hours interfere with women's continuity in the workforce and their earnings. Discrimination and harassment in the workplace are another driver of women having unequal opportunities, including those for advancement. Of course, not just women but people from groups that have been historically discriminated against also suffer wage penalties, and for those who sit at the intersection of two such identities, such as women of color, the penalties compound.

Maya Patel is one of just two partners at her midsize management consulting firm who is a woman of color. She recognized early on that one of the drivers of wage inequality at her company was a lack of transparency in salary levels. So she created a standardized table of salaries for each rank. Employees who excel can increase their salary only by being promoted. Performance appraisals affect one-time bonuses, but not salary. Outside offers and other attempts to negotiate a higher salary are not entertained. This approach runs counter to the "anything goes" aggressive culture of consulting, and indeed, Maya has had difficulty getting other groups at the firm to adopt the practice. But turnover in the division she oversees has become significantly lower than in other divisions. In part, this matched what she saw happening anyway: junior employees were already coming out of performance reviews and openly sharing information about their salaries. We may think we want to maintain the option to negotiate an ever-higher salary on our own, but knowing we are being treated fairly based on our rank is what really matters. This practice removes the potential for supervisor bias and gender-based pay inequity. It also helps those who either dislike the pressure of having to constantly negotiate their salary or carry the fear that others are getting a better deal. Although ensuring wage equality will most help those who stand to lose from inequality, the benefits accrue to all employees.

In many markets, even the taboo of talking about a safe and affordable way of managing monthly menstruation can be an obstacle to female educational attainment and workforce participation. Philosopher Martha Nussbaum has advocated to change the way we measure national prosperity to include equity in health and education, to counter the obstinate prejudice in some societies that women do not deserve the same entitlements as men to basic health, nourishment, and bodily integrity. Grameen Bank, the microlending pioneer founded by Nobel Prize–winner Muhammad Yunus, emphasized lending to women because they were less likely to have access to capital through conventional banks, they often resorted to entrepreneurship because of barriers to traditional employment, and not incidentally, they were more likely to pay their loans back.

All the evidence suggests that when women work outside the home, their work is of comparable quality to that of men, and yet that work is persistently viewed as worth less. This pay inequity points to one obvious conclusion about worth and money: *the money we make is at best an imperfect representation of the worthiness of our work.* The ten wealthiest people in the world as of this writing are all men, reinforcing a convention by which men outperform women in terms of net worth, which says little to nothing about human worth but everything about the persistence of generational wealth in a patriarchal society. Meanwhile, work inside the home is disproportionately done by women. It's economically worthless but societally invaluable. And economic worthlessness constrains the chance for women, and anyone else whose work is economically devalued in the workplace, to experience the satisfying sense of self-worth that comes from working at a well-paid job. Politicians have proposed the possibility of paying stay-at-home parents but unsurprisingly cannot agree on whether or how much to do so. The challenge of valuing work inside the home points to another conclusion about work and money, that *sometimes the worthiest work is paid the least, if it is paid anything at all.*

IS THE PRICE WE PAY TO WORK WORTH IT?

Kathleen Gluck had spent her whole life imagining how good it would feel to be a partner. But Kathleen's life as a partner was substantially one of cognitive dissonance: the feeling of belonging when achieving impossible highs intermingled with equally desperate lows when she missed revenue targets despite her best efforts. Looking back now, Kathleen realizes she was ready for the intellectual component of partner life but not the emotional one. Her day-to-day life was a constant reminder that, despite always pushing herself to work harder than ever, it never felt like enough. Kathleen reflects, "There were daily reminders of my lack of value."

In firms like hers, employees were conditioned to think of value as having one dimension to which everything else was reducible, namely, money. To "create value" meant to make money. People received "credit" for a job well done, a poor performer was a "liability" to the firm, and the employees were their firms' most important "assets."

These turns of phrase are not exclusive to these firms. They are so thoroughly integrated into the lexicon that their origins in accounting might not be immediately obvious. We live and work in a culture in which "spending time" is such a familiar idiom that we may not reflect on how it represents time as a form of money to be spent. This way of thinking is so ingrained in our culture that, in his thirtieth sonnet, Shakespeare reflects on "time's waste" as something we have "paid for." We consume (or spend) our time working within a system in which anything of value is assigned a financial figure, a system that has changed the whole meaning of value for anyone who lives by its rules.

When we assign a monetary value to something, we are saying something about its standalone value. Worth, on the other hand, is inherently relative, involving the comparison of so much of one thing of value for so much of another. Money is just a medium to facilitate exchange. However, the questions we are asking in this chapter tend to be about exchanging things that have monetary value—such as our work—for other things that have nonmonetary value—such as our lives outside of work. We are always making this calculation when we work for money.

The question about whether the price we pay to work is worth the value we get in return involves looking closely at the word we most often use to describe the money we get for working: *compensation*. The notion that we should be compensated for our work implies not only that work can expose us to work-related hazards but also that *work itself is a form of loss, injury, or suffering* for which we need to be compensated.

That loss most obviously pertains to the loss of our time, preventing us from engaging in other worthy activities that we might otherwise do if not for the compensation we receive for work. Economists call this opportunity cost: missing out on the potential benefits of options we do not choose. By the way, the value of that time often does not account for overtime, commuting time, and emotional labor—the psychological toll exacted by our jobs. The pandemic brought the cost of commuting to the fore, as many workers gave up their daily commute to the workplace and grew to appreciate the flexibility of working from home. When the public health emergency ended, employers attempted to mandate their return to the office, only to be faced with what was termed the Great Resistance: employees refused and some quit rather than go back.

As Elizabeth Anderson argues in *Private Government: How Employers Rule Our Lives (and Why We Don't Talk About It)*, the losses we incur from working also include the loss of freedoms. We are expected to obey an unelected superior and follow standards for what we wear, how we style our hair, and even what we are allowed to say at and even away from work. Our communications are surveilled, we are restricted on when we are allowed to enter and exit the workplace, and sometimes in dangerous jobs involving the operation of heavy machinery, we may be subjected to bodily searches and medical testing. Anderson compares the modern workplace to a communist dictatorship, except the workplace she is describing is capitalist. Today, these same mandates may be monitored covertly and even more invasively with the aid of artificial intelligence and the potential to record every movement and keystroke. The prospect of physical injury at work was perhaps more salient in Smith's pin factory than in modern consulting factories, but the health risks of stress and overwork are the same. So is the suffering workers experience, trapped in a repetitive cycle that they cannot escape.

For Kathleen Gluck, this loss of freedom manifested in what she describes as the "machine," a system of evaluation that tracked seemingly dozens of metrics, "any of which could be used to beat myself up." She began to ask herself whether the price she paid to do this work was worth the value she received in return. To answer this question, she relied upon one of the tools of the trade she excelled in: transfer pricing. Although this concept has sometimes been misused by multinational corporations seeking to reduce profits in high tax countries while simultaneously inflating them in low tax jurisdictions, it has a legitimate application to intrafirm transactions. Kathleen imagined how the logic of transfer pricing could be applied to work and life. What if, she wondered, you thought of the domains of your life as divisions that gave and received things to and from each other? Was the joy and pleasure that Mme. Loisel experienced from one night of pretend wealth worth the price she paid—not only the work and wretchedness she suffered to replace the lost necklace but also, if that had never occurred, the misery of returning to her regular life? Was Kathleen's role in the "machine" of self-doubt and contempt worth the not-insignificant rewards?

Kathleen creatively invoked another accounting tool to help us think about the value of working: net present value (NPV). Sometimes, as we explored in Chapter 3, we are not only accounting for trades between one part of our present lives and another; we are also accounting for the value of present transactions or decisions that have an expectation of a future payoff. The high price we paid in our work lives earlier in our careers arguably inspired the evolution of our professional identities, which enabled us to, among other things, write this book. The nearly endless burden of writing a book that is worthy of others to read is perhaps the greatest challenge so far of our careers. It induces us to wake up earlier than we would like to, to write late into evenings and weekends, and to be pulled constantly out of the flow of life when something related to the book occurs to us, which we have to write down immediately. NPV can be a pragmatic planning tool for deciding if an investment in your present career will pay commensurate dividends later on.

If Mme. Loisel had taken an NPV approach to her life, she might have swallowed her pride and admitted to losing the necklace rather than upending her life to earn it back. She might never have indulged in her evening of pleasure had she weighed the risk of losing the necklace in the first place. In practical terms, NPV recognizes that money—or happiness, meaning, time, and so on—is likely to be worth more to us today than tomorrow, so if we are going to give up something that is of value to us today so that we can have more of it in the future, our decision should account for the amount of time we will have to postpone our gratification while discounting the future value in consideration of risk that tomorrow, as we plan for it, may never arrive.

For Kathleen herself, the NPV calculation revealed what she already knew—she was at a breaking point. She had struggled with clinical depression and obsessive-compulsive disorder in the past, feeling that "my worth as a human was tied to what I produce" pushed her over the edge. A major depressive episode was attended by suicidal thoughts. It was only when pushed to this extreme that Kathleen was able to see with clarity that maintaining this path was not worth it in the long run. She "wasn't willing to die for this job." Kathleen called a meeting with the partner in charge of human resources and was granted a restoring leave, time off to reset. She describes the year 2020, when the world locked down due to the COVID pandemic, as the year she "came back to life." Kathleen shared her mental health struggles and her journey to wellness in a blog so that her coworkers would know and understand what happened in the moment, but also so that others going through something similar would know they are not alone, as she so often had felt. Now, years later, her blog has become a valued resource for similarly burned-out professionals wondering what it means to take a step back. Kathleen says not a week goes by when she doesn't hear from someone in a situation similar to hers—often, she notes, a partner or someone on the partner track. People used to ask her if she thought her career would be over after she left her former firm, but she notes the irony that she has more opportunities now.

THE INTANGIBLE VALUE OF WORK

How might you use transfer pricing and net present value to decide whether the trade-offs in your life and career are worth it? If Christopher had done an NPV calculation before purchasing a diamond ring, he would have had to put a price on joy and marital bliss—things that are, and that ought to be, priceless. Accountants refer to this as intangible value, suggesting that the value of some goods are beyond measure—and yet they have a line item for it on their balance sheets anyway, since accountants need to put a number on everything. The first thing Christopher did after buying the ring was to have it appraised and insured, but the insurable value of the ring was incommensurate with what it was worth emotionally, symbolically, and intangibly to him and his wife. When Christopher finally decided on the best diamond ring he could afford, the seller patronizingly invited him to come back after he'd earned his first million to "trade up" to a bigger one. Such is the inability of those conditioned by a system that monetizes the value of everything to recognize other forms of value that may supersede the value of money. Would she have said yes to his marriage proposal had it not been for the ring? She maintains that she would have. But she still wears the ring every day.

The absurdity of putting a monetary value on marriage is only one example of the irony that reducing the value of anything to purely monetary terms impoverishes our lives. There are innumerable other examples of that which cannot be counted and priced. In Elif Batuman's novel *Either/Or*, the main character observes that the prices of books of poetry do not depend on the number of words. The British street artist Banksy's famous stunt of "self-destructing" his painting immediately after it sold at auction for $1.4 million highlighted the absurdity of putting such a high price on art that has aesthetic value in its own right and will then likely be cloistered in the buyer's home, unlike Banksy's street art, which is available for the masses to enjoy, for free. (The irony is that the piece got caught in the shredder before being fully destroyed, which dramatically increased its value.) In her book *Pricing the Priceless Child*, social scientist Viviana Zelizer suggests that perspectives on the value of children have evolved over time, from "economically useless" to "emotionally priceless," leading to the potentially exploitative introduction of children's life insurance policies and illustrating the limitations on the perspective that the value of anything can be monetized.

Work is another good that has a market price that may be incommensurable with its intangible value. People may choose their work based on which opportunity offers the greatest compensation for the least effort. But that approach ignores all of the other reasons to work, including the opportunity to participate in something bigger than ourselves, our emotional commitment to the relationships we form, and the sense of purpose we feel in making a contribution.

It would be easy to decide on our life's work if its worth was equally reflected in its value in the market. But we don't live in that world, and we should be wary of measuring the intangible value of our self-worth in terms of our tangible monetary net worth. And we should be careful of constraining our potential to do work that matters because it does not pay enough. Just as Adam Smith suggests that the market rewards miserable work with greater pay, the flip side of this is that it often seems that the work that feels the worthiest to us is paid the least. This inequivalence helps to explain why many people with otherwise interesting inner lives and aspirations often feel stuck, as though in a metaphorical or literal sweatshop, pursuing uninspiring careers that have little value to them other than the money that compensates them for their daily misery. Yet, as bleak as things got for Kathleen, she found her footing, with a C-suite technology firm position waiting for her when she left the partnership and has since gone on to be a board adviser and executive coach. She had the wherewithal to choose between worth and money—a privilege that neither Mme. Loisel nor Smith's pin factory workers were fortunate enough to have.

CHAPTER 5

IS IT ENOUGH TO LOVE YOUR WORK?

You don't do it for money, or you're a monkey. You don't think of the bottom line, or you're a monkey. You don't think of it in terms of hourly wage, yearly wage, even lifetime wage, or you're a monkey. In the end you don't even do it for love, although it would be nice to think so. You do it because to not do it is suicide.

—Stephen King, *Skeleton Crew*

ROMANCE AND RACHMANINOFF IN WASHINGTON SQUARE PARK

BY ANY ACCOUNT, IT'S AN INCONGRUOUS SCENE: A Steinway baby grand piano sitting in the middle of Washington Square Park in Greenwich Village. The piano bears a "This Machine Kills Fascists" sticker, a nod to Woody Guthrie's famous folk guitar, but the music coming from it is decidedly classical—Chopin, Debussy, Rachmaninoff. Evidence of how the piano made its way to the heart of the park can be found in the thick mover's blanket, now spread on the ground as an invitation for people to lie down underneath the piano, which they do, two to three abreast, in order to fully experience the music as a "wall of sound." At the center of this experience is Colin Huggins, a conservatory-trained former professional accompanist turned full-time busker. He's been at this gig—this piano, this park—for fifteen years, since he got his first taste of public performance.

The extent to which Huggins is consumed by his art is made abundantly clear by his daily lugging of a 900-pound piano to and from a busy New York City park. He coordinates the piano's care, maintenance, and storage in a city that, rather than facilitating any of those tasks, appears designed to do exactly the opposite. Yet, if the standard for professional success is getting paid to do what you love, his is a success story. Huggins makes a living in an expensive city solely by performing for handouts. He gets to do the work he loves every day, interacting directly with those who experience the music, whether from above or below.

His relationship to his work is characteristic of a calling, which Jen and her coauthor, Shasa Dobrow, formally defined as a "consuming, meaningful passion people experience toward a domain" in a 2021 academic paper. In this case, the domain is one's occupation or job. You may remember calling as one of the three work orientations from Chapter 2, along with job and career. Thinking of work as a calling may bring to mind a sense of being called *by* someone or something, most commonly by a higher power. Indeed, early religious thinkers, mostly from the Protestant Christian tradition, wrote and spoke of callings as being explicitly from God to serve in a particular profession: as a member of the clergy. Later, the scope of callings widened to include any kind of work. Callings stemmed from our God-given talents and abilities, the logic went; therefore, following our callings was fulfilling our duty to God. These abilities might be farming, carpentry, or cooking, which all served God and fulfilled our highest life's purpose. This so-called Protestant work ethic stands in contrast to the ancient Greek view that labor is more likely to distract us from such a purpose rather than fulfill it. In modern times, a calling toward work has become secularized, allowing a person to fulfill a perceived higher purpose, whether it comes from within or outside the self.

There is room for disagreement about what qualifies as a calling. Yet, Huggins's story is prototypical of a romantic relationship between a person and their work, in which, among other things, they may believe their calling is their destiny, something they would rather pursue than anything else, without which their existence would be far less meaningful, a worthy end for which they are willing to overcome obstacles and give up a more traditional life. The most obvious example of this kind of calling may be an artist creating art, but someone may also feel called to build, count, sell, teach, or serve.

Romance aside, by the standards of a society that values professional success, earning a steady income, and advancement in a more conventional hierarchy, Huggins's story involves some humbling realities. This existence, though appealingly quirky, is inherently unstable. His ability to work is dependent on the weather, and other activity in the park may distract his audience—not to mention that busking is technically illegal. In an interview for the *New York Times*, Huggins acknowledges this tension: "Most people follow the money, but I don't do that. I'm a street performer. I follow the emotional experience and the ability to give someone a powerful experience. It means I'm poor, but so what." Note that the last sentence is not a question.

The archetype of the starving artist is enduring and often romantic. It calls to mind images of the musician, painter, or writer so engrossed in their work that they forsake all creature comforts. In an inversion of Maslow's pyramid, only self-actualization matters in the form of creativity, energy, and passion. The essential needs to live—food, drink, shelter—will figure themselves out, whether by patronage, grants, or the occasional foraged pizza. In fact, the bald pursuit of fame and fortune can be at direct odds with authenticity and artistic integrity, as any artist who has been called a sellout can attest. Yet, the reality of such a living can wear on a person, even for those who manage to survive in a notoriously tough city. In times of economic precarity, the margins on which people craft their existence become increasingly thin, and both the likelihood and the consequences of failure loom large.

A CALLING IS CALLING?

There are parallels to Huggins for people in nonartistic occupations. While our work opportunities can be constrained by circumstances beyond our control, the work that we ultimately choose can become integral to our identity. We spend a large amount, if not the majority, of our waking lives at work, magnifying the consequences of a poor choice. What we do at least has the potential to represent who we are.

Work's centrality to our lives can be seen in family surnames that literally identify the patriarch's trade: Baker, Carpenter, Smith, and so on. There is some evidence that this correspondence between name and occupation can go in the other direction as well. For example, researchers have found that those named Denise or Dennis became dentists at a higher rate than others, a phenomenon called nominative determinism, even though there is no proof the name drives the occupational decision. Anecdotally, one of the doctors at the practice where Christopher's dogs get their medical care is named Dr. Ruff, but ironically, she pursued her veterinary degree before taking that as her married name. Jen's kids laughed at the surnames among the dentists in their local pediatric practice, including Needleman (a parent-child duo) and Hertzburg ("hurts"). There is also recent evidence that wearing glasses may predispose people to certain careers, like law and education.

Even if your name or eyewear have nothing to do with your job, you may have felt some level of pressure to choose work that defines you. If so, you are not alone. The glorification of the "do what you love" message has recently reached a fever pitch, including, conspicuously, in the business schools where we both teach.

It is not uncommon at such institutions to find platitudes like, "Do what you love, and you'll never work a day in your life" and "Your passion is what drives you," written on the walls. Many colleges assign a common reading for all entering first-year students to read over the summer and arrive on campus ready to discuss. One of the most popular of late is *Callings: The Purpose and Passion of Work* by David Isay. It contains interviews by StoryCorps, the oral history project Isay founded, that touch upon the theme of finding life's calling in work. The implied promise is that through one's collegiate pursuits, one will find a fulfilling occupation and satisfying life. College undergraduates report that the single most common piece of advice they are given when choosing a major is "follow your passions." This is, to put it mildly, a lot of pressure to put on eighteen-year-olds. It may also unintentionally encourage students to choose passions that meet societal norms and expectations, such as around gender. Researchers found that when college students were advised to follow their passions, women disproportionately chose to stay away from traditionally male-dominated fields, like science and engineering—a gap that closed when they were instructed to choose based on either maximizing their income or helping others. Yet, the recommendation to find your passion remains everywhere, including in the memorable advertising campaign for the popular job search firm Monster.com that alleged, "Your calling is calling."

The reason finding work that you love matters so much, the reasoning goes, is that it will not only lead to spiritual fulfillment, but to material fulfillment as well. Pop culture is replete with such messages, from books with alluring if unsubtle titles, such as *Do What You Love, the Money Will Follow* and *Find Your Calling, Love Your Life*, to famous calling evangelists, like the late Apple founder and cultural icon Steve Jobs. In 2005, Jobs delivered a much-shared and oft-quoted commencement speech at Stanford University, which took the "work as one's great love" metaphor to new heights:

> You've got to find what you love. And that is as true for your work as it is for your lovers. Your work is going to fill a large

part of your life, and the only way to be truly satisfied is to do what you believe is great work. And the only way to do great work is to love what you do. If you haven't found it yet, keep looking. Don't settle. As with all matters of the heart, you'll know when you find it. And, like any great relationship, it just gets better and better as the years roll on. So keep looking until you find it. Don't settle.

Let's briefly pause to unpack this metaphor and its message: the "only" way to be satisfied in a life filled with work is to love that work. If you don't love your work, something is wrong, and the onus is on you to keep looking. The parallel between finding a romantic life partner and finding a career path is made explicit. Like the search for a spouse, we are to date around initially, hopping from job to job to see what fits, but ultimately commit, hard and forever, to "the one." The implication, of course, is that this disembodied "spouse" will be just as committed to us. Of course, there are plenty of examples suggesting this is not the case. Early 2023 was rocked by a series of mass layoffs from big tech companies once thought immune, like Google, which cut 12,000 jobs, Facebook, which cut 10,000, and Twitter, 5,500. Employees at Google described being laid off via email, with no prior warning. Having a passion for work is the inspirational stuff of typical graduation speeches, but on the other hand, we see the potential for a shadier reality among those who follow Jobs's words only to find that, as in the title of Sarah Jaffe's book, *Work Won't Love You Back: How Devotion to Our Jobs Keeps Us Exploited, Exhausted, and Alone.*

All of this seems like a distinctly post-twentieth-century message for a potentially alienated urban elite seeking purpose while trying to make sense of the rapidly changing employment landscape. Starting right around 1980, phrases like "find your calling," "find your passion," and "do what you love" start to appear more often in books. And the years since 2005—perhaps not incidentally the year of Jobs's speech at Stanford—have been peak calling.

In the early 1970s, the notion that work could be more than a paycheck was starting to take hold, as the move from farm to factory to office would soon be met with the technology boom and knowledge work revolution. Studs Terkel's book *Working* contains a chapter entitled "In Search of a Calling." In this chapter, Nora Watson, a corporate writer who would rather do creative writing than "writing to order," says: "I think most of us are looking for a calling, not a job. Most of us, like the assembly line worker, have jobs that are too small for our spirit. Jobs are not big enough for people." On the surface, and compared to the alternative, the idea that work would be a source of personal fulfillment, identity, and meaningfulness is alluring. Who among us wants a job that is spirit killing, soul crushing, and "small," which suggests that, by association, we are small as well?

Yet, today, the pressure to find one's calling can be enormous, suffocating those who believe they have identified a calling and making those who haven't feel that they have failed at a fundamental level. We counsel students every year who aren't sure what they want to do for a living. What does it mean when they aren't sure what they love to do? Do they even know themselves? A question of career choice becomes existential rather than simply vocational, and the indictment against those who don't follow their hearts becomes not just personal but societal as well.

It is perhaps no surprise then that sharp critiques of the culture of calling have accompanied its rise. In books with titles like Miya Tokumitsu's *Do What You Love and Other Lies About Success and Happiness* and Erin Cech's *The Trouble with Passion: How Searching for Fulfillment at Work Fosters Inequality*, the authors lay convincing cases for the personal and societal ills that accompany the message to make what we love doing into our paid vocations. These arguments not only question whether "do what you love" is sound advice for any one person, but they equate the cultural obsession with calling as a driver of the ills of capitalism, including overwork, burnout, and economic inequality. Essentially, our love for our work can be co-opted, leaving workers exploited while those in power continue to gain. This leaves us at a confusing point in a society obsessed with doing work we love. All else equal, we would prefer work that is meaningful to that which is meaningless, but viewing calling as the only way to do worthy work raises problems of its own.

FROM ROMANCE TO REALITY

According to a 2006 study by the National Association of Music Merchants, more than half of American households have someone who plays an instrument. Many of those families have more than one would-be musician, and those who do not play an instrument wish they did. There are tens of millions of people bowing, blowing, pounding on, and air-playing instruments with pipe dreams of someday excelling professionally.

Among the elites, the most prized positions will be in a classical orchestra, of which there are slightly over one thousand in the United States. Only the largest ones approach one hundred performers, meaning the maximum number of available seats may be in the low six figures for an aspirant pool numbering in the high eight figures. In other words, a very rough estimate is that one in perhaps every several hundred hopeful instrumentalists has a chance to perform in a professional orchestra. Even those graduating from top conservatories are not guaranteed an in.

Merely a fraction of those orchestras have budgets enabling them to pay their performers anything close to a living wage, reducing the chances of making a living as an orchestral musician to closer to one in many thousands at best. Factor in that only a few chairs are reserved for any one orchestral instrument, and the competition among players in the refined world of classical music is ironically cutthroat. Moreover, only a handful of those orchestras are recognized as world-class. So, it may not be an exaggeration to say that the possibility of a classically trained musician securing a position in a storied symphony orchestra, like the New York Philharmonic or the Cleveland Orchestra, approaches one in a million.

Given these low prospects for success, we are all the more in awe of our friend and academic collaborator Shoshana "Shasa" Dobrow, who early in her academic career as a professor of organizational behavior used to moonlight as a bassoonist in one of the near-elite professional orchestras. Shasa earned her doctorate at Harvard Business School and is now a professor at the London School of Economics, two of the most prestigious educational institutions in the world, meaning she has found success against steep odds not only in the world of music but also in the world of academia, where it is typical for an open position for a single tenure-track professorship to garner hundreds of applications. Fittingly, Shasa's research has for years followed musicians, many of whom persist in pursuit of their callings, often in the face of mounting evidence that their professional aspirations are likely to go unrealized.

Why do they work so hard and sacrifice so much for such a small chance at success? There are numerous romantic reasons why orchestral musicians continue to chase their callings. The body of research on callings across a variety of jobs, occupations, and employers suggests that there are many good reasons to follow a calling: when people view their work as a strong calling, they tend to be more satisfied and engaged at work, more committed to their organizations and occupations, and happier in their lives. They miss fewer days of work, put in more hours at work, and generally go above and beyond in their efforts to perform their jobs. One study found that people in general believe that those with stronger callings should be paid more than their weaker callings counterparts, mostly because they are "the good employees"—some might even say the dream employees. If we ended the story there, we would feel content in Steve Jobs's admonitions to not settle, find that calling, and hold on tight.

However, for all the laurels heaped on those with strong callings, studies that are often embedded in a specific occupation find that callings are a double-edged sword. According to a study of zookeepers, those with strong callings to the work sacrificed just about everything to care for their animals, including their own personal health and well-being. They were more likely to put in unpaid overtime work, ultimately earning lower incomes than their lower-calling peers. Strongly called zookeepers were also more critical of their organization and more likely to do what they personally, rather than their employers, think is best in caring for animals—findings echoed in a study of people working in an animal shelter. The so-called mission of the work, in this case caring for animals, ends up mattering more to these employees than almost all other practical concerns. It doesn't end there: studies show that callings take a toll on personal and work relationships, stress levels, and even sleep. A study of ministers found that those with the strongest callings worked the longest hours, were the least able to psychologically detach from their work at night, and suffered both lower-quality sleep in the evenings and lower energy the following mornings. It is not a stretch to wonder, as some have, whether people with strong callings are targets for exploitation by employers who know that these employees will go to any lengths to perform their work well, even at their own personal expense. To that end, one study found that people felt justified paying others less for work that was their passion, because their passion compensated for the pay.

Going back to the musicians who experience strong callings toward music, their relationship to their work has been described as a kind of career "tunnel vision" in which they feel they have to pursue their callings at any cost. This becomes a literal pursuit at any cost, given that orchestra musicians are not very highly paid. They may also hold on to the irrational hope of becoming one of the few who not only rises to first chair but also breaks through to a successful solo career, which only a fraction of performers realize. One study found that strongly called musicians rated their own virtuosity higher than did objective experts rating an audition (which tends to be a blind rating where musicians perform behind a curtain). Strong callings in musicians were also accompanied by a single-mindedness in which they tacitly ignored or even deliberately rejected evidence contravening their wishes. Musicians with strong callings toward music were also more likely to reject the advice of a trusted mentor or music teacher telling them not to pursue music professionally. All of this means that a disproportionate number of people who feel called to a profession will cling to an inflated self-appraisal of their own talent and to the hope that they are only one break from making it big, yielding a lifetime of unfulfilled expectations. Meanwhile, they live in a society that romanticizes not only artists but even starving artists, while not fully understanding or experiencing firsthand what that all-consuming calling entails.

THE MAN WHO TRADED HIS FAMILY FOR A PAINTBRUSH

Perhaps the quintessential example of the romance of calling is the apocryphal legend of Paul Gauguin, the French postimpressionist artist whose work hangs on the walls of the world's most prestigious art museums. His story also paints him as an awful human being, demonstrating with dramatic effect the extreme reality of the trade-offs he was willing to make to pursue that calling.

Gauguin is reputed to have abandoned his wife and five children and set sail for the South Seas to pursue his passion to paint. There, he fathered still more children with underage girls, whom he also used as subjects for his paintings. He made little money as an artist while he was alive, falling short of his promises to send money back to the family he left. Ironically, well after his death, his painting *Nafea Faa Ipoipo* was reported to have set, in 2015, a record for the most expensive canvas ever sold. If only there had been a futures market for Gauguin's paintings, he might have compensated his family for the misery he inflicted upon them. Does his achievement as a painter excuse his self-indulgence?

Before he was a painter, Gauguin provided for his family in a more workaday manner as a reluctant stock trader. He toiled away in obscurity in a conventional job to maintain a respectable life, including a wife he resented who cared for their children. Every morning, he donned the uniform of the office worker that marked him as a member of Parisian, middle-class economic standing, and in the evening, he came home in restless frustration. For his position in the family in a patriarchal society—breadwinner, father, provider—he endured the same daily boredom experienced by many workers who can contemplate no way out of their routine dependence on an unfulfilling job.

Gauguin's escape from his daily suffering, which to those around him must have seemed surprising, shocking, and sudden, was actually years in the making. He had, for a long time, envisioned a future in art, painting and collecting artwork on the side. Early in his career, his two occupations were satisfyingly complementary. The considerable earnings from his day job supported not only his collecting habit, but also earned him entry with art dealers who sold a few of the pieces he painted on weekends. Perhaps he hoped someday that he could make a viable career in the art world without having to leave everything else behind. After the stock market crashed, his primary source of income contracted and the dealerships closed. The economic conditions worsening at the same time his young family was growing combined to create an all-too-familiar predicament: both money and time became scarce.

For years, Gauguin equivocated about his future, like many people in early-to-mid career, trying to figure out how to balance work and life. He moved his family to a smaller city, where it would be less expensive to live, but his plans there did not pan out. They moved again, depending upon the help of family and friends, but he could not find steady employment. He returned to Paris alone, intending to reunite with his family once he found his financial footing once again. He lived in relative poverty while subsisting on a series of menial jobs, such as posting advertisements for local businesses on kiosks and walls around the city, unable to set aside thoughts of how far and fast he had fallen. Financially, Gauguin was more constrained than he had ever been. Yet, the loss of his job unleashed him spiritually to channel all of his energies toward his passion to paint. Thus began his move toward a permanent and extreme separation from the family he had supported and the life that he had loathed.

First, Gauguin sailed westward, to the Caribbean, where he developed his obsession with subjects and landscapes that must have seemed exotic to his urban sensibility. His subsequent visit to the south of France, provoking an ongoing competition and correspondence with his fellow misanthrope, Vincent Van Gogh (another legend who was driven crazy by the frustration of being under-appreciated and in whose demise Gauguin played a not insubstantial role), suggests that Gauguin was always a day late and a franc short of making it big before he could send money back home, much less return and resume his responsibilities as a head of household. He later made a break for Tahiti, where he embraced the lifestyle of a self-proclaimed "savage," a self-contradictory sign of his low regard for an alien civilization in which he sought total immersion. He caroused and he painted, wild eyed and unkempt. News from abroad that his favorite child had died unsettled but did not deter him from his destiny. To give Gauguin a probably unwarranted benefit of the doubt, he may not have planned to make a permanent break from his past life, but that is how things turned out. He never returned permanently to his former life or his family, painting in relative obscurity and far from home until his dying day.

Perhaps the story of Gauguin, as it is told, is so compelling because it seems to be such an extraordinary example of sacrifice—of his family, his character, and his security—one that ordinary people might only dream of and discard as impractical and selfish. His colorful life has been dramatized in at least two novels: W. Somerset Maugham's *The Moon and Sixpence* and Mario Vargas Llosa's *The Way to Paradise*. The former compares his compulsion to paint to that of a man who has fallen into the water and needs to swim: "He's got to get out or else he'll drown"—and Gauguin was drowning in his dull life as a trader and family man. Be that as it may, the latter concludes that Gauguin, by putting his need to paint ahead of the material needs of his children, was a great artist who nonetheless was "an enemy of God and everything that is decent in this world." Both novels paint a picture of a "genius" and miscreant who could not have it both ways in his fateful choice between his calling as an artist and his responsibilities as a husband, father, and human being.

Moral philosophers whose imaginations also have been captured by the legend of Gauguin have differed on whether his success as a professional was worth his failure as a person. Most of us are inclined to agree that being a good person is integral to human perfectibility, no matter how good a painter you may be. Yet one ongoing debate concerns whether we ought to accept that there is such a thing as "admirable immorality"—laudable achievements that could not have been realized without the unseemly actions that rendered them possible, a question that might come to mind as yet another of your favorite works of art, music, or film are revealed to have been created by monstrous people. In a related line of inquiry, philosopher Bernard Williams considers that the only possible justification for Gauguin's awfulness as a person could be his awesomeness as a painter, but if he had not succeeded as a painter, failure would "unjustify" his project. Williams's line of argument suggests that Gaugin's abandonment of his family might have been worth it because he became a master of modernist art, but his work would not have been worth it if his sailboat had encountered a sudden squall on the journey to Tahiti that swallowed him up, along with all his potential as a painter. In other words, Williams concludes, most importantly, that Gauguin was lucky to have an artistic legacy at all.

Chances are, most of us who choose our personal passions over our obligations to others will not be so lucky—or talented—to see our legacy justified by artistic immortality. Yet, the stakes for us in the battle between meaning and money may seem no less significant than they were for Gauguin, only perhaps less extreme. It just happened that he bet the whole house, literally and figuratively, on his wanderlust. The inconclusive moral of his story is that he probably should have lost his bet, and he and others lost a lot even though, arguably, against all probability, he won.

Gauguin's trade-offs are the same as ours; only his legendary insouciance about his responsibility to be a decent human being might be different. What we do, the status we seek, and why we do it are all signifiers of who we are, what we value, and which values we are willing to trade for others. We work more than we wish we had to while worrying that we may not be able to find enough work to pay for our material needs. We impatiently wait for a better opportunity, but when it arrives, our sights are already set on the next one. We wish for work that is consistent with our moral values, while making do with the reality and compromises that work sometimes requires. We yearn for work we love, yet we wonder whether we will still love it if it becomes our work. We spend the largest share of our waking hours working to live, leaving us to contemplate whether we are merely living to work. We sacrifice our loved ones and our lives for the sake of work, yet work is the sacrifice we make so that we can take care of them. We never stop to ask: If our work were worth living for, would we want to work even more? And so it goes, until and unless we make a break for a distant beach and do not look back.

DO YOU HAVE—OR WANT—A CALLING?

At this point, you might reasonably wonder whether you have a calling. Do you even *want* a calling? A 2021 study looked at people in a variety of occupations—pastors, physicians, international aid workers, and teachers—who felt their current work was their calling to find out how they got there. It found that people tend to arrive at their callings through one of two paths.

One path, the *discerners*, sought their one true calling, the Jobsian ideal marital partner. Some knew their callings from early childhood and sought to enact these callings. Others didn't find their callings right away but knew what that they were doing professionally wasn't it and were certain that "it" was out there, and then journeyed to find it. Sometimes this clarity came from within, as in a former doctor who fasted to find his calling, in this case to become a pastor. Other times, the clarity came from a trusted adviser, as in the case of a physician whose high school teacher told him, "Don't be a high school teacher, focus on the doctor thing."

Those on the other path were the *explorers*, whose stories were marked much more by luck, happenstance, and a sense that they had stumbled into their callings, rather than looking specifically for them. Often people in this category described being personally unfulfilled in their work and wanting a change, such as an international aid worker who said, "'I did feel a calling to figure out how to make my work life, family life, and spiritual life come together because they ended up in three different camps. You know, how do you draw those circles so that they overlap more? I didn't have an answer." He described not even knowing that the world of international aid work in non-governmental organizations (NGOs) existed until he did volunteer work abroad; this work would eventually become his calling. Others described events that "changed everything" in terms of identifying their callings: the job that fell in their lap, the conversation that opened a door, or other chance encounters and coincidences, sometimes stemming from undesirable events, such as injury, illness, or loss, that clarified everything. While people who are smugly working in their callings seem to have figured it all out, the reality of how their stories played out, even in retrospect, is often quite messy.

Of course, we need to acknowledge here that some people have far rockier paths to a calling. Some people may search for a calling unsuccessfully, not being able to determine what they feel called to do. Jen has examined such people across a number of research studies, concluding that searching for a calling is a psychologically precarious state, marked by stress and discomfort. Another way the pressures of "calling culture" might manifest is making people feel like they *should* have a calling. If the call does not come easily, however, we see people struggle with what should be compared to what is. As the explorer paths reveal, sometimes callings come when we least expect them, even when we are not outwardly searching at all, suggesting that an openness to work being more meaningful and/or personally satisfying might yield better results than a desperate search.

Another reality of any given labor market is that people might know what they feel called toward but are unable to find work that answers the call. Much like unrequited love, the experience of what organizational psychologist Justin Berg and colleagues termed "unanswered occupational callings" is psychologically undesirable, marked by stress, regret, and feelings of failure. In fact, research has found that people with unanswered callings are worse off than if they don't have a calling at all. Jen and Shasa (and later with coauthor Hannah Weisman) studied musicians with strong callings who were unable to work as professional musicians—a career outcome that is of course statistically most likely. They found that these would-be musicians experienced lower overall psychological well-being and lower income compared to both those who were working in music or those with weak callings working in any other occupation. This same study also looked at those who remained active in music by doing amateur music work without pay, such as those who play in garage bands for fun. The prediction was that, by virtue of still being able to perform music, even if not as their primary occupation or source of income, these amateur musicians would be better off than those who didn't remain engaged at all. Surprisingly, this wasn't the case; amateurs experienced the same low levels of well-being and income as those who weren't active in music at all. This finding led Jen, Shasa, and Hannah to wonder whether exposure to music reminds these amateur musicians very acutely of what might have been, highlighting even more the discrepancy between their desired occupation and their actual one. It raises a very real question of what the consequences are, both personal and societal, of unanswered callings in highly selective labor markets. It also reveals that callings can be closer to a curse for those who are not lucky enough to find work in them and those who do not have the means to pursue them.

DO CALLING STORIES HAVE HAPPY ENDINGS?

In the classic novel that he completed on his deathbed, *In Search of Lost Time*, Marcel Proust contends that an artist's determination and willingness to sacrifice is necessary to create enduring art. Proust legendarily spent most of the last fifteen years of his life shut in a cold room writing feverishly by night and sleeping by day. He could have been foreshadowing his own end when he wrote of the narrator's hero, an author named Bergotte: "His books . . . kept vigil like angels with outspread wings and seemed, for him who was no more, the symbol of his resurrection." Proust's "indifference to the idea of death" once he began working on his novel is characteristic of artists, among others, who have seen their work as worth dying for. However, whether those callings end happily or unhappily is complicated. Proust essentially forsook his life while he was alive so that he would live on after his death.

Another writer, Joan Didion, recalls in her memoir, *The Year of Magical Thinking*, the night her husband, John Gregory Dunne, also a writer, died at the dinner table. She describes how he always carried note cards with him to avoid losing an idea that occurred to him in the course of ordinary life, his way of answering his calling while not missing out entirely on daily pleasures. Didion herself doubled down on writing after he passed away to retain her memories of him and of their daughter, Quintana, who lost her life in the same year. She would envision conversations with him that she was never able to have in reality, explaining, "I am a writer. Imagining what someone would say or do comes to me as naturally as breathing." Like other artists' stories that reinforce the ineluctable pull of calling, these ones depict calling as a destiny. Yet, they are inconclusive about whether following one's calling is destined to end happy or unhappily.

Callings can lead to ambiguous endings in more conventional professions, too. In her farewell letter to her employees, retiring PepsiCo chairman and CEO Indra Nooyi shared both lessons and regrets. For one of the most powerful women in the world, her work was "the honor of a lifetime," though she had relatively little power in her own household to raise her two daughters, delegating many responsibilities to other family members and professional childcare workers. She wrote, "I've been blessed with an amazing career, but if I'm being honest, there have been moments I wish I'd spent more time with my children and family."

The celebrated passion of Steve Jobs for his calling, which in the speech quoted previously he compared to a marriage that "gets better and better as the years roll on," was reputed also to be the cause of many broken relationships. He was forced out of Apple once because of creative and strategic differences with other leaders. Even after he returned in an acquisition, employees both feared and admired his passion. His personal life was messy—for example, he had a child for whom he did not initially acknowledge paternity and whose memoir recounts their troubled relationship—until he met and married Laurene Powell, a relationship that lasted as the years rolled on. His fervent conviction that his own gut instincts were right, along with his unbreakable focus on his work, were even believed by some of his close confidantes to have caused his avoidable premature death when he opted for alternative treatments rather than the surgery prescribed for his treatable form of pancreatic cancer.

The stakes of calling can be as high as life or death, but more often they entail trading one form of life for another—living to work or working to live. Some of the most romantic examples of calling are those of the rich and famous, but the reality of callings is that they are pursued or forsaken by ordinary people every day. They may involve mature artists and executives at the peak of their talents and earning power, but they might also pertain to uncelebrated laborers choosing between what is best for themselves, their families, and society.

The year 2021 witnessed the Great Resignation, during which both the number of people quitting their jobs as well as the number of job openings in a given month hit record highs in the United States—reaching the tens of millions. Justin Jones was part of that wave, even though early in their career as a dancer, they had experienced archetypal signs of having a calling. Back then, when they had auditioned for a noted choreographer, they "felt like . . . what I wanted to do with my life was dance in his work." They joined the company even though it paid poorly and was gig to gig, proof that even those who are good enough to beat the odds to become professional dancers in New York City can barely make ends meet. Three years into their time with this company, Justin was shocked when they were asked to leave. They recall, "I dreamt about being in [the company's] work after being let go," as a way of processing that early professional disappointment, which did not deter them from continuing to dance professionally for fifteen more years.

During those years, Justin also moved around with their wife, getting teaching positions to "support my life as an artist." After they had children, they were able to send the children tuition-free to the preschool where Justin taught by day, while they choreographed, composed music, and taught dance on evenings and weekends. "I remember teaching [dance classes] while wearing my children in a carrier." They lived with the mind-set that they were a performer who taught, not a teacher who performed. Although callings are characteristically all-consuming, Justin observes that being a dancer is uniquely so: "When you're a dancer, you are like the process. Your body, yourself is the process. You are the material. You are the product, and then it can be really tricky if you move on from that and there comes a moment when you have to really reimagine yourself."

The pandemic was that moment when Justin reimagined everything. They got divorced. "It just felt like in a time of flipping over a bunch of tables in my personal life it just felt like it was time for me to flip over a couple more tables in my professional life." They departed the dance company where they had been the artistic director and decided to resign from the preschool as well. Newly single, they were consumed with parental responsibilities, and they had also been spending more time composing music for other artists' work, earning a positive mention in the *New York Times*. They had saved enough money to take a few months off to "just feel like a human being for a while" and consider "if I'm not a dancer, what am I?" Leaving that identity behind is only one step toward figuring out what is next. For now, they are back to a temporary position as a full-time early childhood educator, and "when the time comes I'll figure out how to make the rest of the ends meet."

One more word about pursuing callings: it may seem that the question of whether to pursue a calling or not is already a privileged one. Most people are trying so hard just to make ends meet, working more than one job not because they want to, but because they have to. It's not wrong to say that the ability to choose what one does for work is a luxury not afforded to everyone. Certainly people who come from privileged backgrounds, have higher levels of education, and access to higher-status personal networks will have different opportunities available for work than those who do not. However, to presuppose that only these people are able to pursue work as a calling or come to feel that their work is meaningful is inaccurate. As we mentioned in Chapter 2, each work orientation—job, career, calling—can be found across types of work, job titles, and occupations. Some occupations are more prototypical of a calling than others—for example, those that clearly provide a social good or a venue for self-expression. Shasa and Jen's research has shown that musicians and artists on average report stronger callings than both business students and managers. However, these averages don't tell the whole story in that there are musicians with very weak callings and managers with very strong callings.

A particularly vivid example of finding calling in unexpected places comes from a seminal study on people who do custodial work in hospitals. The setting is a dismal one, even prepandemic, with cleaners doing literal "dirty work" in rooms people would rather not find themselves. Yet, the study shows the incredible and somewhat inspiring resilience some cleaners demonstrated in wanting to elevate the work they do. The study separates the passive cleaners, who simply tidied one room and then the next, with little interaction with either patients or other hospital staff, from the proactive ones, who seemed unconstrained by their job titles and assigned duties and simply tried to do the best job possible to help patients. The authors coined the term *job crafting* to explore the process by which cleaners made the job they wanted from the job they had.

For example, rather than seeing themselves as cleaning staff who happened to work at a hospital versus hotel or office, these cleaners viewed their role as integral to the patient care team of doctors and nurses. They saw the work of cleaning as making things better for patients and potentially helping to speed their recovery. This study, which has generated much subsequent research on job crafting, is meant to be inspiring for workers, as it suggests that we can make any job more meaningful and need not be overly constrained by a job title or task list. However, on the flip side, its message can be interpreted that if we feel our jobs are meaningless, perhaps we are not trying hard enough.

WHERE DO WE COME FROM? WHAT ARE WE? WHERE ARE WE GOING?

Part of our attraction to calling is that it says something about who we are, our personal identity, which is often different from what we do for a living, our professional identity. Those who have realized their personal callings in professional life hold a kind of romantic fascination because they have supposedly "figured it out." Their callings, however, often come at a cost. Studying others' stories of work and calling can help us figure out our own stories but also the consequences they might entail.

Paul Gauguin's masterwork is a giant canvas depicting a Tahitian paradise on which he inscribed, in the upper-left corner, its title, which asks three simple but profound questions: *D'où venons-nous? Que sommes-nous? Où allons-nous?* (Where do we come from? What are we? Where are we going?). Not coincidentally, those three questions also encourage us to consider our own past, present, and future.

The background of the painting depicts a lush landscape of blue sky and ocean and green forests, putting the human scene in the foreground in sharp relief. A placard on the wall of the Boston Museum of Fine Arts, where the painting now hangs, says that Gauguin "intended the composition to be 'read' from right to left, beginning with a sleeping infant, reaching its climax in a standing youth at center, and ending with the crouched figure of a woman nearing death." That plan says clearly what Gauguin believed about *where we come from* and *where we are going*—the values we inherit and the ideals to which we aspire. This book is written for the figure in the center of the painting, who is neither a child nor the woman falling toward death but rather the person in the middle of life, reaching upward—whether toward the heavens or to pick a piece of fruit is not entirely clear. *What are they? What are we?* That figure represents the longest stage of most people's lives, during which we spend a large share of our time working and have a chance to do work worth doing that makes life worth living.

The answers to Gauguin's three questions are no more readily available than the answer to the question of whether the production of his masterpieces was worth the misery he inflicted upon others. However, that shouldn't stop us from asking them of ourselves. Whether we are contemplating our future careers, considering changes to our present careers, or harboring doubts about our past careers, we owe it to ourselves—and to the others who have depended, currently depend, or will depend on us—to ask where we are going, where we ought to go, and what trades are worth making in the present to make the future possible. When we are reflecting upon the working lives we have had, with the wisdom of hindsight, we should reconsider where we came from and what we were—whether the trade-offs that work entailed were worth it and whether we would do them all over again.

If Gauguin had asked us for our advice about his occupation when he was contemplating trading his life and work as a stock trader for his calling as a painter, we might have pointed out that the personal decision to pursue one's own passion may not be as personal as it might seem. Perhaps, in the interest of his family, he could have traded by day and painted by night at least a little bit longer, while figuring out the details. Eventually, he would have had to consider his options and make a decision. Holding down a job to finance a calling is a likely path to overwork and eventual burnout.

Pursuing a calling often involves some form of self-sacrifice, but the benefits need to outweigh the costs, to self and others. A calling that is all-consuming had better be worth giving up everything for, and we cannot imagine a world in which a painting is worth more than the people in one's life. We would have cautioned him to be conservative about his expectations for his painting prospects, conscious of the human tendency to be overconfident in our chances of success and to discount the effect of factors beyond our control—such as market conditions and the direction of the prevailing winds as we sail toward our destination. He was hell-bent on becoming a painter rather than a trader, but ironically he proved himself to be the kind of trader who risked it all at once rather than building a balanced personal and professional portfolio over time.

Had he accepted our advice, perhaps the world would be that much poorer for being deprived of a master painter. That loss might constitute a price society would be willing to pay for the price that those around him unwittingly paid. However, we doubt he—or anyone in the throes of passion—would have taken any advice. Ironically, Gauguin's nonartistic legacy for us was to prompt us to ask ourselves his questions, even though he arguably did an inadequate job of answering them himself.

For almost two decades, Christopher has asked three simple questions of students—from young undergraduates to seasoned executives—to help them figure out what their work story will be. The first is: One year out of this program, what do you think your job will be? This question addresses the urgent present: their motivation for their schooling leading to a particular position that will enable them to pay their bills, including the student loans they may have taken out to study. It elicits practical answers, much as Gauguin became a trader to support his family, Indra Nooyi took a position at PepsiCo because it was only a fifteen-minute commute from her baby at home and her daughter's grade school, and Steve Jobs used his technical skills to find work designing video games after he dropped out of college. Our students typically aim for a conventional position that utilizes their experience and education.

Among those already employed in a corporation, the answer to the question would be the next step up the ladder from their present position.

The next question is about the past, namely, the values students have inherited: What kind of job contributes the most to general well-being? The phrasing of this question is intentionally broad and impartial. Whereas the "one year out" question prompts consideration of particular positions—associate in a public accounting firm, consumer insights executive for a food company, for example—that fit an individual's skill set, the "general well-being" question elicits answers in the form of occupational categories, such as teaching, medicine, or farming, that may have little to do with the career path of the respondent. This question is meant to elicit answers motivated by the social contribution that work can make, often irrespective of whether the work is financially lucrative, like the hospital cleaners who cited their desire to help the patients they served as a motivation for working.

The third question pertains to the future and is not necessarily about work at all: Practicality aside, if you could be doing anything ten years from now, what would it be? Some students, young and old, want to be retired from work within that time period. When pushed for what they will be doing with their ample free time, they often imagine themselves traveling or playing golf. More often, students unwittingly announce unfulfilled callings that they may believe, right or not, are too late to realize (be a rock star like Bowie) or too impractical to attempt (be a writer like Didion). Those who plan to continue working in their field, even if they do not need to, typically envision themselves freed from the shackles of organizational hierarchy: they plan to be a CEO like Nooyi, on top of that hierarchy, or an entrepreneur like Jobs, outside of that hierarchy.

Students' initial reaction to this exercise is often to remark how different their collective answers are to the three questions. Some characterize the first set of answers as what they *expect to do*, the second as what they *ought to do*, and the third as what they *wish to do*—prompting them to wonder why they are studying so hard and paying so much to earn the job they expect when it is neither what they ought nor wish to do. Although this realization once led one of Christopher's students to announce that she was leaving business for medicine—only to change her mind a few months later—it is not necessarily the goal of the activity to convince students to change course. One point is, rather, to emphasize how improbable it can be to have it all—a "market fit" between one's skills and employers' needs, service to others, and self-realization—in one position. Another point is to promote balanced awareness between the reality of the present and the romance of the past and future and to take a longer view, seeing one's working life as a portfolio of positions that enable one, over time, to "have it all." A final point is to encourage them to consider how to render one's present reality more ideal, to seek to discover those aspects of their "one year out" positions that contribute to general well-being and meaningfulness.

CHAPTER 6

WHAT WORK CAN'T SOCIETY DO WITHOUT?

I believed in small jobs, like raising children, picking
fruit, cleaning. They were the jobs I considered the most
valuable, the jobs that struck me as deserving the most
respect of all.
　　　　—Sally Rooney, *Conversations with Friends*

FROM THE FRONT LINES TO THE FOUR SEASONS

WHEN THE US GOVERNMENT DECLARED A NATIONWIDE emergency in March 2020 due to the COVID-19 pandemic, consumers crowded grocery stores and online marketplaces to stock up on food and other essentials. There, they were likely to find shelves already lacking the necessities they were searching for, including hand sanitizer, disinfecting wipes, and rubber gloves. Some of the shortages were caused by arbitrageurs who rationalized that they were correcting market inefficiencies, such as two brothers who had road-tripped across Tennessee and Kentucky buying up all the hand sanitizer they could get their hands on and selling bottles online for up to seventy dollars. In the months ahead, the public would be forced to cope with shortages of basics they had previously taken for granted, from lumber to computer chips to baby formula. They learned more than they had ever wanted to know about supply chain disruptions caused by, among other things, factory shutdowns, customs delays, and just-in-time manufacturing.

However, the essential product that they seemed more desperate for than anything else was toilet paper. To prepare for an anticipated increase in home-based bathroom use, as workplaces and public venues closed, consumers overcompensated in a surge of panic buying. The flow of bidet sales increased, though not enough to stem a steeper increase in toilet paper sales to 71 percent ahead of the previous year. Stores imposed quotas to distribute the remaining supply more equitably. Office employees at Procter & Gamble helped out on the Charmin factory floor. When a Kimberly-Clark executive left his corporate headquarters on Friday, March 13, he stopped on the way home at the local Walmart to find them already out of the Cottonelle and Scott brands he oversaw. Like many desk workers, that was the last he would see of his office for a long time.

Many of those who stayed at work through the weekend and beyond had been classified as essential workers, without whom the production of necessary goods and provision of important services could not continue. Often, essential workers worked on what was called the front lines, a military analogy associated with protecting others. To be designated a front-line essential worker may have been a duty, such as to literally keep the trains running on time because public transportation systems were often integral to enabling other essential workers to get to their jobs. It may have been an honor, punctuated by nightly applause in cities across the world for health-care workers in hospitals where beds overflowed with gravely ill patients. Being considered essential could have been a sign of recognition for systems maintenance work that was sometimes invisible to its beneficiaries. It might have been a relief to be declared essential as it assured a continued income, such as for food processors who continued to produce food, unlike restaurant servers who were summarily laid off.

Essential work may have been all of these good things, but at the same time it was a curse. These workers were forced to risk personal well-being to carry out professional responsibilities that ranged from the grandiose, developing a vaccine, to the mundane, operating a cash register—which was, under the circumstances, no less heroic. It also was sometimes cause for confusion: in some jurisdictions teachers were told to pivot indefinitely to online learning, while in others, they were ordered back to the classroom. Sometimes, being essential was a backhanded compliment, signifying low status in the organizational hierarchy. After all, as when Napoleon in Tolstoy's *War and Peace* compares his soldiers to game pieces on a chess board, the higher one ranked in an organization, the farther away one was from exposure to the risks faced by those on the front lines.

Meanwhile, not being an essential worker may have been like being given a snow day of indefinite duration, a privilege for those with desk jobs who learned to work from home wearing carefully curated outfits that melded professionalism for the video camera with off-screen comfort. For some, it was harrowing to fall behind on payments and no longer to be needed, as with some restaurateurs who shuttered their establishments permanently. At the same time, it was worrying for their employees to lose a source of income. Amid headlines communicating the horrors of overcrowded hospitals, it may have felt like some selfish consolation to do the kind of work that could be performed at a social distance. For sales representatives and event managers who stopped flying around the world, instead attending meetings from improvised basement and closet "offices," it was a discovery of a whole new way of working that cast doubt on how much they were needed on-site, or for that matter if they were needed at all. Among the wealthy, being away from the front lines was a sign of social and organizational position, an opportunity to retreat to a bucolic country estate, the mountains, even a superyacht. Lift lines swelled at ski resorts, where a mid-week gondola passenger was overheard remarking on the cause: "No one works anymore." Two other passengers chimed in: "We're at work right now. Morning meeting, afternoon on the slopes." To meet the demands of clients who considered the liquidity of their investment portfolios to be essential, one trading firm moved its workforce to a Four Seasons. There, they could quarantine away from urban congestion, work together as though they were in the office, and take a dip in the pool after work, all the while depending upon the reduced services of essential hotel staff helping them maintain a COVID bubble while a virus ravaged the world outside.

THE "ESSENTIALLY CONTESTED CONCEPT" OF ESSENTIAL WORK

It may seem obvious to suggest that the work that is most worthy to society is the work that is most essential to it, but in practice, it is not always that simple. Essential workers are required to come into work while others stay home. Workplaces have historically used similar terminology in exceptional circumstances to call in "essential employees" during bad weather and "continuity personnel" during disruptive catastrophes. Historically, during wartime, people were pressed into service to support essential wartime functions, while those in occupations considered essential could receive deferments from military service. To consider what work matters most to our society, let's look at what work was most essential during two of the defining crises of our century so far.

The evening of 9/11, all US residents were told it was important to return to work as soon as possible. By contrast, as soon as the country locked down for the COVID pandemic, the terms *essential work* and *essential worker* became part of the general lexicon in the United States. Until the 2020 pandemic, the terms had not been used with any regularity since the two world wars in the previous century. (The terms *key worker* and *critical worker*, which were preferred in some other English-speaking countries, were used with increasing regularity post-9/11 and during the pandemic.)

Similar to Justice Potter Stewart's famous quote about obscenity, most people believe they know essential work when they see it. In the first winter of the pandemic, essential facilities workers prevented the pipes from freezing, essential food workers kept the produce growing, essential first responders still put out fires, and essential health-care workers tried to save patients from dying. These judgments of who was essential and who was not were largely uncontroversial, as were, at first, shutdowns of purportedly inessential workplaces: entertainment venues, schools, and even houses of worship.

However, like many so-called essentially contested concepts—which also include, for example, obscenity, art, and justice—what is essential is not only inherently controversial but also implies a value judgment with real-world implications. The sudden familiarity of essential work during the pandemic belied the political importance attached to it, not to mention the profound philosophical importance of the meaning we decide upon. Essential work should pertain to what society cannot do without, but who decides what we need? Is what we need always—or ever—the same as what we think of as what is most worthwhile? For that matter, does the equation of worthy work with essential work look different from the perspective of the worker?

Those who were classified as essential workers were given the arguably unenviable choice of exercising their right to earn a living while risking infection. People in positions of power declared their preferences by designating what was essential, as when an infamously carnivorous president ordered meatpackers to stay at work. There, the virus spread rampantly throughout the confines of a closely spaced disassembly line. In Florida, World Wrestling Entertainment succeeded in obtaining essential status. As the wrestlers resumed their bouts, the world around them engaged in a battle royale about the essence of "essential work." Politicians tried to help, for example, by introducing an Essential Workers' Bill of Rights, including health and safety protections and what they termed meaningful compensation, as well as the Citizenship for Essential Workers Act that provided a pathway to permanent citizenship for those undocumented workers who served in essential roles during the pandemic. Yet years later, the bills remain in committee.

HOW SHOULD WE VALUE ESSENTIAL WORK?

Early in the pandemic, the US Department of Homeland Security—a fairly new government entity that came into being when it was deemed essential after 9/11—issued a memo that designated "essential critical infrastructure workers." Whereas it had been implied, after 9/11, that any work that kept the economy running was a moral responsibility, the pandemic memo advised that "if you work in a critical infrastructure industry, as defined by the Department of Homeland Security, such as healthcare services and pharmaceutical and food supply, you have a special responsibility to maintain your normal work schedule." The sixteen critical infrastructure industries included a preponderance of hands-on so-called dirty work, which included mortuary services, food farming and processing, petroleum drilling, and waste management. The guidance also emphasized security in nearly every industry, from the physical security of defense systems and nuclear reactors to the technological security of financial institutions and communication systems. Thus, the COVID-19 pandemic not only reawakened us to the meaning of essential work but also showed us that what we determine to be essential cannot be separated from the social context in which we value it.

However, work that was essential to maintain society's critical infrastructure to sustain life was not the same as work that was worth staying alive for. As the pandemic wore on, we began to realize that as much as we needed toilet paper and public health guidance, we also needed to be inspired. On March 12, Broadway announced it would go dark for five weeks. While five weeks stretched into eighteen months, the hottest ticket on Broadway, *Hamilton*, arrived on small screens through the streaming service

Disney+. As playwright and poet Oscar Wilde famously said, "All art is quite useless," but that does not make it any less essential. Rather, John Keating, the beloved poetry teacher played by Robin Williams in *Dead Poets Society*, advises his students, "Medicine, law, business, engineering, these are noble pursuits and necessary to sustain life. But poetry, beauty, romance, love, these are what we stay alive for."

On March 11, Utah Jazz center Rudy Gobert became the first National Basketball Association player to test positive—two days after a postgame news conference during which he made a show of mocking the coronavirus by touching reporters' microphones and tape recorders, a prank for which he soon after apologized. The league became the first major sport in the United States to suspend play and also the first to return to play on July 30, spending almost $200 million to construct a public health bubble at Disney World for players, accompanied by their families, to perform for audiences watching only on television. The pandemic also led to the revival of the drive-in movie, which was possible to watch while isolating within your own car's quarantine pod, and contributed to the explosion in the popularity of pickleball, a sport which could be played while socially distanced.

The work we consider essential can also reveal our political preferences. In Washington, DC, as well as in state houses and city halls, politicians bickered over whether an economic recession or an infectious disease would do more damage, reminding us that whatever the answer, work was necessary for social stability. In Texas, after some malls and restaurants were allowed to reopen on a limited basis, certain bars and tattoo parlors defied orders to remain closed, protected by armed militias of protestors guarding their front doors. In a 5–4 vote, the Supreme Court backed attendance restrictions at religious services in some states, only to flip later in the year after a new justice was sworn in. On May 25, George Floyd, a Black man, was murdered by a white police officer, setting off racial justice protests in Minneapolis and around the world, the importance of which were seen to supersede the containment of the virus. In this way, collective behaviors pointed to a social consensus that even an immediate public health threat should not interfere with the long-term priorities of civil society, even though uncivil division may have prevailed among individuals about which priorities—including economic, entertainment, and equity—mattered most.

HOW DOES SOCIETY VALUE LIFE—AND WORK?

On the eve of the pandemic, nearly twenty years after the 9/11 terrorist attacks and after contentious political debate, the 9/11 Victim Compensation Fund (VCF) was reauthorized. The VCF had originally been established within weeks of the attacks to offer monetary "awards" to victims' families to recognize the extraordinary circumstances and scale of loss and provide financial restitution. For some claimants of modest means, the payments—which ranged from $250,000 to over $7 million, averaging over $2 million—secured their economic futures while they coped with the absence of a loved one, while for the grieving families of some wealthy financiers, the awards made it possible to continue to fund large mortgage payments without disrupting their lavish standard of living. Long after the deaths of 2,977 victims whose lives were claimed on 9/11 itself, the reauthorization of the VCF provided economic relief to workers and residents near Ground Zero, who in subsequent years experienced health problems from breathing in toxic materials from the smoldering ruins. It reinforced the reality that money can never adequately compensate for the loss of life and well-being while revisiting the question of whether some forms of work should be economically worth so much more than others.

In Michael Lewis's memoir about Wall Street in the 1980s, *Liar's Poker*, bond traders were known as "Big Swinging Dicks" and were so rich that they played card games in the office using US currency. In Tom Wolfe's novel about the same time period, *The Bonfire of the Vanities*, bond traders thought of themselves as "Masters of the Universe." These caricatures of bond traders suggested that the ones who lost their lives on 9/11 were often well paid. However, the essentiality of their work to the economic system may have been underappreciated by the general populace. In the days after 9/11, bond and stock trading resumed, but the bond markets reopened several days earlier because they traded on more technologically advanced electronic platforms, and unbeknownst to the average investor, they were more essential to macroeconomic stability. Cantor Fitzgerald showed up for the reopening only two days after losing 658 of 960 New York employees that day, the largest loss by any single employer, its surviving employees resolving to save the firm to take care of victims' families by relying upon a satellite office across the Hudson River in New Jersey. They had set up this disaster recovery site after the World Trade Center had first been bombed by terrorists in 1993.

While bond traders were ready to relaunch their trading platform, New York Stock Exchange CEO Dick Grasso was waking up in the office where he would sleep all that week, supervising and participating in the cleanup of a physical trading floor that at the time was still the primary engine of stock trading in America. Just blocks from the site of the twin towers' collapse, the NYSE was covered in dust and debris as well as other evidence of chaos that froze in time after much of Lower Manhattan had evacuated. While the traders waited to return, the yeoman's work of custodial cleanup took priority. Grasso would later be awarded a controversial $140 million deferred compensation package that made mention of his leadership through the crisis, but that would also lead his critics to question if he was worth that much, leading to his departure two years to the day after the NYSE reopened post-9/11.

Years later, in their research about the work of 9/11 victims, Christopher and Jen would study the workforce in and around the World Trade Center, which was so large that it had its own zip code. Three of the five most common occupations were decidedly unglamorous: accountants, administrative assistants, and facilities workers. When we romanticize the grand challenges society needs to solve, perhaps we forget about the daily challenges before us that are equally necessary to confront. First responders and financiers were the other two of the five most common occupations held by victims in the World Trade Center attacks. The work of first responders was indisputably essential, yet it was also typically underpaid, whereas that of financiers was often the highest paid.

The special master of the VCF, Kenneth Feinberg, who was responsible for determining the formula for deciding the amount of each award, had to consider, among other things, whether everyone should get the same amount. If not, what were good reasons for differentiation? Did heroes deserve more? Could awarding more to those who lost more earning power—present earnings multiplied by time and the potential for future increases—be justified? In the end, the fact that families of first responders who died in the attacks would receive substantially less money—nearly $1 million less, on average, according to an analysis Christopher conducted—than the families of higher-earning financiers added insult to injury. Filings by Cantor Fitzgerald attempted to persuade Feinberg to increase awards for families of income earners above the ninety-eighth percentile but ultimately had to compromise. The firm noted that a bond trader who was three years removed from basic training earned close to $300,000 annually and in five more years would have taken home more than $1 million each year—in turn-of-the-twenty-first-century dollars.

In his book, *What Is Life Worth?*, Feinberg defends the formula that tied the awards to earning power by saying that the "market system and its reliance on individual choice" was "as American as apple pie." As he implies, the association of the market economy with American values can lead us to believe that economic value is a signifier of social value. However, it seems self-evident that the essential workers of 9/11 and the pandemic crossed occupations and economic boundaries. Often, though not always, their work was difficult and dangerous. We might not go so far to suggest that all work is equally valuable, even though Feinberg admits, in the conclusion to his book, "I've become convinced that the 9/11 fund formula was defective" and that "all eligible claimants should receive the same amount." We would not go even further to argue that economic value and social value are clearly inversely related, as we discussed in an earlier chapter. Rather, we would assert, in economic terms, that the use value of essential work—its utility to society—is imperfectly related and often greater than its exchange value—the price it commands in the market. We are not even sure that the most socially valuable work ought to be the most lucrative, only that the least socially valuable work ought not to be the highest paid.

SHOULD YOU WORK FOR YOURSELF OR FOR OTHERS?

If you have the privilege to be able to choose what kind of career to pursue, should you choose work that helps others? In 1984, a felicitously named philosopher, Norman Care, published an underappreciated paper called "Career Choice." It contained pragmatic advice about the work we ought to do if we have a choice in the matter. Care observed the worldwide human condition and noted that millions of people "suffer[ed] destitution" in the form of "malnutrition, homeless[ness], or total lack of education [and] political oppression"; there was a significant disparity in socioeconomic status and associated opportunities; and efforts to ameliorate such suffering and disparities were "meager and inadequate." The problems and inequities present in the world in 1984 are all too similar to those in our world today. Writing for people who had the power and position to choose work that could improve their own lives or make a difference in the well-being of others, he wondered whether we ought to choose, in his words, "self-realization or service to others." In other words, should we prioritize our own benefit or the benefit of society?

Care's examination of this seemingly simple question was informed by millennia of philosophical deliberation about justice. He situates the question between two worldviews, one in which "one has but one life to lead" and another in which we are "in life together." Care comes to the preliminary and perhaps obvious conclusion that the best kind of work is that which enables our own self-realization in the course of serving others. Rather than choose one over the other, we can have both. But what if we don't have that luxury? What if we have to choose between them? That was a question faced by first responders on 9/11 and in the pandemic who put their own lives at risk to save those of others.

This question has roots in the fundamental tension between our egoistic tendency to care primarily about ourselves and our empathetic impulse to also care about others. It is further complicated by our views of, for example, the goal of a good life. Is it enough for everyone to merely survive, or is our goal to promote the egalitarian flourishing of all human beings? In ancient Athenian thought, human flourishing (*eudaimonia*) was taken to be the best kind of happiness, but in Athenian social practice, that happiness was only reserved for the most privileged of landed, male citizens. It may seem selflessly idealistic to suggest that we ought to cultivate a society that is more empathetic, egalitarian, and eudaimonic, but it can redound to our self-interest, too. When Thomas Hobbes performed a thought experiment in which he imagined humans unshackled from the constraints of society and free to pursue their own interests as if they were animals in a state of nature, he famously concluded that such a life would be "solitary, poor, nasty, brutish, and short."

Aesop's fables again shed light on the question of whether to work for ourselves or others. Joanne Ciulla relays the tale of "The Ant and the Bee." The two insects argue over which of them is more hardworking and appeal to Apollo for help. The god makes a distinction between the fruits of the ant's labors, which are hoarded for its own personal benefit, versus the bee's labors, which result in honey produced for all of society to enjoy. The bee works hard like an ant; however, the socially beneficial nature of its output elevates the value of its work. This observation supports the position that one way to judge the worth of one's work is in terms of its ability to serve others.

But that has not always been how the business world decides what work is most worthy. At a World Economic Forum session that

Christopher had a hand in earlier in his career, a panel of business leaders called Charles Darwin's *On the Origin of Species* a classic of business literature, implying that the jungle of capitalism was a self-interested competition for survival. However, in recent years the elites of Davos have increasingly embraced a more socially conscious vision of economic life embraced by the forum's founder, Klaus Schwab. The new story of business, as philosopher R. Edward Freeman describes it, is aligned with management scholar Lynn Sharp Paine's observation of a value shift from an exclusive focus on financial performance to concern with environmental and social performance. Political economist Subramanian Rangan similarly challenges us to consider whether the purpose of business is economic performance or social progress, and strategy scholars Michael Porter and Mark Kramer argue that the goal of business is to create *shared value*—pursuing financial success that yields societal benefits—rather than just increase share value for investors. Even the Business Roundtable, composed of executives from some of the United States' largest business corporations, adopted the perspective in 2019 that executives should lead their companies for the benefit of all stakeholders, not just stockholders.

Although Care's philosophical question is earnestly asking what work we *ought to* choose, organizational psychologist Adam Grant observes that we often in reality choose to act in the interests of others, what he refers to as "prosocial motivation." Grant concludes that our impulses to help others can end up helping ourselves—that "givers" who support the success of others tend to be more successful than "takers" who focus only on their own success. Our own research on close relations' perspectives on the work of 9/11 victims finds that work as a calling may include serving oneself, serving others, or both.

All of which is to say that choosing service to others may be likelier than ever to coincide with self-realization in a career, and vice versa. But should we serve others when doing so may be in tension with self-realization? Given that Care's answer to a seemingly personal question about what career to choose is grounded in contemporary philosophy's most prominent political theories of justice, his answer is axiomatic—that we cannot separate the work we decide to do from the society that needs us to do it. If we cannot have it both ways, if we live in a world in need, we are morally required to choose service to others. What Care did not answer, in the vast gap between the immediate present and the distant future, is whether the work society needs the most is ever the most valued work.

CAN YOU MAKE A BIGGER DIFFERENCE WITH YOUR WORK OR YOUR MONEY?

With a net worth in his prime of more than 1.5 percent of the US GDP, John D. Rockefeller is widely considered to be the wealthiest person in American history. He made his fortune as the founder of Standard Oil, providing a light source before the invention of electricity and fueling transportation after the proliferation of the automobile. But was his most essential contribution to society his work as a businessman? Or was it as a philanthropist, providing the capital to found respected institutions from the University of Chicago to the Rockefeller Foundation?

Will Bill Gates, the wealthiest living American for most of this century until 2018, be remembered for cofounding Microsoft, the world's largest personal computer software company? Or for the Bill and Melinda Gates Foundation, to which by 2018 he was devoting nearly all of his professional life to advance public health, education, and action to address climate change?

Whose work matters more to society: Jeff Bezos or MacKenzie Scott, his former wife? Surpassing Gates in 2018 on the wealthiest Americans list, Bezos founded Amazon.com—which was both revered and reviled during the pandemic for safely delivering essential goods to front porches while gradually replacing warehouse workers with robots and delivery drivers with drones. After divorcing Bezos, Scott became the second-wealthiest woman in America and promptly pledged to give most of her money away to support race and gender equity, democracy, and the environment.

Billionaire or not, one of the questions these examples urge us to ask ourselves is whether we can make a bigger difference to societal causes by contributing our professional time, skills, and expertise directly, or by trying to get rich and subsequently giving away our money. Even if you have modest means, if you are a passionate environmentalist, do you need to do work that directly impacts the environment, or can you keep your day job and then donate to charities you support? Peter Singer—who acknowledges that typical philosophers earn a pittance compared to some financiers—urges people who can afford it to give away upward of one-third of their incomes. A noted utilitarian—the school of philosophical ethics that measures impact in terms of the greatest good for the greatest number of people—he particularly advises that money be redistributed from developed to developing markets as this increases the marginal utility of each dollar. This is the logic behind microlending, which seeks to direct modest donations to places where they can make big differences, often facilitated by online giving platforms. Singer's philosophy arguably launched a movement of "effective altruists" who go beyond the conventional largesse of billionaires by committing to maximizing social benefit through their wealth, whether to help someone dying in front of them or suffering in a distant place or time.

Effective altruists think about society's needs both in the immediate present and the unforeseeable future. They worry about people who experience malnutrition now as well as when the possible far-off misappropriation of artificial intelligence enables totalitarian regimes. As an undergraduate student, Sam Bankman-Fried thought he might want to be an animal welfare worker. Yet, he became convinced that he might be able to make a bigger difference indirectly, as a philanthropist. He achieved dubious notoriety for the rise and fall of his cryptocurrency exchange FTX and was convicted of fraud and conspiracy. Bankman-Fried's plan to give the majority of his money away to good causes seemed to be working until FTX's collapse cost effective altruism's beneficiaries millions of dollars. While becoming a billionaire philanthropist may be a laudable aspiration, Bankman-Fried's downfall is a cautionary tale that such plans, like most get-rich-quick schemes, often go awry.

Most of us will never have the good fortune to choose how best to distribute our economic fortunes. But we may still ask ourselves whether we can make a bigger difference with our money than with our work. It may be that we can do more to better align our current jobs with the societal causes we care about. Research has shown that when employers allow employees to take actions in line with causes that are important to them at work, like proenvironmental behaviors, employees are more committed to the organization. This means employers must go above and beyond the typical days per working year that companies reserve for PR-driven volunteer work or outreach days, which cynically smack of greenwashing. What matters is that employees have the flexibility to explore causes that matter to them through their work, as applicable, and are assured that their employers support these causes as well.

Of course, the trade-off between contributing to causes indirectly, through monetary contributions, versus directly, through socially valuable work, must be taken into account, as the latter often pays poorly. The work of philosophers is arguably an example of poorly paid, socially valuable work. Socrates was famously destitute and unkempt as he held forth on the street corners of Athens about things he considered more important than money, while his wife and children practically starved. It would be naive to disregard the harmful effects that fossil fuels, the digital divide, and monopolistic behavior have had on society; however, to suppose that oil refining, software development, and online retail have not been valuable to society ignores the indispensable role that some billionaires have played in advancing the quality of life in postindustrial America. Is effective altruism a way for people to have it both ways: amassing millions while claiming noble ends?

Elon Musk, the most recent person to top the wealthiest Americans list as of this writing, has tried to get rich and solve society's greatest challenges simultaneously. Although he has expressed affinity for the aims of effective altruism, Musk has been relatively private about his philanthropic intentions. Instead, his companies have been credited with taking leadership positions in the electric vehicle industry to aid in the battle against climate change and—should we lose that battle—in exploring space and the potential to terraform other planets. In the most favorable interpretation, Musk's work and that of many social entrepreneurs may be evidence that alignment between economic and social value is not logically impossible.

However, Musk's work has plenty of detractors, from Tesla engineers who blame him for making the car's self-driving capabilities less safe, to critics who consider SpaceX to be a vanity project, and social media users who believe his takeover of the social media platform formerly known as Twitter has exacerbated the misinformation epidemic. It is also worth asking whether society should trust billionaires who turned their talent, hard work, and a larger dose of good fortune than they may care to admit into their own business success to be equally talented, hardworking, and fortunate when it comes to solving social problems that affect everyone else. If the jury is still out on whether the work of one billionaire can provide valuable direct service to the world through his work, at least we can agree that economic and social value are not always aligned—even perhaps that they are all too often misaligned. It would be easy to choose which work to do if there were always coincidence between them. However, the very logic of effective altruism, like that of progressive taxation, implies that markets are imperfect. Wealth sometimes needs to be redistributed to address society's needs because, so often, socially valuable work is undervalued, whether it is attempting to solve society's grand challenges or merely to provide a modest service to benefit others.

IS IT BETTER TO CONTRIBUTE TO SOCIETY LOCALLY OR GLOBALLY?

When Lauren Majors was a college student, she thought she was going to go into politics to work on issues related to reproductive health. However, as an intern in the office of US senator Barbara

Boxer, Lauren came to terms with the double-edged sword of youth. Visiting the offices of legislators and lobbyists and being mistaken for a high school student doing a school project, she was not being taken seriously. That experience, along with her realization that political progress was inevitably slow, led her to completely rethink her career path. Having grown frustrated with the possibility of becoming an agent of large-scale change, Lauren asked herself, "Why am I asking others to do a job that I could do?" She began volunteering in a juvenile detention center, learned about the intersection between substance abuse and teen pregnancy, and discovered that she wanted to work directly with the very people whose lives she had been seeking to influence for the better through politics. She became a community health nurse practitioner and now spends most of her professional time working with vulnerable populations. During the COVID-19 pandemic, she worked in so-called homeless hotels, temporary residences that helped to mitigate the spread of the disease among persons who may otherwise have been sleeping in shelters and on streets. Her passion and specialty, however, is working with patients who struggle with substance abuse disorder.

Murisiku "Muri" Raifu also works in health care, but his career trajectory has arguably been the opposite of that of Lauren Majors. Whereas Lauren went from aspiring to work in national politics to working with individual patients, Muri says that when he left Ghana—where his first encounter with work was helping his mother sell odds and ends in the local bazaar—to attend high school in the United States, "My hope was that someday I was going to do something on a greater scale to affect people's lives." Today, he is in private practice as a neurosurgeon, serving individual patients who need him and recognizing that being a practitioner gives him insight into patients' needs. However, another reason he remains a practicing doctor is to generate capital for the venture that now occupies an increasing amount of his energy and time, a medical technology company that seeks to improve public health and empower patients by digitizing medical records in emerging markets. Not only does

Muri hope his company will be "transformational for people's lives," but he also is proud to employ "fifty people in the world [who] . . . for that day, [are] creating something . . . they can use to feed their family."

Marina Kim, who founded Ashoka U, a network of Change-maker Campuses that has included both of the educational institutions that employ Christopher and Jen, distinguishes between four levels of impact. These range from direct service, working directly with individuals who may need help, to framework change, work that alters mind-sets and markets in hopes of a future in which there are no deep divides between those who serve and those who are served. Adam Grant observes that organizational performance improves when workers are connected with the end-user beneficiaries of their efforts, and Kim says that all work along the impact spectrum is worth doing. However, her work also may be taken to suggest that we should ask ourselves the kinds of questions that Lauren and Muri seem to be asking themselves: Should we invest our efforts at work in direct service to those who need it most or in effecting large-scale change—such as through politics and social entrepreneurship? This line of questioning is similar to asking whose work is more essential: the billionaire philanthropists who give their money away, or the recipients of their giving who do the work itself? During the pandemic, politics aside, who mattered more: policymakers who communicated public guidance about critical infrastructure workers, or the critical infrastructure workers themselves, who tended to the patients and kept communication lines open? Did society benefit more from the analysis of executives who forecasted the rising need for toilet paper production or from the factory floor workers who produced it? In general, whose contribution to society is more essential: the efforts of those at the top of the organizational and societal hierarchies, who provide capital, bring resources together, and manage the work of others, or the efforts of those at the bottom of those hierarchies, who actually do the work, specialize in a task or discipline, and perform the labor themselves?

In the world of *Atlas Shrugged*, Ayn Rand's treatise of neoliberal capitalism that happens to be unusually popular among billionaires and one of the longest novels ever written, the answer clearly favors those working at the top. In the novel, frustrated by government intervention and union interference in their work, a coterie of industrial magnates goes on strike, vowing to "stop the motor of the world." Only after their absence contributes to social division and governmental collapse do the striking industrialists return to right the ship. By contrast, in the world of *War and Peace*, Leo Tolstoy's study of human psychology and history, which also happens to be even longer than *Atlas Shrugged*, the answer to that question is those at the bottom. Tolstoy compares a military organization to the shape of a cone, in which the commander in chief occupies the very top position alone, whereas the soldiers at the bottom, who are the most numerous, do all of the "stabbing, hacking, burning, and pillaging" at the behest of their superiors. Tolstoy concludes with the ironic observation that the powerful figurehead at the top of the cone is the least powerful in that "those who command take the smallest part in the action itself."

If we had to take sides, we would undoubtedly recommend Tolstoy as the better novelist than Rand. However, as for who is more essential in a capitalist economy—the industrial leaders or the rank-and-file laborers—we see the question as important to ask and yet ultimately offering up a false choice between interdependent elements of the workforce. The capitalists depend upon the laborers to produce, whereas the laborers require capital investment to perform. However, in a system full of winner-take-all markets—which economic historian Thomas Piketty has shown has given rise to increasing income inequality between those at the top and those at the bottom—we think the essential contributions of those working on the front lines warrant special recognition. When asked whether she thought her work serving one person at a time was having the kind of impact she imagined her work as a politician might have had, Lauren Majors replied, "I would push back and say it's not one person. . . . They're gonna talk to their friends. . . . Addiction affects the whole family." Direct service can be a form of framework change when, as Lauren reflects, "that patient also sees the health-care system" and impacts the perspectives of many patients and providers.

WORK AS MEANINGFUL AND ESSENTIAL

In the long run, essential work may look very different from what we value the most in the immediate present. We can work effectively and indeterminately without contemplating whether our work is meaningful and why it matters. But if we don't reflect on its meaning, then we may be left with a lifetime of regret about who we did or did not work for, the work we did or did not do, working too much or too little, or doing work that seems less than essential in retrospect.

Events like 9/11 and the pandemic lead us to reflect upon the meaning of life in the face of the possibility of death—our own or someone else's. They also urge us to come to terms with the place and priority of work in a life worth living. These opportunities to consider what matters are what Rabbi Marcia Zimmerman called "liminal moments. It's these moments of transition, of identity, birth, death, all of that, [but] mostly death." As the first woman rabbi in the United States to lead a congregation of more than two thousand households, Rabbi Zimmerman pursued her profession even though her father worried that traditional attitudes could make it an uphill battle for a woman. She officiates at least fifty funerals a year, more during the pandemic when the congregation where she is the senior rabbi gathered largely online for services. Although the unpredictability of death means that a call can come any day at any hour, she performs the funerals for everyone she knows whether or not she had planned to be away from work that day. Rabbi Zimmerman reflects, "There's no BS in death, and that's why I love being present to it. None of us get out of this alive, and so we're all gonna experience end of life. And yet we are all shocked when it happens."

In his book *The Road to Character*, David Brooks distinguishes between résumé virtues—"the skills you bring to the marketplace"—and eulogy virtues—"the ones that are talked about at your funeral"—pointing out that most of us spend our years burnishing our résumé virtues, often at the expense of our eulogy virtues, even though "we all know that the eulogy virtues are more important than the résumé ones." Résumé virtues may be the reasons we get hired for the right work, but eulogy virtues are likelier to lead us to work for the right reasons.

Essential work may not always feel meaningful in its execution, as those who still showed up to rote jobs to keep the economy alive during the pandemic could attest. Yet, it is possible for work to be meaningful precisely *because* it is essential, as in the case of Rabbi Zimmerman's work at the end of life or the work of first responders to save lives. It is possible for work to be essential because it is meaningful, as in the case of life-sustaining education and entertainment without which life feels less worth living. We may wish we didn't need a global pandemic—or the threat of death in general—for society to recognize essential work as worthy. Yet, when these threats reveal what matters most, the distinction between higher-status inessential work and lower-status essential work is difficult to unsee. That even relatively high-status, well-paid doctors experienced a crisis of meaning during the pandemic means we as a society need to think critically about how to recognize and protect essential workers of all kinds from burnout and exploitation.

PART III

Work That's Worthy

CHAPTER 7

CAN YOUR WORK HAVE A HIGHER PURPOSE?

I don't want to live in a world where someone else makes the world a better place than we do.

—Big tech CEO Gavin Belson in the
television series *Silicon Valley*

THE SPECIAL IMPORTANT PERSON THAT
EVERYONE THOUGHT I WAS

BESS HARGREAVES GREW UP WANTING TO MAKE THE world a better place while also wondering how she could possibly live up to the success of her father, a distinguished nuclear engineer. She planned to go into law to serve the public interest, but first she had to pay off her student loans. So, after graduating from law school, she followed the path laid out for her by her father, joining one of the top firms in New York City, where she made more as a first-year associate than her father took home as a college professor. She thought, "Well, I finally won. I finally beat him, and I was fucking miserable."

Bess worked long hours for large bonuses on cases she described as soul-crushing, like defending large banks and asbestos manufacturers, and was told in a performance review that her pro bono work should be saved for the hours between 9:00 p.m. and 2:00 a.m. So, she moved to a midsize firm, where she accepted a smaller salary in exchange for fewer billable hours but instead found herself taking on greater responsibility with less support. While she was at that firm, she started working on family law, which she found more satisfying. She left private practice to join a nonprofit organization serving women living in poverty—many of whom were domestic violence victims—providing free legal assistance with matrimonial and immigration law. She thought she had found what she had been searching for professionally: "I felt like I was doing important work that needed to be done." She was also recently married, and felt her new career also seemed to fit with her personal life: "Most of my bosses were parents, all my bosses were women, and so I felt like it was just a great place to be a mom of young kids."

Bess's twelve-year career at this nonprofit was largely successful. She started a new practice defending women who were saddled with debt accumulated by abusive husbands, she was promoted to a supervisory position, she and her husband started a family, and she negotiated an 80 percent schedule to spend more time with her kids. She recognizes that these were personal privileges that she was fortunate to have and that she would never have gotten back the time she enjoyed with her young children if she had not taken it then.

With hindsight, though, there were signs from the beginning that this job would wear on her. She was told that funding was limited so her starting salary was not negotiable, which meant that her salary stayed low throughout her tenure. While her part-time schedule afforded greater flexibility, she still shouldered a full-time workload that she had fewer hours to get done. Family court in New York City was, in her words, a shit-show, made even worse in the pandemic, when it shut down completely except for the most urgent cases. Working remotely, with young children trying to figure out distance learning while her husband was also working was difficult. Bess reflected, "I'm locked in my bedroom listening to these women tell me stories of horrific abuse" and having to tell them that nothing could be done. By the time she left, the end of the pandemic was in sight, but the burnout had built up, "like cholesterol in your veins."

She sometimes feels immense guilt about leaving her clients and no longer being "the special important person that everyone thought I was." What she describes as her field's "cult of self-martyrdom" was not as different as she imagined it would be from the large private practice where she began her career. Whereas in big law, "they own you," Bess's experience with nonprofit law was that it consumes you. She recalls an awards ceremony early in her nonprofit career in which the entire story of the honoree focused on her heroic sacrifice of family and personal time for the sake of her clients. Bess still doesn't know what she will do next, but when she reflected back on it all, she says, "I have a lot of complicated feelings about walking away from a career or, you know, being a do-gooder or being busy or being productive, making money, like all those things I have complicated feelings about, but the thing I never feel complicated about is that it was not a good job anymore." Almost twenty years since her law career began, she is now working part-time advising law students about their careers while she also tries to figure out her own. She says, "Everything is really up in the air, and I'm slowly becoming OK with that."

THE PROMISE OF PURPOSE

Work can confer a sense of purpose that makes life worth living. It can come from within in the form of a calling, as in the legend of the artist whose passion for his work both made him feel alive and drove him toward self-destruction. Or the call can come from outside, as a moral imperative or even a religious summons. All of it has the potential to make martyrs of us, sacrificing ourselves for a higher purpose. As we've discussed, finding purpose at work doesn't need to involve a calling; it could be a means to a worthy end. But what if it is none of these things? What if we lose that sense of calling for work that no longer feels like it is worth the sacrifice, or if our work was never a calling in the first place and yet still demands more than we are willing to give? To paraphrase existentialist philosopher Albert Camus, a purpose worth dying for had best be worth living for. However, when work amounts to "a Monday through Friday sort of dying," in the enduring sentiment of Studs Terkel, rather than conferring a sense of purpose, work takes it away.

It is one thing to define work as purposeful, but it is quite another to declare work to be *full of purpose*. Purposeful work serves a function that has been decided by an organization or economic forces to be worthy of reward. As Bess observed about work, "being busy or being productive, making money" are purposeful— when there is a fit between the labor demanded by the market and the skills we have to supply. But work that is full of purpose is accompanied by the feeling of doing work that needs to be done and is done independent of whatever rewards the person might get. Purpose has the potential to make work worth it.

Philosopher Susan Wolf says of a life of meaning that it exists at the intersection of "subjective attraction and objective attractiveness." This could also apply to work that has purpose. It should feel rewarding to the person doing it, but it should also be worthy of reward. This sense of purpose goes beyond our personal problems and preferences. It has the potential to connect us to something bigger than ourselves, while allowing us to compare and evaluate some projects as objectively more worthy than others. Yet this sense of purpose also goes beyond what society values as a contribution. In other words, some work seems more worthy than other work simply because it is. Our personal feelings and social approval about such work may be aligned with such objective values but are not why the work is worthy; rather, we feel good about such work and receive accolades for it *because* it is worthy. For example, medicine, education, and military careers rank among the most respected or honest professions, whereas politics, lobbying, and sales are among the least. This is not to say that the former are always honorable and worthy, while the latter cannot be, but we may have to work a little harder to find purpose among them, all else being equal.

And yet the objective attractiveness of worthy work is not always aligned with its subjective attractiveness as represented by how much it is monetarily rewarded by the market. This is one reason why Bess is occasionally resentful of her former classmates and colleagues who made partner in their firms, "rich philanthropists who were sort of like, 'Oh, good for you to like go out and do this terrible work, and we'll give you some money once in a while so that you can be paid a pittance, and I'm gonna do this private work and make a ton of money, and then tell you how much I admire you.'"

The idea that human life may have a higher purpose, or even any purpose at all, is very old. It would not be an exaggeration to say that the first and most important philosophical question concerned the meaning and purpose of life. Philosophers from ancient Greece to China and elsewhere were preoccupied with contemplating the good life for human beings (which, somewhat circularly, often consisted of contemplation), considering the role of work in the good life (not surprisingly, most intellectuals preferred to leave manual labor to others), and speculating about the immortality of the soul (more on this later, in Chapter 9, about legacy). If, on the other hand, the proposition that human work may be full of purpose has waxed and waned through the ages, it appears to be waxing in the present century. The popularity of Rick Warren's curiously profitable books and products about "the purpose driven life," the evidence behind Aaron Hurst's claim that we work in "the purpose economy," and the characterization by Daniel Goleman, among others, of an emerging generation of leaders as "the purpose generation," suggest that the pressure to find purpose at work—much like finding your calling—has never been higher.

HOLDING OUT FOR A HERO

In the classic Pixar film *The Incredibles*, a family of superheroes is forced into a Superhero Relocation Program after public sentiment turns against them because of collateral property damage caused by their crime fighting. As Elastigirl settles into life as a suburban mom, her husband, Mr. Incredible, squeezes into an office cubicle as a sympathetic insurance claims adjuster where—as he tries to "save the world, one policy at a time"—he longs to return to superheroism.

Superhero may not be a viable occupational choice in our world, but our work can still be heroic. Typical characteristics of heroic work include self-transcendence, or an effort to be a part of something bigger than oneself; selflessness, in the form of putting the well-being of others ahead of that of oneself; and courage to put oneself at risk for the sake of ends other than personal survival. By contrast, the stereotypical, workaday insurance claims adjuster is an antihero—a risk-averse follower, unable to prioritize the other's well-being over the bottom line or see the bigger picture other than work as a means to the end of making a living.

Research on conventionally heroic professions, such as firefighters, aid workers, and soldiers, suggests that the romance of heroism is a motivating force for many people. Although heroes are not often compensated monetarily for their sacrifices, the social status they gain through the admiration of others can provide a degree of satisfaction. Most people enter heroic professions for reasons other than monetary compensation. Often a sense of higher purpose provides affirmation for the pursuit of work that is not necessarily materially rewarding.

However, research also reveals that even heroes rarely feel heroic every day, and idealizing the noble ends of these professions may protect against the messy means that constitute the daily reality of their pursuit. Firefighters are likely to spend more time waiting around, cleaning and polishing their engines, than riding them to a fire, and some units receive more calls to respond to drug overdoses and rescue cats than to save people trapped in burning buildings. Aid workers often work far away from home in lonely and frustrating conditions, some of them experiencing a disproportionately high rate of depression and marital infidelity as they aim to make a difference. Soldiers seeking to defend freedom often give up their personal autonomy in command-and-control regiments to determine what risks are worth taking to what worthwhile ends. Perhaps the most awe-inspiring aspect of heroism is also the most sobering: the very real potential to sacrifice not only one's life, but one's overall well-being for the sake of others.

In spite of—or perhaps even in light of—these realities, the higher purpose of heroism can be alluring from the vantage point of an office cubicle. Seeking to capitalize on an emerging generation of workers' fervor for making the world a better place, businesses that may previously have been fixated on making money have carefully crafted statements of purpose that promise heroic possibilities. At PwC, Christopher's former firm, employees "build trust in society and solve important problems," while at Accenture, Jen's former firm, they "help our clients become the next and best versions of themselves." These firms' competitors claim to be, among other things, "building a better working world" (EY), "creating trust and confidence in a more equitable society" (Deloitte), and "unleashing human energy through technology for an inclusive and sustainable future" (Capgemini). In a 2015 article, called "How an Accounting Firm Convinced Its Employees They Could Change the World," a KPMG partner wrote about his firm's purpose statement, describing the firm's role in certifying Nelson Mandela's election in 1994 with taglines like, "We Shape History" and "We Champion Democracy." At the same time, so many technology companies were claiming that their main purpose was to save the world that it became a running joke on the satirical television program *Silicon Valley*.

FUNCTIONAL PURPOSE AND HIGHER PURPOSE

Evolutionary biology tells us that the purpose of life is to grow, reproduce, and survive. But when that is all there is to life, there is little sense of purpose. If we assert that there must be some higher purpose to human life beyond biological functions, then we run into the logical problem of infinite regress. For example, if the purpose of your life is manifested in your achievements and progeny and the longevity of yourself, your achievements, and your progeny, what is the foundation for their significance, other than the longevity of your progeny's achievements and *their* progeny's achievements— and so on? At some point, any scientific attempt to explain the higher purpose of life is destined to beg the question: What is the ultimate purpose that confers purpose upon everything else?

Philosopher and proponent of stakeholder capitalism R. Edward Freeman makes a distinction between ends and means to explain the purpose of business. Profit is necessary for the survival of business. It can support the capacity for business to carry out its purpose. It can also be an outcome of having served its purpose well. But the ultimate purpose of business is not simply to make a profit. Rather, it is to supply the world's demand, to solve an important problem, or to make the world a better place. Freeman writes, "the purpose of business is usually determined by a passionate entrepreneur chasing a dream to change the world." This idea replaces the relentless focus on profit maximization that Milton Friedman popularized in the 1970s and that remains influential in the working world. It also means we should distinguish between substantive versus marketing-based attempts to save the world when we see them.

Sometimes, it takes a life-changing event to lead us to recognize that there might be more to our working lives than making money. In the weeks and months after the 9/11 attacks, several survivors' stories came out in the media that credited a common savior, a man who guided them to safety wearing a red bandana covering his nose and mouth. Efforts to discover the identity of the man coalesced around Welles Crowther, who may in those moments have traded his professional purpose as an equities trader for what he saw as a higher purpose as a first responder. *Man in Red Bandana*, a 2017 documentary film made in Crowther's memory, follows a boy who always carried a red bandana in his back pocket, a gift from his father. He helped clean fire trucks at age seven and became a volunteer firefighter as a teenager, at the Empire Hook and Ladder Co. No. 1 in Upper Nyack, New York. The fire station was about thirty miles up the Hudson River from the World Trade Center where, after college, he worked at investment bank Sandler O'Neill. He is believed to have died alongside New York City firefighters on their way up to the 78th floor sky lobby of World Trade Center 2, where he has been credited with saving at least ten lives. The account of his final minutes concludes that, rather than follow coworkers out of the building, he tied his red bandana around his face to fend off smoke inhalation and joined firefighters to lead others to safety. In the film, Crowther's father said his son had told him of his intention to leave finance for firefighting, leaving behind a partially completed application for the Fire Department of New York (FDNY).

After 9/11, there was an uptick in people seeking work with a higher purpose. Applications for the Peace Corps reached a thirty-year high, some New Yorkers decided to join the FDNY, and many Americans answered a call for military service. They included Pat Tillman, a professional football player who put his career on hold to enlist and then died in 2004 from friendly fire while providing cover for his fellow soldiers when they were ambushed in eastern Afghanistan. Some of the silver lining after 9/11—if there could be such a thing—proved to be temporary, however. Within two decades, the sense of national unity had devolved into declining trust in government and political division.

The effects of the pandemic on working for a higher purpose has been even more complicated. In health care, an estimated 1.5 million workers who were not directly involved in COVID patient care lost their jobs involuntarily. After multiple waves of infections, nurses reported record levels of burnout and the intention to leave patient care in a profession that already was associated with high turnover. A survey by a health-care staffing firm found that nearly half of physicians changed jobs during the pandemic, with better work-life balance being the number-one motivator. However, the exodus from health care is coinciding with an influx of new entrants. Surveys of educators and students point to rising numbers of students considering health-care professions, though the reasons may involve pay and stability as much as purpose. Workers across professions who could afford to risk unemployment participated in the Great Resignation, a twenty-year-high wave of job departures that were motivated more by self-interested factors such as opportunities for pay, advancement, and flexibility than by a perceived higher purpose.

THE PROBLEMS WITH PURPOSE

One popular conception of purpose at work locates it at the intersection of four questions:

- What do you love to do?
- What will the market pay for?
- What are you good at?
- What does the world need?

The idea that purpose is somewhere between passion, pay, skill, and society's needs has been tied to several traditions. The four questions have been attributed to the traditional Japanese concept of *ikigai,* or "reason for being," but they have also been associated with the teaching of Christian theologian Frederick Buechner. The two questions about love and the world's needs are aligned with Care's ethical distinction between self-realization and service to others, whereas the two questions about skill and pay are consistent with the economic logic of the labor market. The four questions have infiltrated the advice of everyone from contemporary career counselors to modern management gurus and have appeared everywhere from office swag to meeting-room walls.

It might be easy to dismiss this conception of purpose as pop psychology, but we believe each question is well worth asking. And yet it is difficult enough to answer one of them, much less all four. It is even more difficult to find coincidence among our answers to multiple questions. As you think about any given job, it is likely that its ability to answer one (or more) of these questions to your satisfaction will be lacking. That's natural. Most jobs will require trade-offs, and many careers will involve compromises about which of these questions is satisfied when, as Bess Hargreaves's career story suggests. What follows are a few stories of people at different career stages who have sought purpose at work but found that even if they could not "have it all" in one particular job, they could hope to have a lot over the course of their changing careers.

YOU DON'T LOVE THIS WORK

After Linnea Komba Dahl graduated from an expensive East Coast university, she felt fine spinning her wheels, waiting tables at a restaurant in Harvard Square and not knowing what was next. However, her father, a well-connected businessman who had earned his way up from the wrong side of the tracks in Oslo, was alarmed. She suspects it was he who orchestrated a job offer for her that came from a television producer in Norway, but after a year of doing that, funding dried up and she was back to waiting tables.

When she returned to the United States, she met with a career counselor, read the self-help classic *What Color Is Your Parachute?*, and took personality tests that all pointed her toward religion and theology. She tried applying her language skills at a translation firm in Boston, but after being sexually harassed to the point that she carried a plastic bag on the T every day in case she threw up on her commute, she was relieved to take an entry-level position at an investment firm where the work was "mind-numbingly dull." The hours were good, the people were nice, and she got an enormous bonus after only two years.

However, even though she was not raised in an overtly religious home, she could not continue in a career that felt soulless to her. From a young age, she had been drawn to spiritual engagement by the story of two influential women in her life: her mother, Regina, and her stepgrandmother, Agnes. Agnes was a lay missionary in Tanzania when she met Regina, just four years her junior and one of only four women in the country who passed the Cambridge Exam in her class. However, as a biracial orphan female being raised by German nuns, Regina's prospects appeared bleak. Agnes legally adopted Regina, provided food, love, and shelter, and acted as the only mother she had ever known. She helped her get a college scholarship in the United States. Several years later, when Linnea was born to Regina, Agnes became Grandma Agnes to the girl as well as a spiritual role model.

Inspired by this story and granted the funds by the most lucrative job she ever had, Linnea finally had the freedom to pursue the path that her role model and career advice had all pointed her toward. "I used my bonus money to pay for Divinity School even though I didn't know exactly how I would find paid employment." While taking a unit of a clinical pastoral education program in which she worked with patients under the supervision of a hospital chaplain, she knew within the first week that this is what she wanted to do with her life. She is now a Buddhist chaplain at a large hospital in Boston and an instructor in ministry studies at Harvard Divinity School. She reflected, "It's absolutely that I need this work; the connection feeds me. It's not, as people sometimes say, that I'm such a good person for doing it. I heal from it, and I feel lucky to be doing it, and very, very blessed. And I just get to meet the most wonderful people who let me into their lives and trust me."

THE WORK DOESN'T PAY ENOUGH

Like many graduating college seniors, Sawyer Michaelson—Christopher's oldest child—was uncertain about whether college would really lead him toward a career. He could not help being curious about the fates of childhood friends who had chosen different paths, like one who lived in his parents' basement after high school trying to make it as a professional video gamer (after a while, he went back to school) and another who left college after one year to declare for the NBA draft (he was drafted). Like many students who pursued a college education, Sawyer felt pressure to find not only gainful employment but also work in which he would "feel that I'd be contributing in a positive, meaningful way to others' lives." While in college, he had majored in neuroscience. As a student-athlete, he discovered that neuroscience connected, among other things, his fascination with the human mind with growing societal concern about the brain health of athletes.

But when he was looking for a full-time job, a part of him envied his peers who studied economics. Some of them had received job offers and signing bonuses after interning the summer of their junior year at banks that marketed credit cards with high interest rates to their debt-burdened classmates. On average, students who major in pragmatic disciplines like business and computer science stand to earn around 50 percent more in their first jobs out of college than those in the humanities. On the typical college campus, students studying to make the world a better place see their professionally dressed peers as sellouts, while they in turn are perceived as bleeding hearts.

Most of the jobs Sawyer interviewed for were lower-paying positions in research laboratories. One was an Alzheimer's study, a worthy project—but his role would have been to euthanize hundreds of rats, or, as he described it, "my purpose would just have been to be the grim reaper." Instead, he found a position as a psychometrist, derived from the words *psychology* and *metrics*, who measures psychological effects and processes. He works directly with patients to help them manage brain disorders that can arise from head trauma. He thinks he is probably making about half of what his banker friends are bringing in but has been exhilarated to be using what he studied to work directly with patients who need help. He doesn't expect to get rich quick, but he hopes his education and experience will someday enable him to continue into clinical practice or influence health policy.

YOU'RE NOT GOOD ENOUGH AT IT

Several of the classmates with whom Dennis Curley shared a stage in college went on to fame and fortune. So, when he had no more prospects in Chicago theater after one gig as a pianist, he wondered if he wasn't a good-enough performer and settled for a corporate job as a paralegal. Working on intellectual property cases reminded him of his work-study job in the classics department, where he learned he could still dream about what he really wanted to do— acting—because his day job was dull and did not require his full attention.

Five years and a few moves later, he knew what he didn't want from work but had no reason to believe that the work he wanted to do wanted him. On a lark, he auditioned for a show in a smaller market and ended up with a choice: $425 a week plus benefits and paid time off for a stable position at a law firm, or $425 a week to perform with no guarantee of how long it would last and whether he would land another show after that. He said to himself, "'This is the chance. This is the window.' That was sort of how I got from thinking I needed a 'job job' to realizing I could be [a] self-employed contractor, which is what I've been ever since." His return to theater was an exhausting ninety-minute show he performed ten times a week—never leaving the stage, no intermission—for two years.

He says, "To do the same thing over and over again . . . you learn a lot about yourself. You learn how to do a performance when you are sick, you learn how to do a performance when you just don't give a crap, and you learn how to go through these waves of, 'Oh, I'm so excited, this is so interesting, I love what I'm doing, I hate being here with every fiber of my being, but the audience cannot know that, so I have to let them feel like it's the first time I've done this.'"

For more than twenty-five years, Dennis has cobbled together gigs as a wedding singer ("I've probably sung 'YMCA' seven hundred times"), church pianist ("People don't need to know that [I'm not religious]. . . . They just want good music"), residuals from a musical series he cowrote (passive income is "the holy grail of music"), corporate entertainment (his medical technology client "would be having a big meeting in San Diego where they're rolling out a new set of urinalysis tests, and then need singers to come sing about it"), and performing a John Denver show that he wrote and continues to book several years on at supper clubs and regional theaters ("I grew up with that as the background noise of my life"). Although he has not made it to Broadway, film, and television like some of his college classmates, his success story, to him, is simple: "I always wanted to be a musician, and I am currently a musician."

THE WORLD DOESN'T NEED YOUR WORK

When Shawn Wong (no relation) transferred to University of California, Berkeley, from San Francisco State University (SFSU), he noticed that his peers were preparing to save the world. Students around him agitated to end the Vietnam War, ethnic studies programs were starting up on college campuses, and, he wryly observed, most of the Asian American premed students were acquiescing to their stereotypical "tiger mothers," majoring in biology or chemistry so they could become doctors. But Shawn, the only Asian male English major out of 1,100 students at UC Berkeley, wanted to be a novelist. He continued to take classes at SFSU because the university had an Asian American studies department and a creative writing teacher he admired, even though he worried he might be expelled from both schools if they found out.

Shawn recalls, "I realized I was the only Asian American writer I knew in the entire world" until his mentor, Kay Boyle, introduced him to Jeff Chan, a creative writing graduate student. Through Chan, Shawn met two other Asian American writers. It was at a book launch party that they had their first exposure to multicultural literature in the flesh, meeting writers like Ishmael Reed, Alex Haley, and Victor Hernandez Cruz before they became household names. The four friends went on to coedit the first anthology of Asian American writing, *Aiiieeeee!*, which was published by a small university press. Mainstream publishers, and even conventional university presses, did not yet know that the world needed Asian American literature.

While Shawn was still a college senior, the anthology garnered reviews in *Rolling Stone* and the *New Yorker*. Five years later, he published his first novel, *Homebase*, the story of his father, who died when Shawn was seven years old, and his mother, who died when he was fifteen. He reflects, "I was responsible for their story. Nobody was going to write their story unless I wrote it." But Shawn couldn't live off proceeds from the book. He made ends meet reviewing restaurants—he once visited fifteen Chinese joints in twenty-one days—and working part-time adjunct teaching positions at colleges for more than a decade without health insurance. He even rented a room in Boyle's Haight-Ashbury home before he got his first tenure-track job offer at the University of Washington in Seattle, where he has been a professor for more than forty years.

It was not until his second novel that he knew at least someone in the world needed his work. He and his wife, who was battling cancer, had planned a vacation to Hawaii, and she was looking for something to read on the trip. "Why can't you write a book I can read at the beach?" she asked. He realized that she was half-joking, half-challenging him to write the kind of book he considered himself too serious of a writer to write. He remembers, more than twenty-five years after she died, "As a caregiver . . . you're really powerless, you know. You don't know [what you can do] other than driving her to her appointments. You're powerless, and you just feel adrift. And so [writing the book] gave me a purpose. My job was to make her laugh, you know, and so I decided to write an entire novel for one person, and I wrote *American Knees* just for her." The book was also well received by readers and critics and adapted into a film.

PURPOSE AND WORTH

As the previous examples illustrate, it can be practically impossible to find our purpose at the intersection of all four questions at any given time in our working lives. But it need not mean that we cannot find any purpose at work at all. It may mean that we discover our purpose among the portfolio of activities that we undertake in the course of a career rather than in one perfect position that has it all. Some of these stories of searching for our purpose at work suggest that work does not need to be heroic to make a worthy contribution to the world. Others affirm that working for a higher purpose can be heroic. Still others imply that a higher purpose alone cannot sustain us without also fulfilling our functional purpose of staying and feeling alive. They all propose that asking these questions of ourselves can be worthwhile, even if we do not arrive at clear answers.

Purpose involves the hope that work can be something beyond daily growth, production, and survival and that life is more than Macbeth's absurdist despair about "a tale told by an idiot, full of sound and fury, signifying nothing." However, to have that hope, we need reasons to believe that work and life can have purpose, not just the sentimental wish that "everything happens for a reason"— attributed to everyone from Hollywood star Marilyn Monroe to Athenian philosopher Aristotle. Although Aristotle does not clearly indicate where the standard for a life full of purpose comes from, he is clear that it includes, among other things, striving for excellence in works and deeds, valuing relationships with others for their own sake and not just the utility or pleasure they confer, and engaging in virtuous behavior. Philosophers of the Middle Ages who inherited Aristotelian purpose-driven teleology solved the logical problem of infinite regress by giving the source of purpose a name—God—and tended to claim that a life of purpose is one lived in accordance with *God's* purpose. Rather than accept the conclusion that only a higher power can confer purpose on our lives from the outside, atheist existentialist philosopher Simone de Beauvoir asserted that moral freedom enables and empowers us to look to ourselves and our relationships with others to give our lives meaning and fill them with purpose. Whichever school of thought most appeals to you, they all share a set of claims. They include that human life has a purpose, that some purposes are higher than others, and that the purpose of human life is greater than the functional purpose of growth, reproduction, and survival.

The stories and questions in this chapter suggest that discovering our purpose at work is not entirely within our control. Indeed, philosopher Thaddeus Metz tells us that much of what makes life valuable is beyond our ability to determine in relation to the things that may create what he calls "disvalue." However, Metz contends that what is within our control is our ability to make something significant out of the circumstances we are dealt—much as Viktor Frankl, the Holocaust survivor who went on to found the psychiatric method of logotherapy, retained his conviction that life could be meaningful even in conditions of despair. As with Bess Hargreaves, who is "slowly becoming OK" with not knowing her purpose at work, we can still do work worth doing that is part of a life worth living while we figure it out.

CHAPTER 8

WHAT WOULD MAKE YOUR LIFE WORTH LIVING IN A WORLD WITHOUT WORK?

Seems that I was busy doing something close to nothing
But different than the day before.
                            —Prince, "Raspberry Beret"

THERE'S A GREAT BIG BEAUTIFUL TOMORROW

VISITORS TO WALT DISNEY WORLD CANNOT HELP BUT
be confronted with founder and visionary Walt Disney's obsession with the future. Evidence is all over the park, from Tomorrowland in the Magic Kingdom to the geodesic dome presiding over the
Experimental Prototype Community of Tomorrow, better known as
Epcot. The "It's a Small World" ride gets outsize attention and for
good reason, with its dubiously diverse children swaying to an ear-
worm tune as visitors meander through a psychedelically rendered

global tableau (as in Epcot's World Showcase, European countries are oversampled), ultimately arriving at a heavenly room where the children are all together and, inexplicably, dressed in white. But it's Tomorrowland's Carousel of Progress attraction that perhaps best links Walt's vision of the future to how the actual future has played out—and continues to play out today. A narrator informs the audience that the show they are about to see was originally created for the 1964 World's Fair as part of the "Progressland Pavilion" and has staged more performances and been viewed by more people than any other show in American history.

The production, we are told, was Walt's own creation, "from beginning to end," featuring a stationary circular stage with a seating area for the audience that revolves around the stage—hence, carousel. The stage has four sections, each approximately two to three decades after the previous section, which together trace the whole of the twentieth century. We open on a turn-of-the-century household where the father lists the merits of the new icebox, the mother has a new washing machine that enables her to "only" spend five hours doing the wash, the son entertains himself with a stereoscope, and the daughter prepares for a Valentine's Day dance in town at which she will arrive via the new horseless trolley. We follow this same family over the years until we arrive at the conveniences of today. Mom is programming the smart home devices on her computer, which Dad tests out by using voice commands to raise the oven's temperature and lower the lights, Junior is playing a video game on a virtual reality headset with Grandma, and so on.

The themes of the Carousel of Progress are, as Disney themes tend to be, unsubtle. The characters remind us that each generation believes that things couldn't possibly be any better than they are today. The song "It's a Great Big Beautiful Tomorrow," which repeats with each revolution and rivals "It's a Small World" in both its utopian optimism and its ability to haunt the listener's every waking minute, reminds us that this beautiful tomorrow "is just a dream away." In the present, we can't imagine a better world but thanks to a combination of human ingenuity and technological advancement that better world will come.

The carousel does manage to work in a few potentially dystopian angles. The 1940s-era Dad decries his new automobile-enabled trip to work:

> Oh, and *here's* something else that's new. I just heard a new term today on the radio. Fella says we've got something now called the "rat race." Did you ever hear that one? Sure describes my life. I'm involved in something now called "commuting." I drive into the city for work all day and then turn right around and drive all the way back. And the highway is crowded with fellow rats doing the same thing!

Meanwhile, present-day Dad manages to inadvertently turn the smart oven up so high that he burns the Christmas turkey, while Grandpa voices offstage complaints about the smart toilet. Still, the most foreboding element of the proceedings may be the simple fact of the thirty-two "audio-animatronic" robots who comprise the cast of Carousel of Tomorrow. In a posted version of the script dated 1994, the narrator proudly highlights that these actors are able to perform consistently all day long without needing a break. Sound familiar? Interestingly, in more recent performances, that part has been omitted. Whether or not this was a deliberate decision informed by its potential to strike fear in the hearts of Disney guests who acutely feel the threat of themselves being replaced by similar automatons, the implication is clear: the robots are coming for at least some of our jobs in the great big beautiful tomorrow.

Economists from Adam Smith to John Maynard Keynes have been predicting for centuries that machines would free us up for lives of leisure, a condition Keynes described as "technological unemployment," and estimated that by 2030 people would only need to work fifteen hours per week. More recently, World Economic Forum founder Klaus Schwab coined the term Fourth Industrial Revolution to portray a future in which machines might usurp manual labor and artificial intelligence (AI) could render knowledge workers jobless, bringing about an existential crisis and survival angst. Reports from the World Bank and McKinsey estimate that somewhere between 45 and 65 percent of jobs are at risk from automation, with the number highest for the lowest-paid jobs and those in developing countries. Speculation abounds on which jobs will eventually be outsourced completely, how any given job might be altered by advances in sentient AI, and whether this is good news or bad news for human lives worth living.

Whether or not prognosticators are right this time about a future world without work, it is worth wondering what we would do with our ample leisure time if work were not essential to our economic opportunity to live. This would represent a radical change from the way we have looked at work and life for centuries—a view in which most of us expect to spend a substantial period of our productive lives working for a living. In this imagined utopia, intelligent machines would do the work for us, and a universal basic income would alleviate the need to make a living. Many thinkers through the ages have believed leisure time allowed people to achieve their worthiest purpose, pursuing a life of the mind filled with creative and intellectual pursuits.

Yet, in today's society, filling our time with work allows us the luxury of not having to decide what it is we truly want to do with our lives. A lifetime of leisure brought on by the end of work portends a different kind of pressure. This new state of affairs gives rise to the dystopian tension to live a meaningful life devoid of the kind of work that we may not previously have realized gives structure to our days and an implied worth to our existence. If our work gives our lives more meaning, what happens when it goes away? Can something fill this void? Whether forced upon us because our work has been taken away or because unemployment has been given to us as a gift, our ideals about how to live in a potential future *without* work can inform our thinking about our reality of how to live in our present world *with* work.

DOING SOMETHING CLOSE TO NOTHING

In Prince's song "Raspberry Beret," what upon first listening seems to be an upbeat pop presentation of love and longing reveals itself to also be a song about workplace refusal. The protagonist is initially bored on the job at a five-and-dime store, much to the discontent of his boss, Mr. McGee, who finds his employee "a bit too leisurely." He then appears to bail on the job altogether when the beret-ed object of his affection "walks in through the out door," and he hops on his bike to take her for a spin past Old Man Johnson's farm. Although our protagonist appears to have no regrets about his carefree approach to work, choosing love and leisure over mindless toil and not looking back, in our work-obsessed American culture, the idea of being merely underemployed seems unacceptable and a fate to be avoided, to say nothing of not working altogether.

Tales of slackers populated film and television in the 1990s, giving voice to a generation that felt uninspired by their initial forays into the world of steady employment—from the convenience store cashiers of *Clerks* ("I'm not even supposed to be here today") to the midlevel cubicle denizens of *Office Space* ("I'd say, in a given week, I probably do about fifteen minutes of real, actual work"). In this view, being underemployed, bored by routine, and a cog in the demoralizing wheel of capitalist machinery seemed an inescapable reality, a realistic preview of life on the job, especially for those in their early-to-mid career stages. The main characters are both relatable and repellant, as they cycle through emotional reactions ranging from casual resignation to a desire to rebel. Peter, in *Office Space*, chucks his corporate office job and becomes a construction worker, a choice we see him struggling to reconcile at the film's end: "This isn't so bad, huh? . . . Getting some exercise, working outside. . . ." Sure, Peter has left a job that drained him and in which, by his telling, each new day was worse than the one that came before, but is he better off?

Despite the recent cultural prominence of slackers (including a 2002 film actually titled *Slackers*) around the turn of the millennium, both this specific term and general concept are in fact neither new nor passé, as the postpandemic phenomenon of so-called quiet quitting or doing the bare minimum at one's job shows. Tom Lutz's excellent 2007 contemplation of slackerdom, *Doing Nothing*, traces how un- and underemployed characters have persisted over the arc of the American republic itself, with a special focus on their evolution in the twentieth century. The term appears, for example, in H. G. Wells's 1898 novel *The History of Mr. Polly*, in which the titular character wonders: "Was he really just a 'lazy slacker' who ought to 'buck up'?" It then gained popularity during World War I as a term for someone dodging the war. "Are you a slacker? If not, enlist," read the recruiting signs of the day. As Lutz aptly puts it, "A disinclination to work is as old as work itself."

Yet, the notion of not working was not always so culturally fraught. The thrust of 1930s films on work refusal glorified the state of unemployment, with titles like *Hallelujah, I'm a Bum, Holiday*, and *You Can't Take It with You*. Work was a mantle to be thrown off in search of one's more authentic self, to pursue not what the employer wanted you to do but what you wanted to do all day. People were portrayed as being unequivocally better off without work, and though there was a voice given to making ends meet, their daily expenses appeared to take care of themselves.

A prime example of this is in Frank Capra's 1938 film *You Can't Take It with You*. Employees at the local bank are literally sick from working, suffering from ulcers, tics, and heart attacks. By contrast, a character named Grandpa Vanderhof presides over a freewheeling family in which, rather than work for someone else, "everybody does just what [they] want to do," from dancing to painting to making fireworks. Upon learning that his bank teller, Mr. Poppins, has a passion for building toys, Grandpa implores him to leave his job and come join their happy crew. When Poppins asks who takes care of the family, Grandpa replies, "The same one that takes care of the lilies of the field, Mr. Poppins, except that we toil a little, spin a little, have a barrel of fun. If you want to, come on over and become a lily too." In fact, the family subsists on passive income from investments, lives in a beautiful mansion, and even employs servants; yet they happily take in anyone with a dream to their bohemian commune. These Depression-era films espoused American values of freedom, self-expression, and innovation, but interestingly work was not the supplier of these values, as it might be today, but rather the impediment to them. Work takes us away from ourselves, and leisure is when we get ourselves back.

By contrast, in today's society, choosing not to work—in fact not to do much of anything at all—isn't held up as a glorified existence but as a cautionary tale. Imagine someone in peak working age and good health telling you they don't work. There would be an implicit question: *Why not?* Working is the default activity during our prime years, and the alternative is practically inconceivable. An ex-consultant turned stay-at-home mom told Jen recently that she took on several hours a week as a personal trainer for a company whose program she enjoyed, "mostly just so I could say I had a job." Although work is not the only way one can productively make use of time, to not work is tantamount to being lazy, and to be lazy is the ultimate insult, almost equivalent to being a person of no worth at all.

In *Doing Nothing*, Lutz outlines the paradox of our cultural obsession with slackers: we simultaneously envy and loathe them. We can consider our own slacking both a justified reprieve from a workaholic culture and evidence of our own indolence. The slacking of others might enrage us as unfair, someone getting away with something—see the endless debates over the merits of welfare—but also can seem energizing. Flight attendant Steven Slater ended his twenty-eight-year career by announcing he was quitting over the intercom, grabbing a beer, and exiting the plane through the evacuation slide. He was heralded as a cult hero standing up to passengers who treated him badly and an airline that didn't do enough to protect him. His story went viral, and a fan page built in his honor quickly garnered 250,000 members.

Every generation tends to paint the ones that come after it as lazy, self-interested, and, well, a slacker. But studies that compared young people of different eras at the same stage of life reveal that there is no evidence that this is the case. In fact, today's young people seem to be steadily gaining in time spent at work and spending less time in leisure to the point where they are reporting being burned out at record levels. In other words, they appear to be quite the opposite of slackers.

Still, there will always be people who opt out of the workplace voluntarily. One of the more acceptable cultural narratives is a parent who leaves the workplace either permanently or temporarily to care for young children. Barriers to getting and affording quality child care put increasing pressure on a parent to provide care, as many would not earn enough to cover the cost of the child care that would allow them to work. Though things are shifting, mothers rather than fathers are still typically the ones who opt out of their careers.

Interestingly, even high-profile women in the prime of their careers whose success and high income would seem to dictate that they keep working have opted in recent years to step down. Among them is Serena Williams, who announced her retirement from tennis in no uncertain terms to spend time with her daughter: "Believe me, I never wanted to have to choose between tennis and a family. I don't think it's fair. If I were a guy, I wouldn't be writing this because I'd be out there playing and winning while my wife was doing the physical labor of expanding our family." Prime minister of New Zealand, Jacinda Ardern, at age forty-two and a mother to a small child, resigned similarly abruptly from her position, saying she "no longer [had] enough in the tank to do it justice."

During the pandemic, when schools went remote and many parents lost jobs, we witnessed an interesting shift in who worked. One parent, again often the female one, might leave a job to supervise young children at home, as 5.1 million women did, resulting in the lowest percentage of women working for pay since 1986. Meanwhile, teens still in high school entered the workforce, sometimes full-time, because they felt compelled to help their families, which put their ability to continue in school in jeopardy. What is considered an appropriate career pause versus slacking is determined in part within these cultural norms.

WE ARE THE ROBOTS

This book was not written by robots. It was painstakingly labored over by two humans as we sat at our keyboards 1,300 miles apart. Later, our editorial and publishing team, located another few hundred miles away, got involved, but they too aren't robots as far as we can tell. Did we use AI in any part of this book? We used search engines that run algorithms to deliver results sorted with the best match to our terms, including for academic papers about which our knowledge is better but still not encyclopedic, relying often on our limited and fallible memories. We occasionally clicked on those little squiggles under our writing that indicated that something was misspelled or grammatically incorrect, and our word-processing program (talk about an antiquated term) would suggest a replacement. Most of us probably have used similar aids during electronic communication, whether email, texting, or instant messaging, and may not have even noticed what was going on—if you ever wonder how reliant you are on your texting app's autocorrect feature, try turning it off. AI in some form has integrated so gradually into our daily lives that what at first seemed scary has become so useful that we have ceased to notice it—which has become scary all over again as AI's potential to disrupt society expands. Of course, there is some AI that is deemed undesirable or unhelpful, and so it goes by the wayside and never enters mass acceptance—remember Google Glass?

A few years ago, a global team of high-performing staff at one of our former firms undertook a project to study how to make their work more meaningful so they could attract and retain the most promising talent. The team's recommendations included outsourcing most of the mundane, repetitive tasks with other mechanical chores to the firm's development centers in India. When asked whether delegating the most unpleasant tasks to their counterparts overseas would reduce the meaningfulness of those colleagues' work, the team rationalized that it was not their problem: They claimed that the scope of their project was to address a labor challenge in their own developed markets, not in developing ones. Moreover, they presumed, the staff in Bangalore were just happy to have any work at all.

Their outsourcing proposal continued a trend motivated originally by margins rather than meaning. In a twenty-first-century version of a global, virtual assembly line, high rate-per-hour staff in the United States and Europe would leverage the time zone difference by assigning detail work to inexpensive development center staff in India, with the assurance that it would be ready in time for the Westerners to resume work the next morning. In an ironic and innovative turn, over time, the development center staff in turn outsourced those mechanical tasks to machines. They avoided meaningless work by automating the dull work they had been delegated, though in doing so they may also have invoked the specter of their own technological unemployment.

When outsourcing frees up the time of busy people whose primary job is not to do mundane tasks that are nonetheless necessary, it represents progress, a time-saving hack we will eventually take for granted, like GPS assistants in our cars. When outsourcing takes over someone's job, it represents an existential threat. Of course, this brings up the question, seemingly asked ad nauseam by a nervous populace that simultaneously fears and denies that their job could be next: "How much will AI affect my job?" The World Economic Forum in 2023 estimated that almost one-quarter of jobs are expected to change by 2027. They estimate that technology will eliminate 83 million jobs by 2027, while 69 million jobs will be created, for a net loss of 14 million jobs representing 2 percent of current employment. Machines currently account for 34 percent of labor, a balance that should shift to 42 percent by 2027. Technology on balance should add to the global GDP estimated in the tens of trillions and create both jobs and wealth; however, any single person's job is in jeopardy.

The techno-futurist documentary film *The Future of Work and Death* takes on this topic head-on by asking what will become of our work—and our lives—in the near future. The consensus in the film was that tasks that involve creativity or interpersonal skills will be the hardest to replace because they are the most difficult to automate effectively. A *New York Times* writer's attempt to have a deep conversation with Bing's chatbot got very weird, very quickly. A transcript of the conversation, which is disturbing and not surprisingly immediately went viral—the author was so upset after it that he was unable to sleep—demonstrates its failings. Not only did the bot get some things flat-out wrong, but when it tried to be more human—for example, taking on a secret persona, admitting to dark thoughts—its emotional regulation went off the rails. The author reflected that this experience made him realize that what was his biggest fear about chatbots—that they will be factually wrong—was not actually what he was most concerned about for humanity. In fact, he was most concerned about generative AI's ability to influence human users in a way that speaks to our darkest and most destructive impulses. As others have noted, chatbots tend to be radically overconfident no matter what they are actually saying and do not seem to take kindly to being corrected. Over twenty-five thousand people, including tech leaders like Elon Musk, signed an open letter to AI developers asking for a moratorium on further development, citing "profound risks to society and humanity." Google's "Godfather of AI" resigned, in part so he could freely speak about the threats coming from unmitigated AI development. It may be the case, then, that new jobs aimed at monitoring, correcting, and controlling AI's potential for societal harm will emerge. Are these better jobs than the ones AI stands to replace? They might involve creativity in trying to outsmart the robots, forecast their likely use, and communicate a plan to the populace at large.

For all the robot baristas and food servers, Robin Sloan in the satirical novel *Sourdough* presents an alternative view of automated food production, humorously identifying "the egg problem," where robots struggle to cleanly crack eggs for baking without getting shells in the dough. Millions of dollars can be poured into getting this one task right, if it serves as the sole barrier to fully automated baking, omelet making, and the like. Tasks that require this kind of attention to detail and minute correction-making may in fact be just a matter of getting technology advanced enough to perform them. At some point, the question becomes not whether a job can be outsourced to technology but whether the technology can perform the job as well as a human. Eggshells in our food may be one area where there is no in-between, but lots of other areas might thrive on good enough.

A different question is whether certain jobs *should* be outsourced. We have crossed this Rubicon as assembly-line jobs once done under dangerous conditions in loud factories, as portrayed in *Modern Times* and *Norma Rae*, have been replaced by machines—jobs that labor unions once worked to protect and ensure were safe. Arguments have been made that, as dangerous as self-driving cars seem to us now in their early days, they will one day reach a point of ubiquity, reliability, and safety that will benefit society and have us rethinking why we let humans drive their own cars for so long. Another argument adding to the rise of sentient AI is that it will save us from boring jobs. Peter and his cubicle mates in *Office Space* would then be spared from endlessly preparing reports that, though technically performed on the computer, nevertheless required filling out endless software templates in a painstaking manner. In the ideal presentation of this future, the more mindless elements of our jobs will be gone, freeing us up for more creative, stimulating pursuits. Herein lies the crux of the argument that technological automation will be net positive for meaningful work.

But if AI takes over someone's "bullshit job," in the Graeberian sense, a job composed primarily of boring tasks, that person may then question their value. Put another way, by historian Louis Hyman: "If a macro can generate your daily report in five seconds rather than the five hours it takes you, what is your value?" Further complicating our assumptions about which work is worth outsourcing is how workers see themselves. What if they *like* their mindless jobs that provide security, stability, money, and other benefits, which allow them to live their fullest lives outside of work? Or they may find positive meaning in what may appear to others as a mindless job. This view is brought into startling clarity in *The Future of Work and Death*, when a long-haul truck driver is asked what his plans are should self-driving trucks replace him. There is no plan, he says. He wants to, in his words, "die in the truck." Undoubtedly, some workers will find that their jobs have been outsourced who don't want those jobs to go away. What, then, will become of their lives?

WHEN WORK GOES AWAY

When the unemployment rate is cited in news periodicals, reporters typically say something about the health of the economy and business prospects. Yet, a reality underlies those statistics. As writer Walter Kirn notes, "the unemployment rate is an abstraction, an aggregation of bodiless data, but losing a job is a lived experience, written on the nerves." Unemployment is harmful, not only for business and society, but especially for the individuals who find themselves unemployed. Losing a job can be a devastating experience, causing both physical and psychological suffering. Job loss and unemployment are among the most stressful life events, comparable to the death of a loved one and illness. Several factors make job loss even more difficult: for example, if the loss was involuntary rather than by choice, such as someone being forced to resign. Things are also more difficult when a worker is fired, which the worker may internalize as their fault, versus being laid off because of economic downsizing, which can be more readily externalized.

A seminal study of unemployment showed that when a large number of people simultaneously lose their jobs, whether through downsizing or other economic factors, the result can be fundamentally destabilizing. In the 1930s, a group of sociologists traveled to Marienthal, a small village outside Vienna, Austria. Marienthal was a company town, having built up around a textile mill that served as its primary employer. When the mill closed in 1929, practically every family in the village experienced unemployment. The researchers arrived at Marienthal nearly two years after the factory's closure to confront a grim reality. At that point, only one in five families had steady employment of any kind. Three-quarters still received unemployment benefits from the government, which were meager. The research team conducted interviews to understand how the village was coping, this far into their extended unemployment. The findings will be counterintuitive to the notion of desperation as a motivating force; rather than becoming politically active or trying to rebel, the researchers wrote that "prolonged unemployment leads to a state of apathy in which the victims do not utilize any longer even the few opportunities left to them." The people of Marienthal were so drained and despondent, the authors reflected that they hope to never see the likes of this situation replicated again. The villagers had lost their work, and along with it their personal worth, their essence, and their personal will.

Later research has, however, upended the notion that the solution to not having a job is to simply get a new job. The quality of the new job matters: people's well-being was worse if they got jobs that they weren't satisfied with than if they remained unemployed. Not all people are as stuck as the residents of Marienthal were. If they are relatively fortunate, they know there may be numerous jobs out there, but that potentially makes them choosier about the ones they ultimately take. Of course, finding a good job is easier if one is not unemployed for long. The longer unemployment persists, the harder it is to keep up a job search, and the lower the expectation that one will become successfully reemployed.

Part of what we mean when we talk about poor-quality jobs and unsuccessful reemployment is the condition of underemployment. The term typically applies to people who are overqualified for a job, based on their level of experience or education, or who are employed in jobs that are substandard in some way, which could include salary, benefits, or managerial level. Underemployment is prevalent—between 10 and 30 percent of the workforce is estimated to be underemployed. It is also harmful, affecting both job satisfaction and overall well-being. Perhaps worse, underemployed people can get trapped in a vicious cycle: their employment in undesirable jobs prevents them from being hired for jobs for which they are better qualified. Again, while searching for a new job, it may be better to hold out for one that is worthy of one's time; however, as the Marienthal story reminds us, we cannot languish in unemployment for too long.

So we have established that unemployment is not desirable. Even if we choose it, we shouldn't languish there too long. The maxim that it is easier to find a job if we have a job rings all too true. But some people, even though they were upset about losing a job, ultimately come to view it as a blessing in disguise, allowing them to change careers or find a job within their current career that is a better fit. So what factors help people become successfully reemployed? Having people in your social networks that support you is key, both emotionally and instrumentally. They can help you find a new job and help you with career exploration and planning. Not surprisingly, the people who have more resources, both social and financial, can likely weather job loss the most easily. But what about the people who are most vulnerable to technological unemployment?

WHEN WORKING LIFE ENDS

Ends can be equivocal. When we wish for the end of work, we ordinarily do not wish at the same time for the end of life. Rather, we want work to end so life can begin, as the saying goes. In this worldview, work is daily pointlessness, and the worst fate imaginable is that of Sisyphus, rolling the boulder up a hill day after day—the "endless pointlessness," as philosopher Richard Taylor calls it.

Philosophers from St. Augustine to Franz Kafka have suggested that death gives meaning to life, whether they believed in an afterlife, like Augustine, or not, like Kafka. Somewhat similarly, the end of one's working life can give meaning to work. Christopher remembers on a recent trip to China visiting public parks packed with retirees whose working lives had been ended by the government's mandatory retirement age, which for most workers was imposed in their fifties (meaning that, by association, at age thirty-five some workers are considered too old to bother hiring). Some park-goers played mah-jongg, one played a bamboo flute to accompany his friends singing Chinese opera, but many of them seemed to be wandering aimlessly, unsure of what to do with their retired selves.

Christopher's stepfather, who was with him on the same trip, wrote about a recurring dream that he'd had after he retired from forty years at the same law firm:

> In some versions, the Firm had moved and I wandered around downtown trying to find it, or I found it often in a different building but I forgot the floor, or I knew the floor but the elevators would not stop at that floor . . . or I got to the Firm but couldn't find my office or it was only a desk in an open area, or in some way it was difficult to get to, or I had access to an office that was mine or was only shared, or the layout of the new offices was unfamiliar, or almost no one I had known was there. . . . I knew I had completely adjusted to retirement when I quit having those dreams—after three or four years!

The pattern of this dream may be familiar to anyone who has lost a place, a person, or even a job that was once so integral to their sense of belonging and identity that it retrospectively gave their lives meaning and a sense of worth. After you retire, when you are asked the ubiquitous question, "What do you do?" how do you think you will answer? What will that say about who you are if you no longer do what was once your work—until and unless you are able to form an identity away from work that feels worthy?

A BRAVE NEW WORLD OF WORK

Our interview with Robert Guest was obviously going to be different from the others we did for this book right from the start. His Zoom screen opened to reveal Robert seated in his (stationary) Honda SUV. Robert bought this car specifically to rent out on the app Turo, an alternative to car rental agencies where people rent someone's actual vehicle, like an Airbnb for cars. He got the idea to earn money on Turo through social media. He was scouring TikTok for inspiration from people who, like himself, wanted to earn passive income, making money with little effort. The Honda is popular on Turo, meaning that it is usually rented, so Robert rarely drives it, but that's OK because he mostly doesn't need to drive anywhere. His home is a bus he has been renovating to live in. The renovation is almost complete; he had just added a porch off the back shortly before we talked. His expenses are few, mostly gas money, since he can plug the bus into a generator or a friend's house. He currently has a part-time gig as a street sweeper, a job he enjoys for its two main perks: being a short bike ride from the bus and requiring only four hours of work at night.

Robert is a self-proclaimed night owl whose perfect day involves watching the sunrise then sleeping in. He does not fit into the traditional world of nine-to-five work and has absolutely no qualms about it. He just turned forty, has no permanent attachments, and prioritizes adventure, novelty, and continual learning above all else. Once the bus is fully renovated, Robert plans to drive it down the Pan-American Highway from Charleston to Costa Rica, where friends await on a Pacific coast beach. Those friends run an outdoor sports company, renting hang gliders and the like to adventurous tourists. But Robert has no plans to join them. Rather, his plan is to live on a combination of income from Turo rentals—which he can manage remotely, outsourcing the cleaning and delivery of the car—coupled with disability payments from his time in the military, where he went on multiple tours to Afghanistan. He is considering adding a second car to be able to earn even more.

While we talked, Robert's story appeared to simultaneously represent a bygone era as well as representing our app-enabled present day. He would fit in with Grandpa Vanderhof from *You Can't Take It with You*—if Grandpa and his crew lived in a tiny mobile home. For all the social media glorification of #vanlife, Robert is not diligently photographing the renovation of his bus for public consumption like many peers and seems to have no interest in self-promotion in general. He was indifferent, at best, to being profiled in this book. Yet, he is otherwise emblematic of the twenty-first century, specifically the trend toward so-called gig work, which has been a defining change in the first part of the new millennium.

A Pew study of gig economy workers conducted in 2021 estimated that 16 percent of the workforce had earned money on an online gig platform in the past year, with greater participation among workers who were younger (age eighteen to twenty-nine), non-white (30 percent of Hispanic adults reported working on a platform within the last year), and from a lower income bracket. The majority of workers take these gigs as a side hustle rather than as a full-time job and primarily to earn extra money—although wanting to be one's own boss and set one's own schedule rank highly as motivators as well. Of course, there is a lively critique of gig economy self-employment as something that sounds good for workers while ultimately making them even more reliant on the corporations that run the platforms—hence, the ongoing debate about whether drivers for ride-share companies like Uber are contractors or employees. Indeed, the Pew study revealed that the majority of gig workers felt they were treated fairly by their employers regarding pay and job assignment, but when it came to benefits they received, about half felt they were not treated fairly. Other complaints about the jobs included feeling unsafe, being harassed, or being treated rudely—complaints that were more frequent among younger, non-white workers. And most of these workers don't have a safety net or much in the way of savings.

The majority of people in the Pew report spent less than ten hours per week working on gig platforms, including time spent waiting for job assignments. The time spent waiting meant they were unable to do anything else, however, and so amounted to unpaid work time. These workers made the calculation that the additional money they made from this work was worth their time waiting for job assignments. Presumably, this calculation was or felt rational; otherwise, they would not have kept doing it. Amazon's Mechanical Turk platform takes this time-versus-money calculus to an even further extreme: people are able to be paid down to the minute for "microtasks," many of which are designed to take fractions of an hour and pay little but add up. We have used MTurk—named, incidentally, for a computerized chess-playing machine developed in the late eighteenth century that competed against the likes of Ben Franklin and Napoleon Bonaparte—to recruit participants for our own research. Platforms like Uber, MTurk, and Taskrabbit raise the potential for our every waking minute, almost down to the second, to be spent in the service of making money. Is it worth giving up our precious leisure time?

Robert Guest believes it is not. During our interview he asked very provocative questions about the worth of work explicitly compared to everything else we would want to do. In his case, a longing since his itinerant childhood for even more travel, adventure, and novelty supplanted any desire for stability and security provided by the workaday world. Robert's high school yearbook quote was, "I want to die fighting lions." He recently heard that pirate activity has ticked up in Costa Rica and was practically giddy at the notion of being kidnapped by pirates.

Robert described watching the people around him work without end to pay an increasing number of bills to fuel their own consumption. He recognizes that these status symbols, like houses and iPhones, are sources of pride for people, but he also sees them as deep sources of stress, stress that he believes is not worthwhile. He laments that he has to work harder to escape this system than to stay in it:

> It's really that people don't want to put the work in to get out.
> So they just stay in it, and they get comfortable, and they get

complacent, and structure is good for most people, and they say they like that and next thing you know, you're 70, and that's it. You don't have anything to look forward to so much as looking back on the things you have, and I don't want that. I want to be having new experiences until I die.

While in the military, Robert's paid work was about as adventurous as one can imagine: he went undercover wearing Afghan clothes, met native warlords as well as high-level officials from NATO and the United Nations, and witnessed the country's national elections. In his postmilitary life, much as he dreams about going back to help the Afghan people, work and living life as he chooses— a life of adventure and bravery—are at distinct odds. To Robert, his choice has taken on a moral imperative: "People always want peace and security and safety, but a part of our essence gets dulled when there's nothing to sharpen it on."

In Robert's view, peace and security are affiliated with work, while bravery and adventure are the hallmarks of his desired leisure time. Aristotle saw it differently: peace, virtue, and an appreciation for the arts allowed us to have leisure, while courage was required for work. Our goals, according to Aristotle, were to create a society that would free us from the needs that necessitate work and therefore allow us to perform the real work of being human. Without work telling us who we need to be in the world, we could rediscover our basic virtues, as well as the liberal arts—music, reading, writing, drawing, and so on—as valuable pursuits in their own right. Unfortunately, however, Aristotle did not live in the age of robots, and since somebody had to do the dirty work, the intellectuals often employed slaves.

As Joanne Ciulla explains in *The Working Life*, the unemployed citizens of Marienthal could not enjoy their so-called leisure time because their lives were just as constrained as when they were working. Rather than the alleged goal of the sharing economy making workers freer than traditional employment, the opposite is often the case: they end up being even more dependent on others and under their control. For victims of technological unemployment, a similar fate may await. Will we truly be freed up by AI to live the lives of our choosing, or will we be more dependent than ever, unable to enjoy our newfound leisure time?

WHAT SHOULD—OR COULD—WE DO IN A WORLD WITHOUT WORK?

Being obsessed with the future makes a strange sort of sense. The future is always so close, yet so far away, looming just ahead of us, yet fundamentally unknowable in advance. The concept of "the future" will therefore always hold a combination of fear and dread alongside optimism and hope. For founder-CEO types, who are used to controlling so much of the world around them, or at least attempting to, the future world remains alluringly outside their sphere of influence. We see echoes of Walt Disney's obsession with the world of tomorrow in the forward thinking of modern-day entrepreneurs like Howard Hughes and Steve Jobs and in the quasi-space-race among Elon Musk, Richard Branson, and Jeff Bezos. Critics ask, with good reason: Why spend so much time, money, and effort trying to get to the moon or Mars when we have so much that needs fixing here on Earth? Moon shots may inspire: companies have taken over this term, which has come to mean an extremely ambitious project or goal that a company strives to achieve by looking to the future and working backward, devising a strategy to get there, rather than anchoring in the present and working forward. There might be an analogy to an individual career: What would it look like if you started with the future, even with retirement, whenever that happened, and worked backward? What would your ideal future look like if you could design your career as you wished? What does this understanding mean for your work choices today?

Of course, when we attempt to make plans, the universe often laughs in response. The biggest disrupter to both the global economy and individual jobs in the twenty-first century so far has not been sentient AI or any other technological innovation run amok, but rather a humble virus, which brought our world to a grinding halt. Much like the overconfident chatbots, future prognosticators often are the most declaratively certain about the precise things they are likely to get the most wrong.

Seriously contemplating what a future world might look like—specifically one in which we choose which work to do ourselves and which to automate—is, nonetheless, useful in our current world. Quite simply, our current world of work often means, by necessity or choice, that we find ourselves so busy with work that we truly don't know what to do with ourselves when we're not working. Aristotle, who posited that we find our basic virtues in leisure, would say that this is an existentially precarious position. Most of us have probably forgotten how to be at leisure, to relax, to choose what we want to do. For those who have dependents who need their attention at home when they're not at work, or others who treat every hobby like it's a job, this difficulty to be at leisure may be especially pertinent. However, even if we have forgotten how to make the most of leisure time, that (hopefully) doesn't mean we can't remember. To perform leisure tasks on purely our own terms, we must be free from need, which necessitates the conditions of safety, security, education, and peace. This might take the place of a universal income to provide for our basic needs to be met, as well as the simultaneous realization that work is itself not always a basic need. It may also require us to deprogram the parts of our brains that can't imagine life without a smartphone and all that it enables and demands of our cognitive energy and disposable income. Partly this takes us off the hook: the problems of ensuring enjoyable leisure versus desperate unemployment are society's burden to bear, needing government interventions and regulatory controls, as much as they are ours. Yet, our collective failure to address these issues as the great big beautiful tomorrow looms will likely have a human toll.

Change is always hard, even as we accept that it is inevitable in the best of times and jarring in the worst, as in the chaos that seems all around us coming out of a pandemic, facing social unrest, and contemplating a warming planet. We fear change, regardless of it being able to help us. However, many people convincingly argue that we feel most alive when presented with change, when we are learning, growing, and undergoing a process that leaves us different from before. The earliest work of humans was fundamentally that of change—to create life, to grow food, to build shelter. The new era of work—whether it is ushered in by robots, unemployment, or retirement—will require change, for better and worse, which will require us to grow, stretch, and reinvent, any of which could provide an opportunity to get closer to our hunter-gatherer forebears or toward a bold new, previously unimagined tomorrow.

CHAPTER 9

WHAT LEGACY WILL YOUR WORK LEAVE?

I didn't mean to say I'm not excited to be in a book. I'm just saying I mean it's like that's cool. That's neat. But I don't have a desire to leave a legacy behind.
　　　—Robert Guest, army veteran and street sweeper

LEGACY MECHANIC

CHAD SOKOLOVSKY'S POEMS ABOUT CHILDHOOD, collected in his first book, *Prophecy Mechanic*, might resonate with many fellow teenaged boys' experience of sexual awakening:

> Girls were mushroom clouds blooming towards
> the shallow trenches of our sunken chests

They also remind readers of their own childhood games, running around in "our dishtowel capes." You may not realize from reading his poetry that Chad—who publishes under the familial surname that his grandfather simplified after emigrating from Russia but goes by Sokol—was raised in what he refers to as "an eschatological religious cult." By the time Chad graduated high school, his future was foretold. He was promoted at age eighteen to minister, and like the elders he was raised to look up to, he would live a life of poverty and work as a manual laborer because there was no point in building a career when the end time was near. He operated the drill press machine for $4.95 an hour inside a Modesto, California, warehouse where the temperature regularly topped 100 degrees, helping to build wooden pallet bins for tomato season.

Chad's autobiographical poems about youth hint at what was to come in the poet's own life, expressing skepticism about having been "born on a flat earth" and being himself "a failed prophecy." At eighteen, his mother is cutting his hair for "the last time":

> when I finally understood she wasn't
> going to get better or that we would
> never be as close as those afternoons
> when I confessed I didn't believe in God
> and she pretended not to hear me.

He went through the motions for a few more years, giving Sunday sermons, preaching door-to-door, getting married, and having a daughter. At nineteen, he worked the parking lot at Costco, pulling carts for nine dollars an hour with medical benefits, and he thought, "'Oh, my God, I'm gonna be set!' I really didn't have any other goals beyond that."

Two experiences "opened [his] eyes." One was junior college. Chad was discouraged from getting an outside education, but as he watched his father and the other church elders face struggle with physical work as their bodies aged, he thought that being a teacher would have better long-term prospects than being a manual laborer. A Western civilization class challenged "everything I thought I knew about history, chronology, and by the end of that first semester the doubt started to set in, and that was the first time I started to question my belief system, and I pretty much left that religion pretty quickly. After that it all started falling into place." He divorced, with custody of his daughter, and he and his daughter left the community they had lived all their lives in. Chad was estranged from his parents because he believed:

> I don't need ministers or monks to see the divinity
> in the faces of my children who are dreaming
> of a bigger world to play in.

The other experience that opened his eyes was working at Costco, which he continued to put himself through college and keep health insurance for his daughter. While waiting to hear about his law school applications, Chad was offered a job in the company's regional buying office, which led him to believe he could make a career there that would provide the financial security he never had growing up. He left law school behind and was promoted from assistant buyer to buyer and continued to rise up the ranks. As Chad remembers it:

> Fast forward 20 years later after I finished college and was working as a food commodity buyer for Costco, I was in charge of the canned tomato program and was in Fresno . . . visiting a canning facility and we went to the fields of Roma tomatoes during harvest. I rode on top of one of the harvesters . . . and as we got to the end of the first furrow, I saw stacks of empty tomato pallets . . . the same ones I used to build. It was an existential moment for me thinking that I came full circle after 20 years and was now the buyer in charge of a multi-million dollar program. That was one of the most defining moments of my life, and I remember thinking that all along the way over the previous 20 years I was never unhappy at any stage of my life and career even though I was barely scraping by financially until the last few years since moving to Washington and being

promoted. I never started off with a specific goal to end up where I am today, or ever imagined as I worked that drill press that I would do much else for a career.

Five years before we spoke with him, Chad Sokol moved to Seattle with his second wife and stepson—his daughter is now grown—to take a corporate executive position with Costco that he had applied for five or six times before getting what some of his colleagues describe as the best role in the company: vice president over wine and spirits. It entitles him to wine tastings and interesting travel. However, it is stressful and involves working over fifty hours a week and receiving text messages from the CEO and CFO at any hour. "So I'm kind of always on," he says. In any case, it's a role that would have been unimaginable to younger Chad and was never contemplated by the church elders of his insular community because it was anathemic to their way of life. Yet, it is now the life he has cultivated and claimed as his own, so much the better for being his choice versus inheritance.

Few of his professional colleagues are aware that, every weekday, Chad rises by 5 a.m. to write poetry at a coffee shop that opens at 6 a.m. before arriving at the office at 7 a.m., because when "I've given . . . 150% of myself to my career . . . and I'm just working . . . a little bit of my soul starts to disappear." His poetry has won multiple awards. He competes nationally in poetry slam competitions and also performs music. He was three-quarters of the way through a new book when we spoke. *Prophecy Mechanic* concludes with "An Imaginary Legacy," a sarcastic take on the self-importance with which legacy is sometimes imbued:

> I'll be a head of state
> behind a mountain
> of decrees awaiting
> the precision of my signature
> and processions of black
> sedans marching like ants.

They'll pile tulips and lilies
beside my river of speeches,
and I will fall like loose change
from the pockets of
children along the tracks,
my copper minted face
flattened on the rails.

A prophecy is a prediction about the future, often concerning an afterlife. A legacy typically involves taking stock of what is enduring about past events and actions that took place in this life. Chad's story suggests that it may not be any easier to plan a legacy than it is to predict a prophecy, which seems to be what philosopher Søren Kierkegaard had in mind when he lamented in his diary: "Life can only be understood backwards, but it must be lived forwards." As a famous refrain from *Hamilton* suggests, our legacy is not always a happy ending that is within our control to write as we wish, but rather it is ultimately in the hands of "who tells your story."

Chad seems more pragmatic than prophetic about his story: "I work with people who have very specific goals they want to get to. And they're struggling, or they're trying to get there. And I look at myself, and I feel like I've always stumbled across things. . . . I think the music and the poetry and other things I'm into all seem a little disparate for me. It's like it all comes together to make a whole . . . each part benefits the other one, so I see it as coming together. But I do have these moments where I look at them, and I take a step back, and I can't figure out how I got to where I am, because it really wasn't a plan."

THE UNEXAMINED WORK IS NOT WORTH WORKING

Philosopher Robert Nozick observes that, in the notable life stories of figures like Socrates and Joan of Arc, their deaths are integral to their lives' legacies. Socrates was famous for saying, "The unexamined life is not worth living," though we would like to believe that he would have also assented to, "The unexamined work is not worth working." Given the opportunity to escape a death sentence that was by all accounts—including even, perhaps, that of those who sentenced him—undeserved, the father of Western philosophy declined to do so. A scene reproduced in Jacque-Louis David's famous painting shows a muscular and righteous Socrates surrounded by his grief-stricken followers. Using what we now call the Socratic method, he bade them to accept why defying his sentence would be a greater injustice than the sentence itself—and to contemplate the immortality of the soul. At just seventeen years old, Joan of Arc was sent to Orléans to reinforce a French army under siege. With a patriotic banner and a claim of divine inspiration, she was credited with bringing about an English retreat and the eventual coronation of King Charles. Barely two years later, English partisans betrayed her, accusing her of blasphemy for dressing as a man and heresy for her religious visions and burning her at the stake. She was later canonized by the Roman Catholic Church and acknowledged as a martyr and patron saint of France. Nozick writes, "death does not always mark the boundary of a person's life as an end that stands outside of it; sometimes it is a *part* of that life, continuing its narrative story in some significant way." As novelist Haruki Murakami observed in *Norwegian Wood*, "Death exists, not as the opposite but as a part of life."

Why are so many stories about legacy also stories involving death? One important reason that we care about leaving a legacy is to overcome our natural fear of death. William James referred to immortality as "one of the great spiritual needs of [humanity]." Unique among animals, humans must carry on with the work of living while being constantly and simultaneously aware that they will one day die. According to terror management theory (TMT), there are several mechanisms that we employ to cope with our evolutionary concern about oblivion. Some of us are motivated to live on through having children. Others turn to faith, particularly those that promise a form of immortality in the afterlife. We seek to identify ourselves with a cause that transcends our time and place. We endeavor to write a great book or create an enduring work of art. These coping mechanisms are not the only reasons that we might engage in these behaviors, nor are they mutually exclusive.

In relation to work, these mechanisms might justify why family business owners hope to pass ownership and organizational values down through the generations. They suggest one motivation for why religious institutions are often the recipients of legacy gifts and why larger bequests are often associated with the naming rights for a building or other semipermanent fixture. They may help to explain the trend among employers to articulate a purpose with which employees can identify and take pride in. They seem to imply the significance of what we call our life's work, and perhaps even have something to do with the existence of this book and our hope that this is not the last one we write. Concern about legacy does not need to be motivated by egoistic obsession with our own personal legacies. Indeed, the *New York Times* "Portraits of Grief" were written out of consideration for people whose opportunity to author their own legacies was taken away suddenly and prematurely.

According to Kim Wade-Benzoni, a Duke intergenerational behavior researcher who worked at NYU on 9/11, there was a forecasted "baby boomlet" after the attacks, which may have been motivated by legacy or a temporary reprioritization of family life over work. Wade-Benzoni's research distinguishes between two responses that people have when primed by experimental or experiential conditions to consider the general possibility of or even heightened risk of death. *Death anxiety* is an emotional response to death awareness that can lead to panic and dread. *Death reflection* is a cognitive response to death awareness that leads us to put our lives in the context of a bigger picture and contemplate meaning. In a paper written by Wade-Benzoni and Adam Grant, the authors examine the implications of "death awareness at work." They find that death anxiety can contribute to tardiness, absenteeism, and other behaviors that can harm work performance. Death reflection, on the other hand, can contribute to prosocial behaviors, such as mentoring others, changing jobs in the interest of serving others, and even doing or contributing to work that benefits future generations.

One way in which our work can directly benefit future generations is through work itself that improves society, preserves the environment, and creates employment opportunities. Some consequentialist philosophers assert that future people have contingent rights that present people have a binding responsibility to respect, much as the seventh-generation principle attributed to Native American thought urges us to think ahead about how our decisions today will support the well-being of our descendants. But perhaps the most familiar way in which work benefits the next generation is when it supports the well-being of your own children. There are entire books on the topic of work and family balance, and nearly all of them recognize that career advancement has the potential to come at the cost of time with children and other dependents. Conversely, caregiving poses an obstacle not only to how well you perform as a professional but even to the work hours you choose and the pay you receive.

If you choose to be a parent who works outside the home principally to support your family, there may be no worthier legacy than your children. But when you have to make trade-offs between your commitment to your career and your family, perhaps another way to think about work is not as detracting from your legacy but rather integral to it. That is to say that the choices you make today—about what work you do, when and how much you do it, and for what purpose—will shape the choices your children make about the same things. Moreover, the world you leave them will affect what work still needs to be done. How will your present example as a working role model positively influence the next generation's future choices about what work is worth doing? How might the work you do now make their lives better today and tomorrow—while they are children and later when they are part of the working world?

HOW WILL YOU MEASURE YOUR LIFE?

By any measure, Clayton Christensen was a successful professional. After receiving an MBA from Harvard Business School, he spent time as a management consultant before becoming a CEO. He went back to Harvard for a doctorate and then joined the faculty there, teaching a popular strategy course called "Building and Sustaining a Successful Enterprise." His 1997 book, *The Innovator's Dilemma*, was named by the *Economist* as one of the six most important books ever written about business, advancing his theory of "disruptive innovation," which pertains to transformative inventions that create new markets or upend established orders. In 2011, he was named in a poll of business leaders as the most influential business thinker in the world.

In 2010, Christensen's success story was disrupted by a cancer diagnosis and subsequent stroke. A deeply religious member of the Church of Jesus Christ of Latter-day Saints, he coauthored a new book that was published in 2012 called *How Will You Measure Your Life?* while he was still learning how to speak again. The book applied ideas from his strategy course, consisting of advice he usually gave in a lecture on the last day of his class, to address three goals: finding happiness in your career, finding happiness in your relationships, and staying out of jail. *The Innovator's Dilemma* might end up being Christensen's professional legacy as a business expert. However, *How Will You Measure Your Life?* might be his most fitting legacy to his career as a teacher, showing how to apply research about planning for and measuring business success to plan for and measure life success.

In relation to the first goal, Christensen drew on motivation theory to counsel that money and other material rewards will only take us so far and that what we really require to be happy at work is meaning. To find happiness in relationships, he said that just as we need empathy to understand our customers' problems, we need to think about what is important to others and not just to ourselves. Regarding the third goal, he warned that "the marginal cost of doing something 'just this once' always seems to be negligible, but the full cost will typically be *much* higher." Some of his former classmates, including disgraced Enron CEO Jeffrey Skilling, had ignored "the trap of marginal thinking."

But it can also be a trap to think that we can plan and measure success in life in the way that we plan and measure success in business—to consider time to be a "resource," relationships to be an "investment," and lives to be something to "measure." This way of thinking is familiar in a contemporary working world in which we keep score of assets and liabilities to build equity in our success. It employs cost-benefit analysis, in which good decisions are determined to be those with the greatest prospective net benefit.

However, there are at least two familiar problems with this kind of utilitarian thinking. One is that it requires us to measure everything on the same scale, even though value is pluralistic, meaning not all forms of value can be reduced to economic or other quantitative measures. This incommensurability among valuable things, as philosopher Martha Nussbaum refers to it, may help to explain why we sometimes are willing to work harder for less money than we could otherwise make doing a job we love.

That was one reason Neil Hill left a relatively lucrative career in restaurant management to become a youth tennis coach who often has to work seven days a week. Neil learned from the tragic example of his father, who felt he only briefly tasted professional freedom as a minor league baseball player before he was injured. He returned home to become an electrician at the same dreaded Pennsylvania steel mill where his brothers worked, succumbing to alcoholism and depression. As if to further reinforce the idea that there are some things that money cannot measure, following the death of their patriarch, the Hill family received a payout from a life insurance policy that purported to place a measurable value on life. The money gave the Hill family more financial security than ever before, enabling Neil and his brother to go to a better school and escape the steel mill. Their father's work may have indirectly killed him. But in doing so, it enabled his family to flourish, even though nobody believed that the "death benefit" from the insurance company was worth the cost of a life.

Another problem with so-called consequentialist thinking is that we cannot plan with certainty for and predict the future. As a case in point, after "hitting a wall" in her legal career doing "the same thing over and over," Kristine Enea had finished ninth of twenty-two candidates in her campaign for county supervisor and was not sure what to do next. She had happened to read an article on living organ donation and decided to give a kidney to a stranger, "a pure good thing to do and that I would succeed at." Shortly thereafter, she started taking premed classes on her circuitous path toward earning a medical degree at age fifty-seven. It might have been tempting to think that, if at that point her legacy had been written, even if everything she had done in her work to that point had been value neutral, donating a kidney tipped the balance net positive and even implanted Kristine's legacy in the life of another human's being. But what if the body of the recipient of her kidney had rejected it? Would her donation have been any less valuable?

Business executives can be constrained by the consequentialist thinking of the financial markets, which typically measure CEO performance in terms of quantifiable results. For the tenth anniversary of PwC's Global CEO Survey, the production team, of which Christopher was a part, asked CEOs to articulate the lasting legacy they wished to leave behind. Even so, one-third of the respondents prioritized market performance—defined as "long-term financial success, market domination, defense of current position"—begging the question: What would it do to their legacy if circumstances beyond their control led to poor financial performance? Would that mean that their legacy was a failure?

In full disclosure, neither of us knew Clay Christensen personally, but of course we knew *of* him, and the people we know who did know him had nothing but kind words to say about him. Yet, we think it is telling that his book is called *How Will You Measure Your Life?* rather than *How to Measure Your Life*, because the former, unlike the latter, encourages us to ask about the value of our lives without promising that it is measurable. It concludes with an epilogue about the importance of purpose, in which Christensen reflects on his own achievements. He could not have known, at the time, how yet another idea in which he played an early part would catch on with the so-called purpose generation of future business leaders operating in a purpose economy. He might not have anticipated a world in which affluent younger workers spiritually identified more with work than with conventional religion. He could not have foreseen that he would succumb to complications from leukemia shortly before the most disruptive pandemic in a century set in. The unstated irony in *How Will You Measure Your Life?* is that, when Christensen reflects upon his own life, he recognizes that he cannot plan for when his "interview with God" will occur and realizes that the value of life is beyond measure, that "God, in contrast to us, does not need the tools of statisticians or accountants." He concludes, "while many of us might default to measuring our lives by summary statistics, such as the number of people presided over, number of awards, or dollars accumulated in a bank, and so on, the only metrics that will truly matter to my life are the individuals whom I have been able to help, one by one, to become better people."

WORK AND DEATH

When professor of Russian language and literature Gary Jahn served on Christopher's PhD committee, he was just beginning what would be the final major research initiative of his career. It was a fully annotated electronic edition of *The Death of Ivan Ilych*, Leo Tolstoy's short novel that Gary considers to be about as perfect as it is possible for a work of art to be, and yet it remains underappreciated, because who would want to read a book with a title like that? The story of a dying man preoccupied with his career, *Ivan Ilych* is a profound consideration of one of the most clichéd contemporary questions about whether we should pursue our legacy through work: "Has anybody on their deathbed ever wished they had spent more time at work?"

Of course, it's sad—the main character dies—and sobering, but in spite of the subject, it's also funny and beautiful, which may help to explain why Gary came to devote twenty years of his career to a twenty-thousand-word story. The arc of Gary's career is a glimpse into the history of American Russian relations as well as a testament to how circumstances beyond our control can shape our life's work and legacy. He was an undergraduate Russian major during the Cuban Missile Crisis. The year he received his master's degree, the Soviet Union invaded Czechoslovakia, destabilizing Eastern Europe and leading, in the year Gary was awarded his doctorate in Russian literature, to a fragile peace forged between superpowers at the Moscow Summit of 1972. When he was hired by the University of Minnesota, departments of Slavic languages were developed with funding from a state department eager to employ operatives fluent in the vernacular and culture of the enemy. After the collapse of the Soviet Union and the presumptive end of the Cold War, funding for and interest in Russian history and culture precipitously declined. Faculty positions in the field decreased around tenfold, and Gary told Christopher, while sitting in his university office beside a bust of Tolstoy, that after he finished his study of *Ivan Ilych*, his research would be finished. Such was the significance of the great author's legacy, he said, that everything that could be written about him had already been written. Christopher mistook that proclamation for a challenge, publishing three new academic papers—in business ethics, not literature, but still—about what we can learn from Tolstoy about "Work and the Most Terrible Life," the title of his paper about *Ivan Ilych*, which will make sense soon enough.

As an example of the painstaking detail of Gary's annotated edition, the seventh footnote appears on just the tenth line of the first page. It contains a link to a typical Russian death notice of the era, described in the story as "surrounded by a black border." After his colleagues register their initial surprise upon reading the notice of Ivan's death, "the first thought of each of the gentlemen in that private room was of the changes and promotions it might occasion among themselves or their acquaintances," now that their peer had permanently vacated his position on the Court of Justice. Although the narrator informs us that Ivan had been genuinely "well liked," the second unspoken thought among those discussing his death is that it is better that "it is he who is dead and not I." Later, at the wake at Ivan's home, one of them observes that his widow, Praskovya Fedorovna, already understands more than he does what she can expect to be paid by the government in the form of her late husband's pension. Gary remarks in the footnote, "In a way, one might say that the main question of which the reader of the story must judge is: 'How did Ivan Ilich come to be enclosed in such a tiny frame?'" This may appear to be one of those narrow questions that only scholars study until we consider the significance for any of us to have everything that we lived and worked for reduced to a few words enclosed in a tiny death notice—and for one's death to be perceived by one's colleagues as an opportunity for advancement and by one's spouse as a pecuniary event.

The black border is only the final confinement of the dead man's life and work. After the book's opening scenes, the narrative goes back in time. In Gary's introduction to his annotated edition, there is a section called "The Proportions of the Text" in which he carefully counts—as only a scholar would do—the lines of text in each chapter, observing a "general pattern of decreasing length" among the chapters that corresponds with a "parallel decrease in their time frame" and "a parallel decrease in the spatial dimensions of the story." *Ivan Ilych* is about someone who did all the right things at work (entered the right career, befriended the right people, sought the right positions, rose to a high level) for all the wrong reasons (wealth, vanity, approval, and to get away from a family that annoyed him)—which is why Tolstoy describes his life as "most simple and most ordinary and therefore most terrible." When Christopher reviews these facts of Ivan's life with his MBA students—a salary that always seemed to be "500 rubles too little," a home that is "just one room short," decorated exactly as "what is usually seen in the houses of people of moderate means who want to appear rich"—they smile wryly at the familiarity of these insights. They inevitably identify somebody in their workplaces and communities who are just like him and even uncomfortably admit that the somebody they recognize might be themselves.

Just as Gary observes, the chapters describing the rise of Ivan's career are expansive, following him from city to city. Those after his figurative and literal fall—he falls off a ladder while hanging curtains in his house, which precipitates his death—limit him to commuting between home and work, then between the rooms of his home, until his final, agonizing hours in which he is confined to his deathbed, facing a wall—an observation Christopher remembers Gary pointing out in class with sinister laughter. When it becomes apparent that he is terminally ill, Ivan considers the absurdity that his own mortality should come from something as trivial as a fall from a ladder instead of in some heroic battle. When he was a judge, he acted as though his work was worth living for, eschewing family life for the sake of advancing his prestige and professional standing. He cannot countenance the possibility that home decorating could be work worth dying for.

Perhaps another more optimistic moral of the story is the possibility of redemption, that Ivan's slow death gives him some control over his legacy by choosing how to live better in his final moments. The story does not conclusively answer whether Ivan should have spent more or less time at the office. But it may lead us to think about how he should have lived and worked all along, to consider the choices that are within our control that may yet influence our legacy that someone else will write and to appreciate why one story could be worth so much of Gary's life and work.

WHO TELLS YOUR STORY?

At the end of *Hamilton*, the stage belongs to Eliza Hamilton—even though Lin-Manuel Miranda's rap musical is ostensibly based upon the legacy of Eliza's far more famous husband, Alexander, as an underappreciated Founding Father of the United States.

Surviving for fifty years after her husband was killed in an infamous duel, she had been singing about her efforts in that time to secure her husband's legacy. These included her proudest achievement as the widow of an orphan: founding a private orphanage, in which she sees Alexander in the eyes of the children she helps. The song in which she expresses that sentiment, "Who Lives, Who Dies, Who Tells Your Story," explores how both narratives and their narrators shape and reshape history—how *Hamilton* itself has resurrected national awareness of Alexander Hamilton; how America's third vice president, Aaron Burr, is remembered primarily for killing Alexander; and how *Hamilton* morphs into all-but-forgotten Eliza's story in the end. Despite all the notoriety of *Hamilton* and the fame and fortune that it has conferred upon the cast and characters, what seems indisputable is its message that legacy is not about fame and fortune but rather about "who tells your story."

Human beings are "the storytelling animal," as literary scholar Jonathan Gottschall shows in his book of that name. We make sense of experience by arranging information into stories that structure our understanding not only of how the world is but how it ought to be. We derive our ideals about behavior from what we come to expect when we refer to the moral of the story, and we tell life stories that enable us to apprehend what we consider to be a life well lived. The storification of life helps to explain why Clay Christensen measures a good life in terms of individual encounters rather than statistical records, why David Brooks observes that our eulogy virtues matter more in the end than the lists of skills and achievements on our résumés, and why Elizabeth Anderson is a value pluralist who contends that worth cannot be summed up in a singular unit of measure.

The idea that the worthiness of our lives can best be communicated as a story is at least as old as Aristotelian ethics, in which good character is a function of uncountable patterns of behavior rather than countable good actions or credits versus bad actions or debits. Aristotle suggests that we cannot adequately judge a person's character until their story is over—much as he praises poetry and other forms of storytelling with a beginning, middle, and end as a better guide for our moral imagination than factual recitations of history, which only tell us what actually happened. Contemporary empirical research has reinforced Aristotle's claims that stories have the potential to cultivate character. Researchers have sought to show the capacity of the story to nurture empathy, emotional intelligence, elevation, our ability to relate to other people, collaboration, and even longevity, among other positive contributors to a legacy worth writing. This is not to imply that stories automatically make us better people or deny that, in the hands of the wrong storytellers, stories have the capacity to manipulate and distort history. It is rather to say that stories carry our values and legacies and that, much as the arc of history bends toward justice, the arc of the story bends toward truth.

THERE IS NO WHY

The story of the aftermath of the attacks on the World Trade Center traversed the full range of dramatic possibilities. The physical spectacle began with the tragedy of the twin towers' fall and continued on in the heroism of the Ground Zero rescue and recovery effort that was carried out not only by survivors and other locals but also volunteers from around the country working solemnly on the smoldering pile. It involved infighting between the NYPD and the FDNY over who had jurisdiction, especially when remains were found of one of their own. It concerned the grief of families who insisted that the footprints of the towers were hallowed ground never to be built upon again. It gave rise to the perception of greed on the part of Larry Silverstein, the buildings' leaseholder who waged lawsuits over how much he was eligible to receive in insurance payouts. It invited intrigue among New Yorkers about an architectural competition to design the master plan for rebuilding around the towers' footprints, leading to inspiration in the form of Daniel Libeskind's winning design that embodied "life victorious." It provoked squabbling between Silverstein's architect, David Childs, and Libeskind over who actually was entitled to design the central skyscraper of

Libeskind's plan, leading to a compromise that nobody believed was beautiful enough. It saw fearmongering among opponents of a proposed Islamic center near the memorial. It required miraculous feats of engineering and design to realize Michael Arad's vision for a memorial, "Reflecting Absence," that would commemorate death and yet still be part of the life of the city. It necessitated negotiation over how to arrange victims' names on the memorial that allowed for "meaningful adjacencies" that acknowledged where they were and relationships they shared with other victims. As the years progressed, it returned to tragedy once again as health problems caused by the toxic cloud around Ground Zero claimed uncounted additional lives.

Perhaps to provide the happiest ending to the story of the life and legacy of the buildings, we need to go back to the beginning, before they were even finished. One summer morning in 1974, high-wire artist Philippe Petit risked his life for a reckless stunt: walking on a tightrope stretched between the twin towers. He reminisced, "I had to make a decision of shifting my weight from one foot anchored to the building to the foot anchored on the wire. This is probably, I don't know, probably the end of my life, to step on that wire, and on the other hand, something I could not resist, and I didn't make any effort to resist, called me upon that cable."

Few photos survive of Petit's feat. From more than four hundred meters below, the performer looked like a speck of dust. Workers strolling on the sidewalks toward their mundane workdays stopped in their tracks to marvel at the moment unfolding above them.

The best testaments to the remarkable significance of his achievement are in the memories of his accomplices, recalling that day in the documentary film, *Man on Wire*. His friend, Jean-Louis, recalls being "really scared" until the moment Petit had both feet on the wire, at which point Jean-Louis thought, "That's it. He's secure," pausing to choke up at the memory before he can continue. Another collaborator concludes that it was "beyond anything you can ever imagine, mind-boggling. The awe of the event and the overwhelming largeness of the scale of the situation took my mind into a place where I really wasn't that concerned about him. It was just magical." Even Annie Allix, speaking in French through tears of admiration years after her then boyfriend jumped into bed with a groupie in his postperformance euphoria, remembers with a kind of religious reverence and imagery: "I saw Philippe up there; it was extraordinary. It was so, so beautiful. It was like he was walking on a cloud. . . . We were thrilled by this image of Philippe lying down up above."

When asked why he did it, Petit was as evasive as he had been when he avoided the police officers waiting to arrest him at the end of the wire. He said, "There is no why," intentionally or not channeling philosopher Friedrich Nietzsche's definition of nihilism, "when 'why' finds no answer."

According to nihilists, life is meaningless, and so to care about your legacy is pointless. Nietzsche's legacy is often mistakenly conflated with nihilism because of his famous declaration that "God is dead." Misinterpretations of the meaning of his words have led some of his deranged followers to commit murder to prove their superiority over societal norms, embrace unmitigated egoism, and justify fascism. What Nietzsche scholars insist he meant to say, however, was not that society has no rules and life has no point without God. Rather, we should not depend solely upon a supernatural force to confer purpose and meaning upon our lives when it is within our control to choose how to live, aspiring to live a life that matters whether or not there is a higher power. The impressive legacy of ideas Nietzsche left to be misrepresented and misconstrued was mostly complete by the time he suffered a mental breakdown at age forty-four and was considered insane for the last decade of his life. A sensible interpretation of Nietzsche's legacy may suggest that to be overly concerned about our legacies may be egocentric, to be unconcerned is nihilistic, and to live only for pleasure in the here and now is hedonistic. Therefore, we should show the proper amount of concern in our present lives with our future legacies because this is our opportunity to signal to others that life is meaningful and will continue to matter after we are gone.

LEGACIES, LASTING AND LOST

In that spirit, the stories we shared in each of the preceding chapters are hopeful. They keep alive the possibility that a lasting legacy can include doing worthy work.

For example, asked, "What would you like your legacy to be?" David Bowie once responded, "I'd love people to believe that I had really great haircuts." Of course, he was being cheeky—but was he? He did have some great haircuts—and some really bad ones, too—that are part of the enduring legacy of the style icon who never wanted to be "just a rock and roll star."

The last and greatest reunion of three generations of the Wong family was organized in Rio de Janeiro for Wong Jun-Chow's ninetieth birthday. T-shirts were made announcing the occasion on the front, with a family tree—his children and grandchildren forming each branch—on the back. In family photos, the patriarch wore his T-shirt backward, legacy on his chest, believing his way was the way it was supposed to be worn.

The first name on the New York Medical Examiner's list of 9/11 casualties is that of Father Mychal Judge, though he was not the first person to die in the attacks. He had given last rites to victims and was praying for first responders in the North Tower lobby when the South Tower fell. Miraculously, he was not killed by falling debris but by a heart attack. Afterward, it came to be known that he had been gay and a recovering alcoholic. Twenty years after his death, his admirers within and beyond the Roman Catholic Church were still campaigning for his legacy to include canonization.

Part of Michelle Obama's legacy will always be that of the first African American First Lady of the United States. But does remembering her as such say too much about her racial and marital identity—and not enough about her own achievements—as a student at Princeton and Harvard Law School, as a professional lawyer and nonprofit executive, as a mother of two daughters, as an advocate for civility in an era of incivility, as an author of several books, as a fashion model, as a political figure who many hoped would seek the presidential nomination, and so on? She was only forty-five when she entered the White House and fifty-three when she left, which means there remains much she can yet accomplish.

After the major episode of depression that overcame Kathleen Gluck when she was a high-functioning Big Four partner, she had reason to believe that she could manage it like she had success-fully managed other crises. However, an increase in her dosage and an experiment with additional medication failed to provide lasting benefits, so she sat down before the next Thanksgiving to write her own obituary. Instead of ending her own life as her legacy, during her leave of absence from work, she started building her living legacy, publicly sharing her experience "in the hope that perhaps someone will read [her story] and feel that they too can ask for more help."

Toward the end of *The Moon and Sixpence* (spoiler alert), W. Somerset Maugham's novel based on the life and legend of Paul Gauguin—known as Charles Strickland in the book—the painter dies from leprosy. While going blind, he paints his alleged masterwork on the walls of his hut that he entreats his Tahitian common-law wife, Ata, to burn down upon his death. Back in London, his estranged legal wife finally lives in material comfort, ben-efiting from his posthumous fame. Surrounded by reproductions of some of his paintings—which the narrator implies she perceives as mere decorative objects—she remains unaware of the incalcu-lable loss of his greatest legacy. The story raises questions about aesthetic value that are of great interest to some contemporary philosophers, such as who is qualified to judge the worthiness of a painting and how its market value relates to its value as an artwork. In addition, it may lead us to wonder whether a legacy that nobody is aware of matters. To put it in the form of the ancient philosophi-cal question of whether a tree falling in the woods makes a sound, does a painting that burns in the tropical forest leave a trace? Per-haps that is meant to capture the concern we may have when we worry about our own legacy. If, someday, nobody remembers us, will our life have meant anything?

"I've got my shortcomings and my flaws and I ain't better than nobody else," George Floyd told the young men in his neighborhood, whom he implored to "put them guns down." Floyd was admired by his family and friends for his ability to identify with people from all walks of life after working through his own bouts with the law and substance abuse. When he suffocated in police custody, after uttering "I can't breathe" more than twenty times, his words and his death as a Black man under the knee of a white police officer became a part of his legacy. People emerged from pandemic lockdowns around the world to "say his name," rallying for racial justice and law enforcement reform.

Perhaps the most imitated corporate purpose statement of this century was not a statement at all but an operating strategy: PepsiCo's "Performance with Purpose." After she became the first South Asian woman to lead a Fortune 50 company, now-retired chairperson and chief executive Indra Nooyi articulated a strategic plan that was responsive to Wall Street's expectations and responsible to its consumers. Recognizing that much of her company's potential growth was in emerging markets, including her native India, Nooyi sought to expand and evolve the company's product portfolio away from "junk food" and "discarded plastic and wrappers" and "to connect what was good for our business with what was good for the world." Her retirement letter to her employees expressed pride at the company's success at implementing this strategy, but she also urged them to "think hard about time," lamenting how much of her daughters' childhoods she had missed doing such a demanding job. In her memoir, *My Life in Full*, she anticipates her future to include caring for her aging mother and her future grandchildren.

Walt Disney originally intended Epcot to be a literal Experimental Prototype Community of Tomorrow, a utopian city that would solve what he saw as the problems of urban life. In Disney's view, as always, technological innovation in the good old US of A would come to the rescue. Instead of cars, people would travel by monorail. Homes would have smart appliances that could easily upgrade to the state of the art. The community, in Walt's eyes, would "never cease to be a blueprint of the future." However, Disney died before this legacy could be realized. The Epcot park of today is an homage to his vision—presenting visitors with any number of ideas about global harmony, advancement in communication, and the power to harness imagination to tackle life's great challenges—yet clearly falling short of the fully realized livable community this vision foretold. However, the Disney Corporation has evolved in still other ways that might honor Walt's legacy, accepting accountability for past racism, standing up to the Florida governor's anti-LGBTQ+ agenda, and, of course, ever advancing in its animation and theme park capabilities.

Eliza Hamilton's last act before the stage goes dark is to gasp, provoking endless debate about its meaning. Her gasp has been interpreted to signify, among other things, her death and encounter with God; her death and reunion with Alexander; and her discovery that she is still alive as the storyteller "about America then, told by America now," in Lin-Manuel Miranda's words. According to Philippa Soo, who originated the role of Eliza on Broadway, the gasp means all of those things and more. In her imagination while she performed, the gasp meant different things "night to night"— perhaps signifying that Eliza's legacy continues to be written.

What will your legacy be? Although you may not be ready to answer that question until your work is done, we hope that this book has helped you contemplate how you want to live your life and what role work will occupy in defining that legacy. We hope it has made you think broadly about what work is, what you work for, and when you have done enough. We hope it has led you to consider the things you love to do, the work you regard to be essential to society, whether or not they are one and the same, and if they are fairly priced in the marketplace. And we hope it inspires you to think about a higher purpose, a better future, and your lasting legacy. Doing work that is worthy—of ourselves or to society, paid or unpaid, essential or entertaining—may be one of our most important opportunities in life to contribute something of value to a world in which there is no end of work to be done.

ACKNOWLEDGMENTS

Our society's collective awareness of the potential for work to add to or detract from our lives was elevated by both 9/11 and the COVID-19 pandemic. We remember family, friends, colleagues, and strangers who were lost in those tragedies, with particular appreciation for first responders and other essential workers who ran toward danger so others could live.

Those events and exemplars inspired our research about work, but we have also benefited from the insights and expertise of many scholars whose work has influenced ours. These include our colleagues from our academic institutions—the University of St. Thomas and Babson College, in particular, which granted us sabbaticals which greatly facilitated the writing of this book—and New York University. We are also grateful to the academic communities in which we actively participate and that have given us so much in return—notably, the May Meaning Meeting, with a special shout-out to Amy Wrzesniewski; the Melrose and the Toro Company Center for Principled Leadership; the Academy of Management Careers and Social Issues in Management Divisions; European Group for Organization Studies; International Meaningful Work Symposium; and Society for Business Ethics.

There are too many individual colleagues and friends who have influenced our work than we can list here, but the following people formally contributed to this book in a variety of ways, reviewing passages, suggesting research, and providing intellectual and practical resources: Katie Bailey, Lakshmi Balachandra, Bruce Buchanan, Shasa Dobrow, Kristine Enea, Danna Greenberg, Jon Haidt, Gary Jahn, Tae Wan Kim, Bobby Kipp, Adam Kolber, Melissa Manwaring, Fred Price, Laura Sonday, Hannah Weisman, and Nicole Zwieg Daly.

We are also grateful for conversations with the following people who contributed to this book whether or not they knew it: Michel Anteby, Dolly Chugh, Joanne Ciulla, Patty Dahm, Amy Finnegan, Rob Foehl, Tom Forliti, Ed Freeman, Kerry Gibson, Ani Ross Grubb, Luke Hedden, Manuela Hill-Muñoz, Lee Howell, Laura Huang, Jon Jachimowicz, Michele Kerrigan, Marina Kim, N.R. "Sonny" Kleinfield, Sophie Lambin, Eric Lamm, Louise Lawson, Doug Lepisto, Julie Levinson, Evgenia Lysova, Sally Maitlis, Santiago Mejia, Andy Molinsky, Wendy Murphy, Stacy Pervall, Mike Pratt, Pati Provinske, Juan Pujadas, Theresa Ricke-Kiely, Teresa Rothausen, Naomi Rothman, Kira Schabram, Father Martin Schlag, Janny Scott, Harry Van Buren, Molly Weinstein, Yohuru Williams, Brian Wycliff, Larry Yu, and Jackie Zins.

Our students have not only inspired our work but also motivated us to write for them in their quest for work worth doing within lives worth living. A few individual students have assisted with the production of this book or in the development of research discussed in the book: Lavanya Ashok, Joel Gardner, Kody Harris, and Chenkay Li.

One of the greatest unexpected rewards of writing this book was talking with dozens of people about their work stories of success, failure, and resilience, many of which appear in these pages. They spoke with us about the risks and rewards of their busy work lives from their cars, offices, and homes, on screen and off screen. For their generous permission to share their stories and wisdom about work, we are grateful to Dennis Curley, Linnea Komba Dahl (pseudonym), Kristine Enea (again), Kathleen Gluck (pseudonym), Robert Guest (pseudonym), Bess Hargreaves (pseudonym),

Neil Hill, Justin Jones, Lauren Majors, Sawyer Michaelson, Murisiku Raifu, Chad Sokol, Shawn Wong, and Rabbi Marcia Zimmerman.

If Christopher had not by chance bumped into Jon Haidt in an NYU stairwell, Jon may never have generously introduced us to our future agent. Esmond Harmsworth worked patiently with us through four concepts, three titles, and nearly two years of the pandemic to perfect the proposal. And if not for Esmond, we may never have met our editor Colleen Lawrie. She had us at "contemplative" the first time she talked with us about the book and supported and clarified our vision in every communication. Our work with Esmond and his team at Aevitas Creative and Colleen and her team at Hachette/PublicAffairs—including but not limited to Lindsay Fradkoff, Pete Garceau, Kelly Lenkevich, Olivia Loperfido, Kate Mueller, and Jocelynn Pedro—are integral to why you are holding this book in your hands.

Christopher is fortunate to have a large extended family from which to learn about work. It includes his Wong aunts and uncles, who motivate him knowing that no book will be good enough for them until the family saga has been written. Michele Michaelson has shown that satisfaction can be discovered in a second career, while Ron and Dorcas Michaelson made peace with work in retirement. Arlene Winnick cheered on this project while Steve Winnick challenged ideas. Matt Goldman shared publishing guidance and Josh Kaplan provided contract advice. Margaret Wong passed along her father's work ethic and her own commitment to meaningful work to Christopher, and Walter Graff, who passed away before we finished this book, left behind writing and wisdom that live on.

More than anyone, Beth Winnick is the reason this preoccupied philosopher found an occupation, getting me my first internship when we were dating, helping to build my career after we got married, and being the first person I go to with drafts, prototypes, celebrations, frustrations, and everything else. Sawyer not only agreed to an interview but also provided a hopeful perspective from his generation. Reese generated marketing and design concepts while leading me to think twice about style and substance. Esme was the first person in my family to find out about the book deal and is often the last person I speak with every morning before I begin working. My family members have shaped my work and the reasons I do it more than they may know.

Jen feels lucky to be surrounded by people who not only tolerated hearing her ongoing updates about this book, but also responded with genuine enthusiasm and intellectual engagement with the topic. A very incomplete list recognizes the collective brilliance of Sean and Kristie Barry, Brooke Cader, Imogen and Paul Dransfield, Erica Galioto, Hannah Gilbert, Jill Goldenziel, Craig and Heather Hovey, Eric and Andrea (Vaughn) Johnson, Andrea "AJ" Johnson, Anaita Kasad, Deborah Kronenberg, Andi Lipman, Tracy Mahoney, Pete and Andrea Morgan, Hess and Max Norman, Jamie Pina, Roy Roberts, Jessie Souder, Patrick Stern, and Abby Whitbeck.

Greg and Cecilya Kharas are role models for living the good life, in all its forms. Michael Kharas and Tingting Zhang-Kharas took time from their work of finding a cure and parenting Kelly and Kevin to talk through ideas with me. Bob and Sally Tosti always talked about the work they did, its joys and challenges, while glorifying a life of the mind above all. None of this would be possible without them. Last, but certainly not least, Lucy and Theo contributed more to this book than it would appear would be possible for an eleven- and nine-year-old, though I know they are still holding out for their original title choice, *Is Work Worth the Work?* I hope one day they will feel their own work is worth it. Dave Kharas is the most supportive partner I can imagine, even as I know he wishes there were more project management and semiconductors in this, and every, book. My family reminds me daily what it's all for.

Christopher and Jen want to acknowledge the irony that the very work that we think we do *for* our families at the same time takes *from* them in the form of their support and sacrifice. We hope it was worth it to each of them.

BIBLIOGRAPHY

Preface

Bowie, David. "About—David Bowie." Bowie personal website. https://www
.davidbowie.com/about.

Brown, Mick. "David Bowie, 25 years ago: 'I've done just about everything that it's
possible to do'." *Telegraph* (London), January 10, 2021. https://www.telegraph
.co.uk/music/interviews/david-bowie-25-years-ago-done-just-everything
-possible-do.

Walters, Barry. "Review: David Bowie's 'Blackstar' Is Adventurous to the End."
Review of *Blackstar*, by David Bowie. NPR, January 11, 2016. https://www
.npr.org/sections/therecord/2016/01/11/462660569/review-david-bowies
-blackstar-is-adventurous-to-the-end.

Whately, Francis, dir. *David Bowie: The Last Five Years*. Santa Monica,
CA: HBO, 2017. https://www.hbo.com/movies/david-bowie-the-last-five
-years.

Introduction: Is Your Work Worth It?

BBC News. "*New Yorker* Fires Jeffrey Toobin for Exposing Himself on Zoom."
November 11, 2020. https://www.bbc.com/news/world-us-canada
-54912610.

Blanchflower, David G., and Andrew J. Oswald. "Is Well-Being U-Shaped over the
Life Cycle?" *Social Science & Medicine* 66, no. 8 (April 2008): 1733–1749,
https://doi.org/10.1016/j.socscimed.2008.01.030.

Brower, Tracy. "What the Generations Want from Work: New Data Offers
Surprises." *Forbes*, August 28, 2022. https://www.forbes.com/sites/tracy
brower/2022/08/28/what-the-generations-want-from-work-new-data-offers
-surprises/?sh=28581d393f32.

Burns, Ric, dir. "Mario M. Cuomo, New York Governor." Transcript of 3:47 min. clip, from *The Center of the World: New York, a Documentary Film.* Arlington, VA: PBS, September 8, 2003. https://www.pbs.org/wgbh/americanexperience/features/newyork-cuomo/.

Conference Board, The. "Job Satisfaction 2023." https://www.conference-board.org/research/job-satisfaction/US-worker-satisfaction-continues-to-increase.

Empson, Laura. *Leading Professionals: Power, Politics, and Prima Donnas.* Oxford, UK: Oxford University Press, 2022.

Gallup. "State of the Global Workplace 2023 Report." https://www.gallup.com/workplace/349484/state-of-the-global-workplace.aspx.

Ghebreyesus, Tedros Adhanom. "WHO Director-General's opening remarks at the media briefing on COVID-19." World Health Organization, March 11, 2020. https://www.who.int/director-general/speeches/detail/who-director-general-s-opening-remarks-at-the-media-briefing-on-covid-19---11-march-2020.

Goldmacher, Shane. "The Imperious Rise and Accelerating Fall of Andrew Cuomo." *New York Times*, November 10, 2021. https://www.nytimes.com/2021/03/13/us/politics/andrew-cuomo-scandals.html.

Greene, Kelly, and Carlos Tejada. "Workers Deeply Affected by Attacks Decide to Make Changes in Their Lives." *Wall Street Journal*, December 26, 2001. https://www.wsj.com/articles/SB1009236905886354560.

James, William. *Is Life Worth Living?* Philadelphia: S. Burns Weston, 1896.

Karlamangla, Soumya. "A Nurse Without an N95 Mask Raced in to Treat a 'Code Blue' Patient. She Died 14 Days Later." *Los Angeles Times*, May 10, 2020. https://www.latimes.com/california/story/2020-05-10/nurse-death-n95-covid-19-patients-coronavirus-hollywood-presbyterian.

Knoll, Corina, Ali Watkins, and Michael Rothfield. "'I Couldn't Do Anything: The Virus and an E.R. Doctor's Suicide." *New York Times*, July 11, 2020. https://www.nytimes.com/2020/07/11/nyregion/lorna-breen-suicide-coronavirus.html.

Lussenhop, Jessica. "Coronavirus at Smithfield Pork Plant: The Untold Story of America's Biggest Outbreak." BBC News, April 17, 2020. https://www.bbc.com/news/world-us-canada-52311877.

Michaelson, Christopher. "A Novel Approach to Business Ethics Education: Exploring How to Live and Work in the 21st Century." *Academy of Management Learning & Education* 15, no. 3 (2016): 588–606.

New York Times. "Portraits of Grief." 2001. https://www.nytimes.com/interactive/us/sept-11-reckoning/portraits-of-grief.html.

Victor, Daniel. "'I'm Not a Cat,' Says Lawyer Having Zoom Difficulties." *New York Times*, February 9, 2021. https://www.nytimes.com/2021/02/09/style/cat-lawyer-zoom.html.

Chapter 1: What Is Work?

Angelou, Maya. *And Still I Rise*. New York: Random House, 1978.

Anonymous. "Why I'm Planning to Leave My Ph.D. Program." *Chronicle of Higher Education*, August 22, 2022. https://www.chronicle.com/article/why-im -planning-to-leave-my-ph-d-program.

Barber, Lynn. "Bleeding Art." *Guardian* (Manchester, UK), April 20, 2003. https:// www.theguardian.com/artanddesign/2003/apr/20/thesaatchigallery.art6.

Bloom, Nicholas, James Liang, John Roberts, and Zhichun Jenny Ying. "Does Working from Home Work? Evidence from a Chinese Experiment." *Quarterly Journal of Economics* 130, no. 1 (2015): 165–218. https://doi.org/10.1093/qje/qju032.

Boren, Cindy. "How Joey Chestnut Preps for a Stomachful of Hot Dogs." ESPN, July 3, 2018. https://www.espn.com/espn/story/_/id/23977424/how-joey-ches tnut-preps-stomach-full-hot-dogs-nathan-famous-international-hot-dog-eating -contest.

Carney, Scott. *The Red Market: On the Trail of the World's Organ Brokers, Bone Thieves, Blood Farmers, and Child Traffickers*. New York: HarperCollins, 2011.

Centers for Disease Control and Prevention. "Ergonomics and Musculoskeletal Disorders." CDC, March 28, 2013. https://www.cdc.gov/niosh/updates/ergprs .html.

Ciulla, Joanne B. *The Working Life: The Promise and Betrayal of Modern Work*. New York: Currency, 2001.

Crawford, Matthew B. *Shop Class as Soulcraft: An Inquiry into the Value of Work*. New York: Penguin, 2009.

DealBook. "Blankfein Says He's Just Doing 'God's Work'." *New York Times*, November 9, 2009. https://dealbook.nytimes.com/2009/11/09/goldman-chief-says -he-is-just-doing-gods-work/.

Dickens, Charles. *Hard Times*. 4th ed. Edited by Fred Kaplan. New York: W. W. Norton, 2016.

Eurostat. "International Standard Classification of Occupations." Accessed September 18, 2023. https://ec.europa.eu/eurostat/ramon/documents/isco_88 /isco_88_intro.pdf.

Evans, James A., Gideon Kunda, and Stephen R. Barley. "Beach Time, Bridge Time, and Billable Hours: The Temporal Structure of Technical Contracting." *Administrative Science Quarterly* 49, no. 1 (2004): 1–38. https://doi .org/10.2307/4131454.

Gladwell, Malcolm. *Outliers: The Story of Success*. New York: Little, Brown, 2008.

Government of India, Ministry of Labour & Employment. "National Classification of Occupations—2015." National Career Service, 2015. https://www.ncs.gov .in/Documents/National%20Classification%20of%20Occupations%20_Vol%20I -%202015.pdf.

Graeber, David. "Bullshit Jobs and the Yoke of Managerial Feudalism." *Economist*, June 29, 2018. https://www.economist.com/open-future/2018/06/29/bullshit -jobs-and-the-yoke-of-managerial-feudalism.

Hochschild, Arlie Russell, and Anne Machung. *The Second Shift: Working Parents and the Revolution at Home*. New York: Penguin, 2012.

Hustvedt, Siri. "A Woman in the Men's Room: When Will the Art World Recognise the Real Artist Behind Duchamp's Fountain?" *Guardian* (Manchester, UK), March 29, 2019. https://www.theguardian.com/books/2019/mar/29/marcel -duchamp-fountain-women-art-history.

Kawasaki, Guy. "It's Called Work for a Reason." *New York Times*, September 8, 2015. https://www.nytimes.com/roomfordebate/2015/09/08/can -companies-excel-without-making-workers-miserable/its-called-work-for -a-reason.

Krogstad, Jens Manuel, Mark Hugo Lopez, and Jeffrey S. Passel. "A Majority of Americans Say Immigrants Mostly Fill Jobs U.S. Citizens Do Not Want." Pew Research Center, June 10, 2020. https://www.pewresearch.org/fact -tank/2020/06/10/a-majority-of-americans-say-immigrants-mostly-fill-jobs-u-s -citizens-do-not-want/.

Levin, Annie. "How NYU's Grad Student Union Went on Strike—and Won." *Progressive Magazine*, June 2, 2021. https://progressive.org/latest/nyu-grad -student-union-strike-won-levin-210602/.

Lussenhop, Jessica. "Coronavirus at Smithfield Pork Plant: The Untold Story of America's Biggest Outbreak." BBC News, April 17, 2020. https://www.bbc .com/news/world-us-canada-52311877.

Meyer, David, and Oumou Fofana. "Joey Chestnut Manhandles Protester Before Record 15th Nathan's Hot Dog Eating Contest Win." *New York Post*, July 4, 2022. https://nypost.com/2022/07/04/joey-chestnut-wins-15th-nathans-hot-dog -eating-contest/.

Miller, Claire Cain. "How Society Pays When Women's Work Is Unpaid." *New York Times*, February 23, 2016. https://www.nytimes.com/2016/02/23/upshot/how -society-pays-when-womens-work-is-unpaid.html.

———. "Same-Sex Couples Divide Chores Much More Evenly, Until They Become Parents." *New York Times*, May 16, 2018. https://www.nytimes.com /2018/05/16/upshot/same-sex-couples-divide-chores-much-more-evenly-until -they-become-parents.html.

Moses, Edwin. "Interview: Edwin Moses." Interview by Paul Schienberg. *Psyched Online*, 2002. https://www.psychedonline.com/interview-edwin-moses/.

Nettuno, Tyler. "52 Major League Eating Records That Belong to Joey Chestnut." *USA Today*, July 4, 2023. https://ftw.usatoday.com/lists/joey-chestnut-major -league-eating-records-hot-dog-competition.

Perfume Society, The. "Estée Lauder." Accessed June 27, 2023. https://perfume society.org/perfume-house/estee-lauder/.

Pew Research Center. "The State of American Jobs." October 6, 2016. https://www .pewresearch.org/social-trends/2016/10/06/the-state-of-american-jobs/.

Pieper, Josef. *Leisure: The Basis of Culture*. San Francisco: Ignatius Press, 2009.

Piercy, Marge. *To Be of Use*. New York: Doubleday, 1973.

Ransome, Paul. *The Work Paradigm: A Theoretical Investigation of Concepts of Work.* Aldershot, Hants, UK: Avebury, 1996.

Smith, Adam. *An Inquiry into the Nature and Causes of the Wealth of Nations.* New York: Bantam Dell, 2003.

Spar, Debora L. *The Baby Business: How Money, Science, and Politics Drive the Commerce of Conception.* Cambridge, MA: Harvard Business Review Press, 2006.

Suzman, James. *Work: A Deep History, from the Stone Age to the Age of Robots.* New York: Penguin, 2021.

Tagore, Rabindranath. 1931. *The Religion of Man.* New York: Macmillan.

Tate Modern. "Fountain, Marcel Duchamp, 1917, replica 1964." Accessed June 27, 2023. https://www.tate.org.uk/art/artworks/duchamp-fountain-t07573.

Twain, Mark. *The Adventures of Tom Sawyer.* Berkeley: University of California Press, 1980.

US Census Bureau. "The Changing Economics and Demographics of Young Adulthood from 1975 to 2016." April 19, 2017. https://www.census.gov/newsroom/press-releases/2017/cb17-tps36-young-adulthood.html.

US Department of Labor. "O*NET OnLine." Accessed June 27, 2023. https://www.onetonline.org/.

Wallace, David Foster. *The Pale King.* Edited by Michael Pietsch. New York: Little, Brown, 2011.

Weber, Max. *The Protestant Ethic and the Spirit of Capitalism.* New York: Dover, 2003.

Chapter 2: Why Do You Work?

Adams, J. Stacy. "Inequity in Social Exchange." *Advances in Experimental Social Psychology* 2 (1965): 267–299. https://www.sciencedirect.com/science/article/abs/pii/S0065260108601082.

Amire, Roula, and Great Place to Work. "The Best Workplaces for Millennials Offer Meaning and Purpose." *Fortune*, July 18, 2022. https://fortune.com/2022/07/18/best-workplaces-millennials-2022-purpose-meaning/.

Argyris, Chris. *Understanding Organizational Behavior.* Homewood, IL: Dorsey, 1960.

Bellah, Robert N., Richard Madsen, William M. Sullivan, Ann Swidler, and Steven M. Tipton. *Habits of the Heart: Individualism and Commitment in American Life.* New York: Harper & Row, 1985.

Boova, Laura, Michael G. Pratt, and Douglas A. Lepisto. "Exploring Work Orientations and Cultural Accounts of Work." In *The Oxford Handbook of Meaningful Work*, edited by Ruth Yeoman, Catherine Bailey, Adrian Madden, and Marc Thompson, 186–207. Oxford, UK: Oxford University Press, 2019.

Brickman, Philip, Dan Coates, and Ronnie Janoff-Bulman. "Lottery Winners and Accident Victims: Is Happiness Relative?" *Journal of Personality and Social Psychology* 36, no. 8 (1978): 917–927.

Brickman, Philip, and Donald T. Campbell. "Hedonic Relativism and Planning the Good Society." In *Adaptation Level Theory: A Symposium*, edited by Mortimer H. Appley, 287–392. New York: Academic Press, 1971.

Bridgman, Todd, Stephen Cummings, and John Ballard. "Who Built Maslow's Pyramid? A History of the Creation of Management Studies' Most Famous Symbol and Its Implications for Management Education." *Academy of Management Learning & Education* 18, no. 1, (2019): 81–98. https://doi.org/10.5465/amle.2017.0351.

Bush, George W. "Statement by the President in His Address to the Nation." The White House Archives, September 11, 2001. https://georgewbush-whitehouse.archives.gov/news/releases/2001/09/20010911-16.html.

Cho, Yuna, and Winnie Y. Jiang. "How Work Orientation Impacts Objective Career Outcomes via Managerial (Mis)perceptions." *Academy of Management Journal* 65, no. 4 (2022): 1353–1382. https://doi.org/10.5465/amj.2020.0841.

Ferriss, Timothy. *The 4-Hour Workweek: Escape 9-5, Live Anywhere, and Join the New Rich*. New York: Harmony, 2009.

Fiorillo, Damiano. "Do Monetary Rewards Crowd Out the Intrinsic Motivation of Volunteers? Some Empirical Evidence for Italian Volunteers." *Annals of Public and Cooperative Economics* 82, no. 2 (2011): 139–165. https://doi.org/10.1111/j.1467-8292.2011.00434.x.

Forkish, Ken. *Flour Water Salt Yeast: The Fundamentals of Artisan Bread and Pizza*. Berkeley, CA: Ten Speed Press, 2012.

Frankl, Viktor E. *Man's Search for Meaning*. New York: Pocket Books, 1985.

Furaker, Bengt, and Anna Hedenus. "Gambling Windfall Decisions: Lottery Winners and Employment Behavior." *UNLV Gaming Research & Review Journal* 13, no. 2 (2009): 1–15.

Gneezy, Uri, and Aldo Rustichini. "Pay Enough or Don't Pay at All." *Quarterly Journal of Economics* 115, no. 3 (2000): 791–810. https://doi.org/10.1162/003355300554917.

Goleman, Daniel. "Millennials: The Purpose Generation." Korn Ferry. Accessed September 22, 2023. https://www.kornferry.com/insights/this-week-in-leadership/millennials-purpose-generation.

Herzberg, Frederick, Bernard Mausner, and Barbara Bloch Snyderman. *The Motivation to Work*. New York: John Wiley, 1960.

Higher Education Research Institute. "The American Freshman: Fifty-Year Trends, 1966–2015." UCLA, July 30, 2016. https://heri.ucla.edu/the-american-freshman-fifty-year-trends-1966-2015/.

Hume, Janice. "'Portraits of Grief,' Reflectors of Values: The New York Times Remembers Victims of September 11." *Journalism & Mass Communication Quarterly* 80, no. 1 (2003): 166–182. https://doi.org/10.1177/107769900308000111.

James, Harvey S., Jr. "Why Did You Do That? An Economic Examination of the Effect of Extrinsic Compensation on Intrinsic Motivation and Performance." *Journal of Economic Psychology* 26, no. 4 (2005): 549–566. https://doi.org /10.1016/j.joep.2004.11.002.

King, Barbara J. "Feeling Down? Watching This Will Help." NPR, 2014. https:// www.npr.org/sections/13.7/2014/02/27/283348422/that-s-unfair-you-say-this -monkey-can-relate.

Lam, Bouree. "What Becomes of Lottery Winners?" *Atlantic*, January 12, 2016. https://www.theatlantic.com/business/archive/2016/01/lottery-winners -research/423543/.

Maslow, Abraham H. "A Theory of Human Motivation." *Psychological Review* 50, no. 4 (1943): 370–396. https://doi.org/10.1037/h0054346.

Michaelson, Christopher, and Jennifer Tosti-Kharas. "Serving Self or Serving Others? Close Relations' Perspectives on Ethics and Calling." *Journal of Vocational Behavior* 114 (2019): 19–30. https://doi.org/10.1016/j.jvb.2019 .02.005.

———. "Work Worth Dying For?" HuffPost, September 9, 2016. https://www .huffpost.com/entry/work-worth-dying-for_b_11939748.

New York Times. "Portraits of Grief." 2001. https://www.nytimes.com/interactive /us/sept-11-reckoning/portraits-of-grief.html.

New York Times. Portraits: 9/11/01: The Collected "Portraits of Grief" from The New York Times. New York: Times Books, 2002.

Niza, Claudia, Burcu Tung, and Theresa M. Marteau. 2013. "Incentivizing Blood Donation: Systematic Review and Meta-Analysis to Test Titmuss' Hypotheses." *Health Psychology* 32, no. 9 (2013): 941–949. https://psycnet.apa.org /doi/10.1037/hea0000035.

Osterman, Paul, ed. *Broken Ladders: Managerial Careers in the New Economy.* Oxford, UK: Oxford University Press, 1996.

Robinson, Sandra L., and Denise M. Rousseau. "Violating the Psychological Contract: Not the Exception but the Norm." *Journal of Organizational Behavior* 15, no. 3 (1994): 245–259. https://doi.org/10.1002/job.4030 150306.

Saval, Nikil. *Cubed: A Secret History of the Workplace.* New York: Anchor, 2015.

Schabram, Kira, Jordan Nielsen, and Jeffery Thompson. "The Dynamics of Work Orientations: An Updated Typology and Agenda for the Study of Jobs, Careers, and Callings." *Academy of Management Annals* 17, no. 2 (2023): 405–438. https://doi.org/10.5465/annals.2021.0153.

Titmuss, Richard. *The Gift Relationship: From Human Blood to Social Policy.* Crows Nest, New South Wales, Australia: George Allen and Unwin, 1970.

Tosti-Kharas, Jennifer, and Eric Lamm. "What Really Motivates You? A Data-Driven Exercise and Discussion." *Management Teaching Review* 8, no. 2 (2023): 180–196. https://doi.org/10.1177/2379298121104100.

US Bureau of Labor Statistics. "Characteristics of Minimum Wage Workers, 2020." BLS Reports, February 2021. https://www.bls.gov/opub/reports/minimum -wage/2020/home.htm.

Whyte, William H., Jr. *The Organization Man*. New York: Simon & Schuster, 1956.

Wrzesniewski, Amy. "'It's Not Just a Job': Shifting Meanings of Work in the Wake of 9/11." *Journal of Management Inquiry* 11, no. 3 (2002): 230–234. https:// doi.org/10.1177/1056492602113003.

Wrzesniewski, Amy, Clark McCauley, Paul Rozin, and Barry Schwartz. "Jobs, Careers, and Callings: People's Relations to Their Work." *Journal of Research in Personality* 31, no. 1 (1997): 21–33. https://doi.org/10.1006/jrpe.1997 .2162.

Chapter 3: When—and How Much—Should You Work?

Abend, Lisa. "Why 2023 Could Finally Be the Year of the 4-Day Workweek." *Time*, January 19, 2023. https://time.com/6248369/4-day-work-week-2023/.

Case, Anne, and Angus Deaton. *Deaths of Despair and the Future of Capitalism*. Princeton, NJ: Princeton University Press, 2020.

Chernow, Ron. *Alexander Hamilton*. New York, Penguin, 2005.

Ciulla, Joanne B. *The Working Life: The Promise and Betrayal of Modern Work*. New York: Currency, 2001.

Dickler, Jessica. "41% of Americans Say It's 'Going to Take a Miracle' to Be Ready for Retirement, Report Finds." *CNBC*, September 14, 2021. https://www.cnbc .com/2021/09/14/36percent-of-americans-say-they-wont-have-enough-to -retire-report-finds.html.

Dua, André, Kweilin Ellingrud, Phil Kirschner, Adrian Kwok, Ryan Luby, Rob Palter, and Sarah Pemberton. "Americans Are Embracing Flexible Work—and They Want More of It." McKinsey & Company, July 23, 2022. https://www .mckinsey.com/industries/real-estate/our-insights/americans-are-embracing -flexible-work-and-they-want-more-of-it.

Dyer, Geoff. *The Last Days of Roger Federer and Other Endings*. New York: Farrar, Straus and Giroux, 2022.

Ehrenreich, Barbara. *Nickel and Dimed: On (Not) Getting By in America*. London: Picador, 2011.

Fein, Esther B. "Book Notes," *New York Times*, November 20, 1991. https://www .nytimes.com/1991/11/20/books/book-notes-059091.html.

Griffith, Erin. "Why Are Young People Pretending to Love Work?" *New York Times*, January 26, 2019. https://www.nytimes.com/2019/01/26/business /against-hustle-culture-rise-and-grind-tgim.html.

Hautala, Laura. "Amazon Deaths Under Investigation as Warehouse Conditions Draw Scrutiny." *CNET*, September 2, 2022. https://www.cnet.com/tech /services-and-software/amazon-under-investigation-for-string-of-warehouse -deaths-as-scrutiny-grows/.

Hunnicutt, Benjamin Kline. *Kellogg's Six-Hour Day*. Philadelphia: Temple University Press, 1996.

International Labour Organization. "Statistics on Working Time." Accessed July 13, 2023. https://ilostat.ilo.org/topics/working-time/.

Jamieson, Dave. "The Life and Death of an Amazon Warehouse Temp." HuffPost, October 17, 2018. https://highline.huffingtonpost.com/articles/en/life-and -death-amazon-temp/.

Kirn, Walter. *Up in the Air*. New York, Anchor, 2002.

Konnikova, Maria. "Snoozers Are, in Fact, Losers." *New Yorker*, December 10, 2013. https://www.newyorker.com/tech/annals-of-technology/snoozers-are-in -fact-losers.

Kurutz, Steven. "How to Retire in Your 30s With $1 Million in the Bank." *New York Times*, September 1, 2018. https://www.nytimes.com/2018/09/01/style/fire -financial-independence-retire-early.html.

Lepore, Jill. "What's Wrong with the Way We Work." *New Yorker*, January 11, 2021. https://www.newyorker.com/magazine/2021/01/18/whats-wrong-with-the-way -we-work.

Leroy, Sophie. "Why Is It So Hard to Do My Work? The Challenge of Attention Residue When Switching Between Work Tasks." *Organizational Behavior and Human Decision Processes* 109, no. 2 (2009): 168–181. https://doi.org /10.1016/j.obhdp.2009.04.002.

Malesic, Jonathan. *The End of Burnout: Why Work Drains Us and How to Build Better Lives*. Berkeley: University of California Press, 2022.

Miranda, Lin Manuel. *Hamilton: An American Musical*. Atlantic Records, 2015, MP3.

Mr. Money Mustache. "Start Here." Accessed July 13, 2023. https://www.mrmoney mustache.com/.

Murillo, Ana Lucia. "It's Confirmed: The Workweek Is Indeed Longer Now That You're WFH." *Money*, September 20, 2021. https://money.com/work-from -home-longer-hours/.

Ng, Thomas W. H., Kelly L. Sorensen, and Daniel C. Feldman. "Dimensions, Antecedents, and Consequences of Workaholism: A Conceptual Integration and Extension." *Journal of Organizational Behavior* 28, no. 1 (2007): 111–136. https://doi.org/10.1002/job.424.

Northcote, James. *One Hundred Fables: Original and Selected*. London: J. & D.A. Darling, 1850.

Nozick, Robert. *The Examined Life: Philosophical Meditations*. New York: Simon & Schuster, 1990.

Nussbaum, Martha C., and Saul Levmore. *Aging Thoughtfully: Conversations About Retirement, Romance, Wrinkles, and Regret*. Oxford, UK: Oxford University Press, 2017. https://global.oup.com/academic/product/aging-thought fully-9780190600235?cc=us&lang=en&.

Obama, Michelle. *Becoming*. New York: Crown, 2018.

Pandey, Erica. "Axios-Ipsos Poll: Retirement Out of Reach." Axios, July 20, 2023. https://www.axios.com/2023/07/20/retirement-savings-planning.

Pantic, Nina. "The Top Players Who Won Slams After Having Children." Tennis, April 20, 2017. https://www.tennis.com/baseline/articles/the-top-players-who-won-slams-after-having-children.

Pastuovic, Michael. "The NFL Running Back Age Cliff." Northwestern Sports Analytics Group, December 29, 2020. https://sites.northwestern.edu/nusportsanalytics/2020/12/29/the-nfl-running-back-age-cliff/.

Reddit. "f/financialindependence." Reddit thread. Accessed July 13, 2023. https://www.reddit.com/r/financialindependence/.

Robin, Vicki, and Joe Dominguez. *Your Money or Your Life: 9 Steps to Transforming Your Relationship with Money and Achieving Financial Independence.* New York: Penguin Books, 2018.

Rosario, Isabella. "When the 'Hustle' Isn't Enough." NPR, April 3, 2020. https://www.npr.org/sections/codeswitch/2020/04/03/826015780/when-the-hustle-isnt-enough.

Sainato, Michael. "'Lack of Respect': Outcry over Amazon Employee's Death on Warehouse Floor." *Guardian* (Manchester, UK), January 9, 2023. https://www.theguardian.com/technology/2023/jan/09/amazon-employee-death-warehouse-floor-colorado.

Schabram, Kira, Matt Bloom, and D. J. Didonna. "Recover, Explore, Practice: The Transformative Potential of Sabbaticals." Academy of Management Discoveries, November 4, 2022. https://doi.org/10.5465/amd.2021.0100.

Schor, Juliet B. *The Overworked American: The Unexpected Decline of Leisure.* New York: Basic Books, 1993.

Schor, Juliet B., Wen Fan, Orla Kelly, Guolin Gu, Tatiana Bezdenezhnykh, and Niamh Bridson-Hubbard. *The Four Day Week: Assessing Global Trials of Reduced Work Time with No Reduction in Pay.* Auckland, New Zealand: Four Day Week Global, 2022.

Shakespeare, William. *As You Like It.* In *The Complete Works of William Shakespeare.* Project Gutenberg, release date 1994. https://www.gutenberg.org/cache/epub/100/pg100-images.html#chap04.

Shamai, Orit, Itzhak Harpaz, and Raphael Snir. "Towards Advancing Well-Being in Organizations: An Examination of Happiness Underlying Overwork." *Academy of Management Proceedings* 2018, no. 1 (2018): 14443. https://doi.org/10.5465/AMBPP.2018.14443abstract.

Sheehy, Gail. *New Passages: Mapping Your Life Across Time.* New York: Ballantine Books, 1996.

———. *Passages: Predictable Crises of Adult Life.* New York: Bantam, 1977.

Shell, Ellen Ruppel. *The Job: Work and Its Future in a Time of Radical Change.* New York, Penguin, 2018.

Slaughter, Anne-Marie. "Why Women Still Can't Have It All." *Atlantic*, July–August 2012. Accessed July 27, 2023. https://www.theatlantic.com/magazine/archive/2012/07/why-women-still-cant-have-it-all/309020/.

Sonday, Laura. "Examining the Economic Tether and the Meaning of Work." PhD diss., University of Michigan, 2021. https://dx.doi.org/10.7302/3048.

Taylor, Margaret. "The Perfect Number of Hours to Work Every Day? Five." Wired UK, June 15, 2021. https://www.wired.co.uk/article/working-day-time-five-hours.

US Bureau of Labor Statistics. "Labor Force Statistics from the Current Population Survey." Accessed September 22, 2023. https://www.bls.gov/cps/cpsaat36.htm.

US Census Bureau. "National Poverty in America Awareness Month: January 2023." Press release, January 2023. https://www.census.gov/newsroom/stories/poverty-awareness-month.html.

Wilson, Timothy D., and Daniel T. Gilbert. "Affective Forecasting." *Advances in Experimental Social Psychology* 35 (2003): 345–411. https://doi.org/10.1016/S0065-2601(03)01006-2.

Ziebelman, Alexis. "Peaking at 16: The Reality of Female Gymnasts." *Daily Pennsylvanian*, March 13, 2013. http://www.thedp.com/article/2013/03/peaking-at-16-the-reality-of-female-gymnasts.

Chapter 4: Should You Work for Love or Money?

ABC News. "A Sweet Solution to the Sticky Wage Disparity Problem." August 10, 2013. https://abcnews.go.com/Business/companies-follow-ben-jerrys-lead-wages/story?id=19920634.

Anderson, Elizabeth. *Private Government: How Employers Rule Our Lives (and Why We Don't Talk About It)*. Princeton, NJ: Princeton University Press, 2017.

Andresky Fraser, Jill. *White Collar Sweatshop: The Deterioration of Work and Its Rewards in Corporate America*. New York: W. W. Norton, 2001.

Aragão, Carolina. "Gender Pay Gap in U.S. Hasn't Changed Much in Two Decades." Pew Research Center, March 1, 2023. https://www.pewresearch.org/short-reads/2023/03/01/gender-pay-gap-facts/.

Baker, Michael, Yosh Halberstam, Kory Kroft, Alexandre Mas, and Derek Messacar. "Pay Transparency and the Gender Gap." *American Economic Journal: Applied Economics* 15, no. 2 (2023): 157–183.

Batuman, Elif. *Either/Or*. New York: Penguin, 2022.

Berkeley, George. *A Treatise Concerning Principles of Human Knowledge*. Indianapolis, IN: Hackett, 1982.

Bhattacharjee, Yudhijit. "Women Say Stopping Tenure Clock Isn't Enough." *Science*, December 17, 2004. https://www.science.org/content/article/women-say-stopping-tenure-clock-isnt-enough.

Blau, Francine D., and Lawrence M. Khan. "The Gender Wage Gap: Extent, Trends, and Explanations." *Journal of Economic Literature* 55, no. 3 (2017): 789–865.

Bloomberg. "Bloomberg Billionaires Index." Accessed September 22, 2023. https://www.bloomberg.com/billionaires/.

Davis, Pamela B., Emma A. Meagher, Claire Pomeroy, William L. Lowe Jr., Arthur H. Rubenstein, Joy Y. Wu, Anne B. Curtis, and Rebecca D. Jackson. "Pandemic-Related Barriers to the Success of Women in Research: A Framework for Action." *Nature Medicine* 28 (2002): 436–438. https://doi.org/10.1038/s41591-022-01692-8.

Diener, Ed, and Robert Biswas-Diener. "Will Money Increase Subjective Well-Being?" *Social Indicators Research* 57 (2002): 119–169.

Edmonds, Charlotte. "Here's How Much Money the Average NFL Player Makes in 2002." NBC Sports Philadelphia, July 29, 2002. https://www.nbcsportsphiladelphia.com/nfl/philadelphia-eagles/heres-how-much-money-the-average-nfl-player-makes-in-2022/250699/.

Frank, Robert H., and Philip J. Cook. *The Winner-Take-All Society: Why the Few at the Top Get So Much More Than the Rest of Us.* New York: Penguin, 1996.

Fry, Richard. "Some Gender Disparities Widened in the U.S. Workforce During the Pandemic." Pew Research Center, January 14, 2022. https://www.pewresearch.org/short-reads/2022/01/14/some-gender-disparities-widened-in-the-u-s-workforce-during-the-pandemic/.

Fry, Richard, Brian Kennedy, and Cary Funk. "STEM Jobs See Uneven Progress in Increasing Gender, Racial and Ethnic Diversity." Pew Research Center, April 1, 2021. https://www.pewresearch.org/science/2021/04/01/stem-jobs-see-uneven-progress-in-increasing-gender-racial-and-ethnic-diversity/.

Heidary, Fatemeh, Abolfazl Rahimi, and Reza Gharebaghi. "Poverty as a Risk Factor in Human Cancers." *Iranian Journal of Public Health* 42, no. 3 (2013): 341–343.

Jost, John T., Sally Blount, Jeffrey Pfeffer, and Geörgy Hunyady. "Fair Market Ideology: Its Cognitive-Motivational Underpinnings." *Research in Organizational Behavior* 25 (2003): 53–91. https://doi.org/10.1016/S0191-3085(03)25002-4.

Kahneman, Daniel, and Angus Deaton. "High Income Improves Evaluation of Life but Not Emotional Well-Being." *Proceedings of the National Academy of Sciences* 107, no. 38 (2010): 16489–16493. https://doi.org/10.1073/pnas.1011492107.

Killingsworth, Matthew A. "Experienced Well-Being Rises with Income, Even Above $75,000 per Year." *Proceedings of the National Academy of Sciences* 118, no. 4 (2021): e2016976118. https://doi.org/10.1073/pnas.2016976118.

Killingsworth, Matthew A., Daniel Kahneman, and Barbara Mellers. "Income and Emotional Well-Being: A Conflict Resolved." *Proceedings of the National Academy of Sciences* 120, no. 10 (2023): e2208661120. https://doi.org/10.1073/pnas.2208661120.

Latu, Ioana M., Marianne Schmid Mast, Joris Lammers, and Dario Bombari. "Successful Female Leaders Empower Women's Behavior in Leadership Tasks."

Journal of Experimental Social Psychology 49, no. 3 (2013): 444–448. https://doi.org/10.1016/j.jesp.2013.01.003.

Leete, Laura. "Wage Equity and Employee Motivation in Nonprofit and For-Profit Organizations." *Journal of Economic Behavior & Organization* 43, no. 4 (2000): 423–446. https://doi.org/10.1016/S0167-2681(00)00129-3.

Madgavkar, Anu, Olivia White, Mekala Krishnan, Deepa Mahajan, and Xavier Azcue. "COVID-19 and Gender Equality: Countering the Regressive Effects." McKinsey Global Institute, July 15, 2020. https://www.mckinsey.com/featured-insights/future-of-work/covid-19-and-gender-equality-countering-the-regressive-effects.

Marcal, Katrine. "Paid or Not, Women Have Always Contributed to the Wealth of Nations." *Guardian* (Manchester, UK), October 11, 2015. https://www.theguardian.com/commentisfree/2015/oct/11/women-have-always-contributed-to-wealth-of-nations.

Maupassant, Guy de. "The Necklace." In *Fiction 100: An Anthology of Short Stories*, 4th ed., edited by James H. Pickering. New York: Macmillan, 1985.

Michaelson, Christopher. "Literature and the Canonical Values of Capitalism." In *Aesthetics and Business Ethics*, edited by Daryl Koehn and Dawn Elm, 37–50. Dordrecht, Netherlands: Springer, 2014.

———. "Values and Capitalism." In *Normative Theory and Business Ethics*, edited by Jeffery Smith, 195–208. Lanham, MD: Rowman & Littlefield, 2009.

Miller, Claire Cain. "Stay-at-Home Parents Work Hard. Should They Be Paid?" *New York Times*, October 3, 2019. https://www.nytimes.com/2019/10/03/upshot/paying-for-parenting.html.

Murugananthan, Arunachalam. "India's Pad Man." *Undertold Stories*, April 18, 2017. https://www.undertoldstories.org/2017/04/18/breaking-the-taboo-how-one-man-is-trying-to-make-sanitary-pads-affordable-for-women-in-india/.

Nussbaum, Martha C. *Creating Capabilities: The Human Development Approach*. Cambridge, MA: Belknap Press, 2013.

PayScale. "The Most and Least Meaningful Jobs." Accessed September 22, 2023. https://www.payscale.com/data-packages/most-and-least-meaningful-jobs/most-meaningful-jobs.

Pruitt-Young, Sharon. "A Banksy Piece Was Shredded at Auction in 2018. Now, It May Sell for Millions More." NPR, September 7, 2021. https://www.npr.org/2021/09/07/1034962331/banksy-shredder-girl-with-balloon-love-is-in-the-bin-auction-sothebys.

PwC. "Championing Gender Equity." Accessed September 22, 2023. https://www.pwc.com/gx/en/about/diversity/gender-equity.html.

———. "Understanding a Financial Statement Audit." May 2017.

Rainey, Clint. "The Age of 'Greedflation' Is Here: See How Obscene CEO-to-Worker Pay Ratios Are Right Now." *Fast Company*, July 18, 2022. https://www.fastcompany.com/90770163/the-age-of-greedflation-is-here-see-how-obscene-ceo-to-worker-pay-ratios-are-right-now.

Ryan, Richard M., and Edward L. Deci. "On Happiness and Human Potentials: A Review of Research on Hedonic and Eudaimonic Well-Being." *Annual Review of Psychology* 52, no. 1 (2001): 141–166. https://doi.org/10.1146/annurev .psych.52.1.141.

Salles, Arghavan. "COVID Has Worsened Gender Disparities, Especially for Women of Color. Here's What We Can Do Now to Turn the Tide." The Clayman Institute for Gender Research, Stanford University, January 21, 2021. https://gender.stanford.edu/news/covid-has-worsened-gender-disparities -especially-women-color-heres-what-we-can-do-now-turn.

Schneider, Michael, and Joe Otterson. "TV's $1 Million Salary Club: Kevin Costner, Sylvester Stallone, Mahershala Ali and More See Huge Paydays." *Variety*, 2002. https://variety.com/2022/tv/features/tv-salaries-kevin-costner-sylveter -stallone-millions-1235320075/.

Smith, Adam. *An Inquiry into the Nature and Causes of the Wealth of Nations.* New York: Bantam Dell, 2003.

Tiberius, Valerie. *The Reflective Life: Living Wisely with Our Limits.* Oxford, UK: Oxford University Press, 2010.

UN Women. "UN Women Reveals Concerning Regression in Attitudes Towards Gender Roles During Pandemic in New Study." June 22, 2022. https://www .unwomen.org/en/news-stories/press-release/2022/06/un-women-reveals -concerning-regression-in-attitudes-towards-gender-roles-during-pandemic-in -new-study.

Yunus, Muhammad. *Banker to the Poor: Micro-Lending and the Battle Against World Poverty.* New York: PublicAffairs, 2008.

Zelizer, Viviana. *Pricing the Priceless Child: The Changing Social Value of Children.* Princeton, NJ: Princeton University Press, 1994.

Chapter 5: Is It Enough to Love Your Work?

Antique Sound Workshop. "Music-Making in America: Recent Gallup Poll Contradicts Conventional Wisdom." Accessed September 23, 2023. https://aswltd .com/gallup.htm.

BBC News. "Was Steve Jobs' Genius Also a Fatal Flaw?" March 8, 2012. https:// www.bbc.com/news/technology-16157142.

Berg, Justin M., Adam M. Grant, and Victoria Johnson. "When Callings Are Calling: Crafting Work and Leisure in Pursuit of Unanswered Occupational Callings." *Organization Science* 21, no. 5 (2010): 973–994. https://doi.org/10.1287 /orsc.1090.0497.

Bloom, Matt, Amy E. Colbert, and Jordan D. Nielsen. "Stories of Calling: How Called Professionals Construct Narrative Identities." *Administrative Science Quarterly* 66, no. 2 (2021): 298–338. https://doi.org/10.1177/0001839220949502.

Bunderson, J. Stuart, and Jeffrey A. Thompson. "The Call of the Wild: Zookeepers, Callings, and the Double-Edged Sword of Deeply Meaningful Work." *Admin-*

istrative Science Quarterly 54, no. 1 (2009): 32–57. https://doi.org/10.2189 /asqu.2009.54.1.32.

Cech, Erin A. *The Trouble with Passion: How Searching for Fulfillment at Work Fosters Inequality*. Berkeley: University of California Press, 2021.

Chan, Kelvin. "Google Axes 12,000 Jobs as Layoffs Spread Across Tech Sector." Associated Press, January 20, 2023. https://apnews.com/article/technology -business-sundar-pichai-covid-pandemics-c85c45231712709582b1d3fe46be5ffe.

Cheryan, Sapna, and Therese Anne Mortejo. "The Most Common Graduation Advice Tends to Backfire." *New York Times*, May 22, 2023. https://www.nytimes .com/2023/05/22/opinion/stem-women-gender-disparity.html.

Cho, Yuna, and Winnie Y. Jiang. "How Work Orientation Impacts Objective Career Outcomes via Managerial (Mis)perceptions." *Academy of Management Journal* 65, no. 4 (2022): 1353–1382. https://doi.org/10.5465/amj.2020.0841.

Clinton, Michael E., Neil Conway, and Jane Sturges. "'It's Tough Hanging-Up a Call': The Relationships Between Calling and Work Hours, Psychological Detachment, Sleep Quality, and Morning Vigor." *Journal of Occupational Health Psychology* 22, no. 1 (2017): 28–39. https://doi.org/10.1037/ocp0000025.

Didion, Joan. *The Year of Magical Thinking*. New York: Alfred A. Knopf, 2005.

Dobrow, Shoshana R., and Daniel Heller. "Follow Your Heart or Your Head? A Longitudinal Study of the Facilitating Role of Calling and Ability in the Pursuit of a Challenging Career." *Journal of Applied Psychology* 100, no. 3 (2015): 695–712. https://doi.org/10.1037/a0038011.

Dobrow, Shoshana R., Hannah Weisman, Daniel Heller, and Jennifer Tosti-Kharas. "Calling and the Good Life: A Meta-Analysis and Theoretical Extension. *Administrative Science Quarterly* 68, no. 2 (2023): 508–550. https://doi.org /10.1177/00018392231159641.

———. "Calling Attention to 20 Years of Research: A Comprehensive Meta-Analysis of Calling." *Academy of Management Proceedings* 2019, no. 1 (2019). https://doi.org/10.5465/AMBPP.2019.199.

Dobrow, Shoshana R., and Jennifer Tosti-Kharas. "Calling: The Development of a Scale Measure." *Personnel Psychology* 64, no. 4 (2011): 1001–1049. https://doi .org/10.1111/j.1744-6570.2011.01234.x.

———. "Listen to Your Heart? Calling and Receptivity to Career Advice." *Journal of Career Assessment* 20, no. 3 (2012): 264–280. https://doi.org/10.1177 /1069072711434412.

Finney, Martha, and Deborah Dasch. *Find Your Calling, Love Your Life: Paths to Your Truest Self in Life and Work*. New York: Simon & Schuster, 1998.

Foderaro, Lisa W. "City Cracking Down on Performers in Washington Square Park." *New York Times*, December 4, 2011. https://www.nytimes.com/2011/12/05 /nyregion/city-cracks-down-on-washington-square-park-performers.html.

Fuller, Joseph, and William Kerr. "The Great Resignation Didn't Start with the Pandemic." *Harvard Business Review*, March 23, 2022. https://hbr.org/2022/03 /the-great-resignation-didnt-start-with-the-pandemic.

Gerken, Tom. "Meta Lay-Offs: Facebook Owner to Cut 10,000 Staff." BBC News, March 14, 2023. https://www.bbc.com/news/technology-64954124.

Goldwater, Robert. *Gauguin*. New York: Harry N. Abrams, 2004.

Google Books Ngram Viewer. "Find your calling." Google search, accessed September 22, 2023. https://books.google.com/ngrams/graph?content=find+your+calling&year_start=1800&year_end=2019&corpus=en-2019&smoothing=3.

Isay, David. *Callings: The Purpose and Passion of Work*. New York: Penguin Books, 2017.

Jaffe, Sarah. *Work Won't Love You Back: How Devotion to Our Jobs Keeps Us Exploited, Exhausted, and Alone*. New York: Bold Type Books, 2021.

Jobs, Steve. "You've Got to Find What You Love." Transcript of speech delivered at Stanford University, June 12, 2005. https://news.stanford.edu/2005/06/12/youve-got-find-love-jobs-says/.

Kurutz, Steven. "The Real Piano Man." *New York Times*. August 30, 2008. https://www.nytimes.com/2008/08/31/nyregion/thecity/31pian.html.

Maugham, W. Somerset. *The Moon and Sixpence*. London: William Heinemann, 1919.

Michaelson, Christopher. "The Importance of Meaningful Work." *MIT Sloan Management Review* 51, no. 2 (2010): 12–13.

Monster.com. "Your Calling Is Calling." YouTube video, 1 min., August 12, 2008. Posted by Bestadvertising Channel. https://youtu.be/Xam7Dws_UfU?si=Yw32Q2gRibJuUwBg.

Nellie Bowles. "In 'Small Fry,' Steve Jobs Comes Across as a Jerk. His Daughter Forgives Him. Should We?" *New York Times*, August 23, 2018. https://www.nytimes.com/2018/08/23/books/steve-jobs-lisa-brennan-jobs-small-fry.html.

Nooyi, Indra. "Farewell Letter to PepsiCo Associates." Electronic letter, October 2, 2018. https://www.indranooyi.com/farewell-letter-to-pepsico-associates.

Obadaru, Otilia. "Forgone, but Not Forgotten: Toward a Theory of Forgone Professional Identities." *Academy of Management Journal* 60, no. 2 (2017): 523–553. https://doi.org/10.5465/amj.2013.0432.

Proust, Marcel. *In Search of Lost Time*. Translated by C. K. Scott Moncrieff and Terence Kilmartin. Revised by D. J. Enright. New York: Modern Library, 1992.

Robb, Alice. "If Your Name Is Dennis, You're More Likely to Become a Dentist." *New Republic*, January 8, 2014. https://newrepublic.com/article/116140/psychologists-say-our-names-affect-what-careers-we-choose.

Sinetar, Marsha. *Do What You Love, the Money Will Follow: Discovering Your Right Livelihood*. New York: Dell, 1987.

Siy, John Oliver, Adriana L. Germano, Laura Vianna, Jovani Azpeitia, Shaoxiong Yan, Amanda K. Montoya, and Sapna Cheryan. "Does the Follow-Your-Passions Ideology Cause Greater Academic and Occupational Gender Disparities Than Other Cultural Ideologies?" *Journal of Personality and Social Psychology* 125, no. 3 (2023): 548–570. https://doi.org/10.1037/pspi0000421.

Slote, Michael. "Admirable Immorality." In *Goods and Virtues*, 77–107. Oxford, UK: Clarendon Press, 1989.

Spangler, Todd. "Elon Musk Plans to Lay Off Nearly 75% of Twitter Employees, or 5,500 Staffers." *Variety*, October 20, 2022. https://variety.com/2022/digital /news/elon-musk-twitter-layoffs-75-percent-1235410335/.

Terkel, Studs. *Working: What People Do All Day and How They Feel About What They Do*. New York: Pantheon Books, 1974.

Thompson, Jeffery A., and J. Stuart Bunderson. "Research on Work as a Calling . . . and How to Make It Matter." *Annual Review of Organizational Psychology and Organizational Behavior* 6 (2019): 421–443. https://doi.org/10.1146 /annurev-orgpsych-012218-015140.

Tokumitsu, Miya. *Do What You Love: And Other Lies About Success and Happiness*. New York: Regan Arts, 2015.

Tosti-Kharas, Jennifer, and Dobrow, Shoshana R. "When the Stars Align: Career and Life Consequences of Calling." *Academy of Management Proceedings* 2021 (1). Proceedings of the 81st Annual Meeting of the Academy of Management, Boston, August 2021. https://doi.org/10.5465 /AMBPP.2021.230.

Tosti-Kharas, Jennifer, Shoshana R. Dobrow, and Hannah Weisman. "Amateur vs Professional Pursuit: The Impact of Pursuing a Calling (Un)Professionally." Paper presented at "What's New on Calling: Multi-Method Insights on Its Predictors and Outcomes," symposium by Anna Dallas Rosa, Michelangelo Vianello, and Evgenia Lysova. *Academy of Management Proceedings* 2023 (1). Proceedings of the 83rd Annual Meeting of the Academy of Management, Boston, August 2023. https://doi.org/10.5465/AMPROC.2023.11774symposium.

Vadukul, Alex. "It's a Tough Time to Be a Street Musician with a 900-Pound Piano." *New York Times*, July 16, 2020. https://www.nytimes.com/2020/07/16 /nyregion/coronavirus-pianist-washington-square-nyc.html.

Van Dam, Andrew. "Why Are These Groups So Much More Likely to Wear Glasses Than Any Others?" *Washington Post*, May 5, 2023. https://www.washington post.com/business/2023/05/05/glasses-eyes-use-rising/.

Vargas Llosa, Mario. *The Way to Paradise*. Translated by Natasha Wimmer. London: Faber & Faber, 2004.

Voss, Zannie Giraud, Glenn B. Voss, and Karen Yair, with Kristen Lega. "Orchestra Facts: 2006–2014: A Study of Orchestra Finances and Operations." League of American Orchestras, 2016. https://www.arts.gov/sites/default/files/Research -Art-Works-League.pdf.

Williams, Bernard. "Moral Luck." In *Moral Luck: Philosophical Papers 1973–1980*, 20–39. Cambridge: Cambridge University Press, 1981. https://doi.org /10.1017/CBO9781139165860.

Woodie, Maria. "Is This Gauguin Painting Really the Most Expensive in the World?" Artists Network, July 18, 2017. https://www.artistsnetwork.com /art-history/paul-gauguin-painting-lawsuit/.

Wrzesniewski, Amy, and Jane E. Dutton. "Crafting a Job: Revisioning Employees as Active Crafters of Their Work." *Academy of Management Review* 26, no. 2 (2001): 179–201. https://doi.org/10.5465/amr.2001.4378011.

Zhang, Fangfang, and Sharon K. Parker. "Reorienting Job Crafting Research: A Hierarchical Structure of Job Crafting Concepts and Integrative Review." *Journal of Organizational Behavior* 40, no. 2 (2019): 126–146. https://doi .org/10.1002/job.2332.

Chapter 6: What Work Can't Society Do Without?

Ashforth, Blake E., and Glen E. Kreiner. "'How Can You Do It?': Dirty Work and the Challenge of Constructing a Positive Identity." *Academy of Management Review* 24, no. 3 (1999): 413–434.

BBC News. "Twitter Ends Covid Misinformation Policy Under Musk." November 20, 2022. https://www.bbc.com/news/technology-63796832.

Brooks, David. *The Road to Character*. New York: Random House, 2016.

Business Roundtable. "Business Roundtable Redefines the Purpose of a Corporation to Promote 'An Economy That Serves All Americans'." August 19, 2019. https://www.businessroundtable.org/business-roundtable-redefines-the -purpose-of-a-corporation-to-promote-an-economy-that-serves-all-americans.

Cantor Fitzgerald, L. P. "Submission of Cantor Fitzgerald, L.P., eSpeed, Inc., and Tradespark L.P. to the Special Master of the September 11 Victim Compensation Fund of 2001 and to the Department of Justice." September 12, 2002.

Care, Norman S. "Career Choice." *Ethics* 94, no. 2 (1984): 283–302.

Centers for Disease Control and Prevention. "CDC Museum COVID-19 Timeline." Accessed September 24, 2023. https://www.cdc.gov/museum/timeline/covid19 .html.

Ciulla, Joanne B. *The Working Life: The Promise and Betrayal of Modern Work*. New York: Currency, 2001.

Dechter, Aimée R., and Glen H. Elder Jr. "World War II Mobilization in Men's Work Lives: Continuity or Disruption for the Middle Class?" *American Journal of Sociology* 110, no. 3 (2004): 761–793.

Echikson, Julia, and Patricia Mazzei. "No Trading Floor? No Problem. A Financial Firm Quarantines at the Four Seasons." *New York Times*, April 7, 2020. https://www.nytimes.com/2020/04/07/us/coronavirus-citadel-securities-four -seasons-florida.html.

Feinberg, Kenneth R. *What Is Life Worth? The Unprecedented Effort to Compensate the Victims of 9/11*. New York: PublicAffairs, 2005.

Feinberg, Kenneth R., Camille S. Biros, Jordana Harris Feldman, Deborah E. Greenspan, and Jacqueline E. Zins. "Final Report of the Special Master for the September 11th Victim Compensation Fund of 2001. Vol. 1." US Department of Justice, 2004. https://www.ojp.gov/pdffiles1/Archive /208388NCJRS.pdf.

Fernandez, Manny, and David Montgomery. "Businesses Chafing Under Covid-19 Lockdowns Turn to Armed Defiance." *New York Times*, May 13, 2020. https://www.nytimes.com/2020/05/13/us/coronavirus-businesses-lockdown-guns.html.

Forbes Staff. "Forbes Releases 37th Annual Forbes 200 Ranking of the Richest Americans." *Forbes*, October 3, 2018. https://www.forbes.com/sites/forbespr/2018/10/03/forbes-releases-37th-annual-forbes-400-ranking-of-the-richest-americans/?sh=1d7058c85cb1.

———. "The 400 Richest People in America." *Forbes*. Accessed September 24, 2023. https://www.forbes.com/forbes-400/.

Freeman, R. Edward. "The New Story of Business: Towards a More Responsible Capitalism." *Business and Society Review* 122, no. 3 (Fall 2017): 449–465. https://doi.org/10.1111/basr.12123.

Gallie, Walter Bryce. "Essentially Contested Concepts." *Proceedings of the Aristotelian Society* 56 (1955–1956): 167–198.

Gates, Bill. "About Bill." GatesNotes, the Blog of Bill Gates. Accessed September 24, 2023. https://www.gatesnotes.com/Bio.

Grant, Adam. *Give and Take: Why Helping Others Drives Our Success*. New York: Penguin, 2014.

———. "How Customers Can Rally Your Troops." *Harvard Business Review* 89, no. 6 (2011): 96.

Grant, Adam M., and Justin M. Berg. "Prosocial Motivation at Work: When, Why, and How Making a Difference Makes a Difference." In *The Oxford Handbook of Positive Organizational Scholarship*, edited by Kim Cameron and Gretchen Spreitzer, 28–44. Oxford, UK: Oxford University Press, 2012.

Hamilton, Gabrielle. "My Restaurant Was My Life for 20 Years. Does the World Need It Anymore?" *New York Times Magazine*, April 23, 2020. https://www.nytimes.com/2020/04/23/magazine/closing-prune-restaurant-covid.html.

Hernandez, Daisy, and Manasee Wagh. "These 19 Items Are in Short Supply Due to COVID-Related Supply Chain Issues." *Popular Mechanics*, September 23, 2022. https://www.popularmechanics.com/culture/g38674719/covid-shortages/.

Hiltzik, Michael. "Column: The Bezos-Branson-Musk Space Race Is a Huge Waste of Money and Scientifically Useless." *Los Angeles Times*, July 6, 2021. https://www.latimes.com/business/story/2021-07-06/jeff-bezos-richard-branson-elon-musk-space-race.

Hobbes, Thomas. *Leviathan*. London: Routledge, 1894.

Huggett, Thomas D., Elizabeth L. Tung, Megan Cunningham, Isaac Ghinai, Heather L. Duncan, Maura E. McCauley, and Wayne M. Detmer. "Assessment of a Hotel-Based Protective Housing Program for Incidence of SARS-CoV-2 Infection and Management of Chronic Illness Among Persons Experiencing Homelessness." *JAMA Network Open* 4, no. 12 (2021): e2138464-e2138464. doi:10.1001/jamanetworkopen.2021.38464.

Kim, Marina. "Rethinking the Impact Spectrum." Ashoka, May 8, 2015. https://www
.ashoka.org/en-us/story/rethinking-impact-spectrum.

Knibbs, Kate. "As Toilet Paper Flies off Shelves, Bidet Sales Go Boom-Boom."
Wired, March 17, 2020. https://www.wired.com/story/toilet-paper-shortage
-bidet-sales-boom/.

Kulish, Nicholas. "FTX's Collapse Casts a Pall on a Philanthropy Movement." *New
York Times,* November 13, 2022. https://www.nytimes.com/2022/11/13
/business/ftx-effective-altruism.html.

———. "How a Scottish Moral Philosopher Got Elon Musk's Number." *New York
Times,* October 8, 2022. https://www.nytimes.com/2022/10/08/business
/effective-altruism-elon-musk.html.

Lewis, Michael. *Liar's Poker.* New York: W. W. Norton, 2010.

Michaelson, Christopher, and Jennifer Tosti-Kharas. "Serving Self or Serving
Others? Close Relations' Perspectives on Ethics and Calling." *Journal of Vocational Behavior* 114 (2019): 19–30. https://doi.org/10.1016/j.jvb.2019.02.005.

Neate, Rupert. "Super-Rich Buying Up 'Downton Abbey Estates' to Escape Pandemic." *Guardian* (Manchester, UK), November 14, 2020. https://www
.theguardian.com/news/2020/nov/14/super-rich-downton-abbey-estates
-england-country-coronavirus.

Nicas, Jack. "He Has 17,700 Bottles of Hand Sanitizer and Nowhere to Sell Them."
New York Times, March 14, 2020. https://www.nytimes.com/2020/03/14
/technology/coronavirus-purell-wipes-amazon-sellers.html.

Nicholas, Tom, and Vasiliki Fouka. "John D. Rockefeller: The Richest Man in
the World." Harvard Business School Case 815-008, December 2014, revised
March 2018.

Padilla, Alex. "Citizenship for Essential Workers Act." Congress.gov, March 15,
2021. https://www.congress.gov/bill/117th-congress/senate-bill/747.

Paine, Lynn Sharp. *Value Shift: Why Companies Must Merge Social and Financial Imperatives to Achieve Superior Performance.* New York: McGraw-Hill,
2004.

Playbill staff. "Broadway Goes Dark Amid Coronavirus Concerns." *Playbill,* March
12, 2020. https://playbill.com/article/broadway-goes-dark-amid-coronavirus
-concerns.

Porter, Michael E., and Mark R. Kramer. "Creating Shared Value." *Harvard Business Review* 89, no. 1/2 (2011): 62–77. https://hbr.org/2011/01/the-big-idea
-creating-shared-value.

Rand, Ayn. *Atlas Shrugged.* New York: Random House, 1957.

Rangan, Subramanian, ed. *Performance & Progress: Essays on Capitalism, Business, and Society.* Oxford, UK: Oxford University Press, 2015.

Schwab, Klaus, with Peter Vanham. *Stakeholder Capitalism: A Global Economy
That Works for Progress, People and Planet.* Hoboken, NJ: John Wiley, 2021.

Scott, MacKenzie. "Pledge Letter." *The Giving Pledge,* May 25, 2019. https://
givingpledge.org/pledger?pledgerId=393.

Shanafelt, Tait D., Colin P. West, Lotte N. Dyrbye, Mickey Trockel, Michael Tutty, Hanhan Wang, Lindsey E. Carlasare, and Christine Sinsky. "Changes in Burnout and Satisfaction with Work-Life Integration in Physicians During the First 2 Years of the COVID-19 Pandemic." *Mayo Clinic Proceedings* 97, no. 12 (2022): 2248–2258. https://doi.org/10.1016/j.mayocp.2022.09.002.

Siddiqui, Faiz. "How Elon Musk Knocked Tesla's 'Full Self-Driving' Off Course." *Washington Post*, March 29, 2023. https://www.washingtonpost.com /technology/2023/03/19/elon-musk-tesla-driving/.

Stanley, Alessandra. "After the Attacks: The Chairman; Wall Street's Driven Steward Presses for Business as Usual." *New York Times*, September 17, 2001. https://www.nytimes.com/2001/09/17/business/after-attacks-chairman-wall -street-s-driven-steward-presses-for-business-usual.html.

Swanson, Ana, and David Yaffe-Bellany. "Trump Declares Meat Supply 'Critical,' Aiming to Reopen Plants." *New York Times*, April 28, 2020. https://www.nytimes .com/2020/04/28/business/economy/coronavirus-trump-meat-food-supply.html.

Szalai, Jennifer. "How Sam Bankman-Fried Put Effective Altruism on the Defensive." *New York Times*, December 9, 2022. https://www.nytimes.com /2022/12/09/books/review/effective-altruism-sam-bankman-fried-crypto.html.

Thomas, Landon, Jr. "The Man Behind Grasso's Payday." *New York Times*, March 14, 2004. https://www.nytimes.com/2004/03/14/business/the-man-behind -grasso-s-payday.html.

Tolstoy, Leo. *War and Peace*. Translated by Ann Dunnigan. New York: Signet Classics, 1968.

US Department of Justice. "September 11th Victim Compensation Fund of 2001." Accessed September 24, 2023. https://www.justice.gov/archive/victimcompen sation/payments_deceased.html.

Voytko, Lisette. "The Richest Women in America." *Forbes*, October 5, 2021. https:// www.forbes.com/sites/lisettevoytko/2021/10/05/the-richest-women-in -america-2021-forbes-400/?sh=50444e5b1b23.

Warren, Elizabeth. "Elizabeth Warren and Ro Khanna Unveil Essential Workers Bill of Rights." Elizabeth Warren, Newsroom, Press Releases, April 13, 2020. https://www.warren.senate.gov/newsroom/press-releases/elizabeth-warren -and-ro-khanna-unveil-essential-workers-bill-of-rights.

Washburn, Gary. "How the NBA Created a COVID-Free Bubble and Made It the Safest Place on Earth." *Boston Globe*, November 2, 2020. https://www .bostonglobe.com/2020/11/02/sports/with-careful-planning-total-commitment -nba-constructed-safest-place-earth/?event=event12.

Wieczner, Jen. "The Case of the Missing Toilet Paper: How the Coronavirus Exposed U.S. Supply Chain Flaws." *Fortune*, May 18, 2020. https://fortune .com/2020/05/18/toilet-paper-sales-surge-shortage-coronavirus-pandemic -supply-chain-cpg-panic-buying/.

Will, Madeline. "Deemed 'Essential Workers,' Some Teachers Told to Skip Quarantine After COVID-19 Exposure." *EducationWeek*, August 21, 2020. https://

www.edweek.org/leadership/deemed-essential-workers-some-teachers
-told-to-skip-quarantine-after-covid-19-exposure/2020/08.

Williams, Bernard. *Ethics and the Limits of Philosophy*. Cambridge, MA: Harvard University Press, 1985.

Wolfe, Tom. *The Bonfire of the Vanities*. London: Picador, 2008.

World Economic Forum. "Reading Leaders' Minds—Session Summary." World Economic Forum Annual Meeting, Davos-Klosters, Switzerland, January 27–31, 2010.

Young, Ryan. "Rudy Gobert Reflects on Last Season's COVID-19 Microphone Incident: 'I Was Trying to Liven the Mood'." Yahoo! Sports, December 24, 2020. https://sports.yahoo.com/utah-jazz-rudy-gobert-microphone-incident -coronavirus-covid19-pandemic-015904350.html?soc_src=social-sh &soc_trk=ma.

Zaveri, Mihir. "The WWE Is Now Considered an 'Essential Service' in Florida." *New York Times*, April 14, 2020. https://www.nytimes.com/2020/04/14/us /wwe-essential-business-florida-coronavirus.html.

Chapter 7: Can Your Work Have a Higher Purpose?

Allison, Scott T., George R. Goethals, and Roderick M. Kramer, eds. "Introduction: Setting the Scene; The Rise and Coalescence of Heroism Science." In *Handbook of Heroism and Heroic Leadership*, 23–38. London: Routledge, 2016.

Berlin, Gretchen, Meredith Lapointe, Mhoire Murphy, and Joanna Wexler. "Assessing the Lingering Impact of COVID-19 on the Nursing Workforce." McKinsey & Company, May 11, 2022. https://www.mckinsey.com/industries/healthcare /our-insights/assessing-the-lingering-impact-of-covid-19-on-the-nursing -workforce.

Brower, Tracy. "New Data: The Most Respected Jobs and 5 Ways to Gain Respect No Matter What Your Work." *Forbes*, May 30, 2022. https://www.forbes.com /sites/tracybrower/2022/05/30/new-data-the-most-respected-jobs-and-5-ways -to-gain-respect-no-matter-what-your-work/?sh=627d46c441c1.

Camus, Albert. *The Myth of Sisyphus*. Translated by Justin O'Brien. New York: Vintage Books.

Cheng, Michelle. "Nearly Half of All College Students Are Now Considering Careers in Health or Science." *Quartz*, June 4, 2021. https://qz.com/2017005/the -pandemic-is-leading-students-to-consider-jobs-in-healthcare.

Chin, Frank, Jeffrey Paul Chan, Lawson Fusao Inada, and Shawn Wong. *Aiiieeeee!: An Anthology of Asian American Writers*. Washington, DC: Howard University Press, 1974.

DeSimone, Danielle. "Why 9/11 Inspired These Service Members to Join the Military." United Service Organizations, September 7, 2021. https://www.uso.org /stories/2849-why-9-11-inspired-these-patriots-to-join-the-military.

Duffy, Ryan D., Blake A. Allan, Elizabeth M. Bott, and Bryan J. Dik. "Does the Source of a Calling Matter? External Summons, Destiny, and Perfect Fit." *Journal of Career Assessment* 22, no. 4 (2014): 562–574.

Frankl, Viktor E. *Man's Search for Meaning.* New York: Pocket Books, 1985.

Freeman, R. Edward, Kirsten E. Martin, and Bidhan L. Parmar. *The Power of And: Responsible Business Without Trade-Offs.* New York: Columbia Business School Publishing, 2020.

French, Rachel, Linda H. Aiken, Kathleen E. Fitzpatrick Rosenbaum, and Karen B. Lasater. "Conditions of Nursing Practice in Hospitals and Nursing Homes Before COVID-19: Implications for Policy Action." *Journal of Nursing Regulation* 13, no. 1 (2022): 45–53. https://doi.org/10.1016/S2155-8256(22)00033-3.

Friedman, Milton. "A Friedman Doctrine: The Social Responsibility of Business Is to Increase Its Profits." *New York Times,* September 13, 1970. https://www.nytimes.com/1970/09/13/archives/a-friedman-doctrine-the-social-responsibility-of-business-is-to.html.

García, Héctor, and Francesc Miralles. *Ikigai: The Japanese Secret to a Long and Happy Life.* New York: Penguin Life, 2017.

Goleman, Daniel. "Millennials: The Purpose Generation." Korn Ferry. Accessed September 22, 2023. https://www.kornferry.com/insights/this-week-in-leadership/millennials-purpose-generation.

Hurst, Aaron. *The Purpose Economy: How Your Desire for Impact, Personal Growth and Community Is Changing the World.* 2nd ed. Boise, ID: Elevate, 2016.

McGurran, Brianna. "Average Salaries of College Graduates 2023." *Forbes Advisor.* Accessed September 22, 2023. https://www.forbes.com/advisor/student-loans/average-salary-college-graduates/.

Meminger, Dean. "How 9/11 Changed the Police and Fire Departments." NY1, September 9, 2021. https://ny1.com/nyc/all-boroughs/news/2021/09/09/how-9-11-changed-the-police-and-fire-departments.

Metz, Thaddeus. "The Meaningful and the Worthwhile: Clarifying the Relationships." *Philosophical Forum* 43, no. 4 (2012): 435–448. https://doi.org/10.1111/j.1467-9191.2012.00436.x.

Oelberger, Carrie R. "The Dark Side of Deeply Meaningful Work: Work-Relationship Turmoil and the Moderating Role of Occupational Value Homophily." *Journal of Management Studies* 56, no. 3 (2019): 558–588.

Parker, Kim, and Juliana Menasce Horowitz. "Majority of Workers Who Quit a Job in 2021 Cite Low Pay, No Opportunities for Advancement, Feeling Disrespected." Pew Research Center, March 9, 2022. https://www.pewresearch.org/short-reads/2022/03/09/majority-of-workers-who-quit-a-job-in-2021-cite-low-pay-no-opportunities-for-advancement-feeling-disrespected/.

Pat Tillman Foundation. "Pat's Story." Accessed September 22, 2023. https://pattillmanfoundation.org/the-foundation/pats-story/.

Peace Corps. "9/11 Drives Americans to Answer Peace Corps Call to Service." Press release, September 11, 2006. https://www.peacecorps.gov/news/library /911-drives-americans-to-answer-peace-corps-call-to-service/.

Pew Research Center. "Two Decades Later, the Enduring Legacy of 9/11." September 2, 2021. https://www.pewresearch.org/politics/2021/09/02/two-decades -later-the-enduring-legacy-of-9-11/.

Pfau, Bruce N. "How an Accounting Firm Convinced Its Employees They Could Change the World." *Harvard Business Review*, October 6, 2015. https://hbr .org/2015/10/how-an-accounting-firm-convinced-its-employees-they-could -change-the-world.

Pratt, Michael G., Douglas A. Lepisto, and Erik Dane. "The Hidden Side of Trust: Supporting and Sustaining Leaps of Faith Among Firefighters." *Administrative Science Quarterly* 64, no. 2 (2019): 398–434.

Saley, Chad. "Survey: Nearly Half of Physicians Changed Jobs During the Pandemic." CHG Healthcare, June 27, 2022. https://chghealthcare.com/blog /physicians-changed-jobs-survey/.

Sparks, Sarah D. "Student Interest in Health-Care Careers Takes Off During Pandemic." Education Week, March 2, 2021. https://www.edweek.org/teaching -learning/student-interest-in-health-care-careers-takes-off-during-pandemic /2021/03.

Terkel, Studs. *Working: What People Do All Day and How They Feel About What They Do*. New York: Pantheon Books, 1974.

Warren, Rick. *The Purpose Driven Life: What on Earth Am I Here For?* Grand Rapids, MI: Zondervan, 2013.

Weiss, Matthew J., dir. *Man in Red Bandana*. Fort Myers, FL: Rodriguez Productions, 2017. https://www.maninredbandana.com/.

Wolf, Susan. *Meaning in Life and Why It Matters*. Princeton, NJ: Princeton University Press, 2010.

Wong, Shawn. *American Knees*. Seattle: University of Washington Press, 2005.

———. *Homebase: A Novel*. Seattle: University of Washington Press, 2008.

Wood, Johnny. "10 Most Respected Professions in the World." World Economic Forum, January 15, 2019. https://www.weforum.org/agenda/2019/01/most -respected-professions-in-the-world/.

Chapter 8: What Would Make Your Life Worth Living in a World Without Work?

Adema, Willem, Jonas Fluchtmann, Alexandre Lloyd, and Valentina Patrini. "Paid Parental Leave: Big Differences for Mothers and Fathers." OECD Statistics Blog, January 12, 2023. https://oecdstatistics.blog/2023/01/12/paid-parental -leave-big-differences-for-mothers-and-fathers/.

Anderson, Monica, Colleen McClain, Michelle Faverio, and Risa Gelles-Watnick. "The State of Gig Work in 2021." Pew Research Center, December 8, 2021.

https://www.pewresearch.org/internet/2021/12/08/the-state-of-gig-work-in
-2021/.

Anthony, Scott D., and Mark Johnson. "What a Good Moonshot Is Really For."
Harvard Business Review, May 14, 2013. https://hbr.org/2013/05/what-a-good
-moonshot-is-really-2.

Benatar, David, ed. *Life, Death, and Meaning: Key Philosophical Readings on the
Big Questions*. 3rd ed. Lanham, MD: Rowman and Littlefield.

Blacknell, Sean, and Wayne Walsh, dirs. *The Future of Work and Death*. Surrey,
UK: Journeyman Pictures, 2016.

Capra, Frank, dir. *You Can't Take It with You*. Culver City, CA: Columbia Pictures,
1938.

Chuah, Lay Lian, Norman V. Loayza, and Achim D. Schmillen. "The Future of
Work: Race with—not Against—the Machine." Research and Policy Briefs:
From the World Bank Malaysia Hub, no. 16, August 2018. https://documents1
.worldbank.org/curated/en/626651535636984152/pdf/129680-BRI-PUBLIC-The
-Future-of-Work-final.pdf.

Ciulla, Joanne B. *The Working Life: The Promise and Betrayal of Modern Work*.
New York: Currency, 2001.

Future of Life Institute. "Pause Giant AI Experiments: An Open Letter." March 22,
2023. https://futureoflife.org/open-letter/pause-giant-ai-experiments/.

Harter, Jim. "Is Quiet Quitting Real?" Gallup, May 17, 2023. https://www.gallup
.com/workplace/398306/quiet-quitting-real.aspx.

Hobson, Charles J., Linda Delunas, and Dawn Kesic. "Compelling Evidence of the
Need for Corporate Work/Life Balance Initiatives: Results from a National
Survey of Life Events." *Journal of Employment Counseling* 38, no. 1 (2001):
38–44. https://doi.org/10.1002/j.2161-1920.2001.tb00491.x.

Hyman, Louis. "It's Not the End of Work. It's the End of Boring Work." *New York
Times*, April 22, 2023. https://www.nytimes.com/2023/04/22/opinion/jobs-ai
-chatgpt.html.

Jahoda, Marie, Paul F. Lazarsfeld, and Hans Zeisel. *Marienthal: The Sociography
of an Unemployed Community*. London: Taylor & Francis, 2017.

Judge, Mike, dir. *Office Space*. Los Angeles: 20th Century Studios, 1999.

Kachor, Kate. "Former JetBlue Flight Attendant Living the Quiet Life After Quitting His Job During Public Meltdown." 9News, April 30, 2017. https://
www.9news.com.au/9stories/former-jetblue-flight-attendant-living-the-quiet
-life-after-quitting-his-job-during-public-meltdown/dcdee44b-5195-4981
-add8-5d08c8151291.

Kelly, Jack. "U.S. Lost Over 60 Million Jobs—Now Robots, Tech and Artificial Intelligence Will Take Millions More." *Forbes*, October 27, 2020. https://www.forbes
.com/sites/jackkelly/2020/10/27/us-lost-over-60-million-jobs-now-robots-tech
-and-artificial-intelligence-will-take-millions-more/?sh=24077ebb1a52.

Klemko, Robert. "As Coronavirus Took Jobs or Workers Fell Ill, Teen Children
Have Toiled Full-Time, Becoming Lifelines." *Washington Post*, June 3, 2020.

https://www.washingtonpost.com/national/coronavirus-teens-working
/2020/06/03/ff689b28-9c73-11ea-ad09-8da7ec214672_story.html.

Konrath, Sara H. "The Younger Generation Isn't Lazy; They're Burned Out."
Greater Good Magazine, October 21, 2022. https://greatergood.berkeley.edu
/article/item/the_younger_generation_isnt_lazy_theyre_burned_out.

Leana, Carrie R., and Daniel C. Feldman. "Finding New Jobs After a Plant Closing:
Antecedents and Outcomes of the Occurrence and Quality of Reemployment." *Human Relations* 48, no. 12 (1995): 1381–1401. https://doi.org
/10.1177/001872679504801201.

Leswing, Kif. "Google Ends Enterprise Sales of Google Glass, Its Augmented Reality Smartglasses." CNBC, March 15, 2023. https://www.cnbc.com/2023/03/15
/google-discontinues-google-glass-enterprise-end-to-early-ar-project.html.

Lutz, Tom. *Doing Nothing: A History of Loafers, Loungers, Slackers, and Bums
in America*. New York: Farrar, Straus and Giroux, 2007.

Lynxwiler, J. Eric. "Imagineering the Future: Walt Disney's Obsession with Building a Better Tomorrow." *Vice*, January 29, 2016. https://www.vice.com/en
/article/dp59xq/imagineering-the-future-walt-disneys-obsession-with-building
-a-better-tomorrow.

Manyika, James, Susan Lund, Michael Chui, Jacques Bughin, Jonathan Woetzel,
Parul Batra, Ryan Ko, and Saurabh Sanghvi. "Jobs Lost, Jobs Gained: What
the Future of Work Will Mean for Jobs, Skills, and Wages." McKinsey Global
Institute, November 28, 2017. https://www.mckinsey.com/featured-insights
/future-of-work/jobs-lost-jobs-gained-what-the-future-of-work-will-mean-for
-jobs-skills-and-wages.

Marchese, David. "What If Instead of Trying to Manage Your Time, You Set It
Free?" *New York Times Magazine*, May 14, 2023. https://www.nytimes.com
/interactive/2023/05/15/magazine/jenny-odell-interview.html.

McKee-Ryan, Frances M., and Jaron Harvey. "'I Have a Job, But . . .': A Review
of Underemployment." *Journal of Management* 37, no. 4 (2011): 962–996.
https://doi.org/10.1177/0149206311398134.

McKee-Ryan, Frances M., Zhaoli Song, Connie R. Wanberg, and Angelo J. Kinicki.
"Psychological and Physical Well-Being During Unemployment: A Meta-
Analytic Study." *Journal of Applied Psychology* 90, no. 1 (2005): 53–76.
https://doi.org/10.1037/0021-9010.90.1.53.

Metz, Cade. "'The Godfather of A.I.' Leaves Google and Warns of Danger Ahead."
New York Times, May 1, 2023. https://www.nytimes.com/2023/05/01/technology
/ai-google-chatbot-engineer-quits-hinton.html.

Milestone, Lewis, dir. *Hallelujah, I'm a Bum*. Los Angeles: United Artists, 1933.

Miller, Claire Cain. "The Pandemic Created a Child-Care Crisis. Mothers Bore the
Burden." *New York Times*, May 17, 2021. https://www.nytimes.com
/interactive/2021/05/17/upshot/women-workforce-employment-covid.html.

Morris, Chris. "Microsoft's New Bing Chatbot Is Already Insulting and Gaslighting
Users." *Fast Company*, February 14, 2023. https://www.fastcompany
.com/90850277/bing-new-chatgpt-ai-chatbot-insulting-gaslighting-users.

Mullaney, Tim. "Is the Uber, Lyft, and Gig Economy Battle over Workers Nearing Its End Game?" CNBC, October 16, 2022. https://www.cnbc.com/2022/10/16/how-the-uber-lyft-gig-economy-battle-over-drivers-ends.html.

Pope, Hugh. "St. Augustine on Death." *Blackfriars* 21, no. 248 (November 1940): 623–631.

Roose, Kevin. "Bing's A.I. Chat: 'I Want to Be Alive.'" *New York Times*, February 16, 2023. https://www.nytimes.com/2023/02/16/technology/bing-chatbot-transcript.html.

———. "A Conversation with Bing's Chatbot Left Me Deeply Unsettled." *New York Times*, February 16, 2023. https://www.nytimes.com/2023/02/16/technology/bing-chatbot-microsoft-chatgpt.html.

Schor, Juliet B. *After the Gig: How the Sharing Economy Got Hijacked and How to Win It Back*. Berkeley: University of California Press, 2020.

Sherman, Richard, Robert Sherman, and Walt Disney. "Carousel of Progress (Magic Kingdom)—Current Version (1994–Present)." Disney Park Scripts Central, Walt Disney World, 2015. https://www.disneyparkscripts.com/carousel-of-progress-magic-kingdom-1994-version/.

Sloan, Robin. *Sourdough*. New York: MCD, Farrar, Straus and Giroux, 2017.

Smith, Kevin, dir. *Clerks*. Los Angeles: Miramax Films, 1994.

Smith, Linda K., and Caroline Osborn. "Why Parents with Multiple Young Kids Opt Out of Formal Child Care." Bipartisan Policy Center, August 15, 2022. https://bipartisanpolicy.org/blog/why-parents-opt-out-of-formal-child-care/.

Stein, Joe. "The Me Me Me Generation: Millennials are Lazy, Entitled Narcissists Who Still Live with Their Parents: Why They'll Save Us All." *Time*, May 20, 2013. https://time.com/247/millennials-the-me-me-me-generation/.

Stone, Pamela. *Opting Out? Why Women Really Quit Careers and Head Home*. Berkeley: University of California Press, 2007.

Sutin, Angelina R., Paul T. Costa Jr., Elaine Wethington, and William Eaton. "Turning Points and Lessons Learned: Stressful Life Events and Personality Trait Development Across Middle Adulthood." *Psychology and Aging* 25, no. 3 (2010): 524–533. https://doi.org/10.1037/a0018751.

Suzman, James. *Work: A Deep History, from the Stone Age to the Age of Robots*. New York: Penguin, 2021.

Taylor, Richard. "The Meaning of Life." In *Good and Evil*, 319–334. Amherst, NY: Prometheus Books, 2000.

Wanberg, Connie R., Ruth Kanfer, and Maria Rotundo. "Unemployed Individuals: Motives, Job-Search Competencies, and Job-Search Constraints as Predictors of Job Seeking and Reemployment." *Journal of Applied Psychology* 84, no. 6 (December 1999): 897–910. https://doi.org/10.1037/0021-9010.84.6.897.

Weaver, Caity. "I Lived the #VanLife. It Wasn't Pretty." *New York Times*, April 20, 2022. https://www.nytimes.com/2022/04/20/magazine/van-life-dwelling.html.

Wells, H. G. *The History of Mr. Polly*. New York: Penguin Classics, 2005.

Westerman, Ashley. "New Zealand Prime Minister Jacinda Ardern Plans to Leave Office." NPR, January 19, 2023. https://www.npr.org/2023/01/18/1149903191 /jacinda-ardern-resignation-new-zealand-prime-minister.

Williams, Serena, with Rob Haskell. "Serena Williams Says Farewell to Tennis on Her Own Terms—and in Her Own Words." *Vogue*, August 9, 2022. https:// www.vogue.com/article/serena-williams-retirement-in-her-own-words.

World Economic Forum. *Future of Jobs Report 2023*. WEC, 2023. https://www3 .weforum.org/docs/WEF_Future_of_Jobs_2023.pdf.

Wu, Yan, and Sergio Peçanha. "Type in Your Job to See How Much AI Will Affect It." *Washington Post*, May 9, 2023. https://www.washingtonpost.com /opinions/interactive/2023/ai-artificial-intelligence-jobs-impact-research/.

Yuan, Li. "No Job, No Marriage, No Kid: Chinese Workers and the Curse of 35." *New York Times*, June 28, 2023. https://www.nytimes.com/2023/06/28 /business/china-jobs-age-discrimination-35.html.

Zikic, Jelena, and Ute-Christine Klehe. "Job Loss as a Blessing in Disguise: The Role of Career Exploration and Career Planning in Predicting Reemployment Quality." *Journal of Vocational Behavior* 69, no. 3 (2006): 391–409. https://doi .org/10.1016/j.jvb.2006.05.007.

Chapter 9: What Legacy Will Your Work Leave?

ABC News. "Ground Zero Mosque Opponents, Supporters Turn Out to Demonstrate." August 19, 2010. https://abcnews.go.com/US/Politics/ground-mosque -opponents-supporters-turn-demonstrate/story?id=11455698.

Algoe, Sara B., and Jonathan Haidt. "Witnessing Excellence in Action: The 'Other-Praising' Emotions of Elevation, Gratitude, and Admiration." *Journal of Positive Psychology* 4, no. 2 (2009): 105–127.

Arad, Michael. "Reflecting Absence: An Interview with Michael Arad." Interviewed by Harel Shapira. Public Books, August 20, 2013. https://www.publicbooks .org/reflecting-absence-an-interviewwith-michael-arad/.

Aristotle. *The Nicomachean Ethics of Aristotle*. Translated by D. P. Chase. Project Gutenberg, 2003. https://www.gutenberg.org/files/8438/8438-h/8438-h.htm.

———. *Poetics*. Translated by S. H. Butcher. Project Gutenberg, 2013. https:// www.gutenberg.org/files/1974/1974-h/1974-h.htm.

Baatz, Simon. "Leopold and Loeb's Criminal Minds." *Smithsonian Magazine*, August 2008. https://www.smithsonianmag.com/history/leopold-and-loebs -criminal-minds-996498/.

Banvishi, Anvi, Martin D. Slade, and Becca R. Levy. "A Chapter a Day: Association of Book Reading with Longevity." *Social Science & Medicine* 164 (2016): 44–48.

Chernow, Ron. *Alexander Hamilton*. New York: Penguin, 2005.

Christensen, Clayton M. *The Innovator's Dilemma: The Revolutionary Book That Will Change the Way You Do Business*. New York: HarperBusiness, 2011.

Christensen, Clayton M., James Allworth, and Karen Dillon. *How Will You Measure Your Life?* New York: HarperBusiness, 2012.

Countryman, Eli. "'Hamilton' Star Phillipa Soo Explains Eliza's Gasp in the Ending." *Variety*, July 29, 2020. https://variety.com/2020/film/news/hamilton-ending-explained-eliza-gasp-1234720560/.

Dodson, Cy, dir. *Say His Name: Five Days for George Floyd*. PBS, 2021. https://www.pbs.org/show/say-his-name-five-days-george-floyd/.

Dunlap, David W. "Architects' Clashing Visions Threaten to Delay World Trade Center Tower." *New York Times*, October 23, 2003. https://www.nytimes.com/2003/10/23/nyregion/architects-clashing-visions-threaten-to-delay-world-trade-center-tower.html.

Feiler, Daniel C., and Wade-Benzoni, Kimberly A. "Death and Intergenerational Behavior: A Tale of Power and Immortality." In *The Impact of 9/11 on Psychology and Education: The Day That Changed Everything?*, edited by Matthew J. Morgan, 187–200. New York: Palgrave Macmillan, 2010.

Forliti, Amy. "Medical Experts: Floyd's Speech Didn't Mean He Could Breathe." Associated Press, July 9, 2020. https://apnews.com/article/a4300f189d906609560e15caa361566b.

Francescani, Chris. "Anniversary of 9/11 Marked Under Cloud of Health Problems, Funding Fights." Reuters, September 9, 2012. https://www.reuters.com/article/usa-sept11-idCNL2E8K901020120909.

Goleman, Daniel. "Millennials: The Purpose Generation." Korn Ferry. Accessed September 22, 2023. https://www.kornferry.com/insights/this-week-in-leadership/millennials-purpose-generation.

Gottschall, Jonathan. *The Storytelling Animal: How Stories Make Us Human*. New York: Houghton Mifflin Harcourt, 2012.

Grant, Adam M., and Kimberly A. Wade-Benzoni. "The Hot and Cool of Death Awareness at Work: Mortality Cues, Aging, and Self-Protective and Prosocial Motivations." *Academy of Management Review* 34, no. 4 (October 2009): 600–622. https://doi.org/10.5465/amr.34.4.zok600.

Henao, Luis Andres, Nomaan Merchant, Juan Lozano, and Adam Geller. "A Long Look at the Complicated Life of George Floyd." *Chicago Tribune*, June 11, 2020. https://www.chicagotribune.com/nation-world/ct-nw-life-of-george-floyd-biography-20200611-cxmlynpyvjczpbe6izfduzwv54-story.html.

Homans, Charles. "Man vs. Mouse: Ron DeSantis Finds Taking on Disney Is a Dicey Business." *New York Times*, April 26, 2023. https://www.nytimes.com/2023/04/26/us/politics/desantis-disney-republicans.html.

Hurst, Aaron. *The Purpose Economy: How Your Desire for Impact, Personal Growth and Community Is Changing the World*. 2nd ed. Boise, ID: Elevate, 2016.

James, William. *Is Life Worth Living?* Philadelphia: S. Burns Weston, 1896.

Kelly, Mike. "9/11's First Casualty Mychal Judge Is a Legend—Can He Be a Saint?" NorthJersey.com, September 10, 2021. https://www.northjersey.com/in-depth

/news/columnists/mike-kelly/2021/09/10/father-mychal-judge-911-attacks-fdny
-catholic-saint/4939813001/.

Kierkegaard, Søren. *Papers and Journals: A Selection.* Translated by Alastair
Hannay. New York: Penguin, 1996.

Langewiesche, William. "American Ground: Unbuilding the World Trade Center." *Atlantic,* July–August 2002. https://www.theatlantic.com/magazine
/archive/2002/07/excerpts-from-american-ground-unbuilding-the-world-trade
-center/302542/.

Lynxwiler, J. Eric. "Imagineering the Future: Walt Disney's Obsession with Building a Better Tomorrow." *Vice,* January 29, 2016. https://www.vice.com/en
/article/dp59xq/imagineering-the-future-walt-disneys-obsession-with-building
-a-better-tomorrow.

Mar, Raymond A. "The Neural Bases of Social Cognition and Story Comprehen-
sion." *Annual Review of Psychology* 62 (2011): 103–134.

Marsh, James, dir. *Man on Wire.* New York: Magnolia Pictures, 2008. https://www
.magpictures.com/manonwire/.

Maugham, W. Somerset. *The Moon and Sixpence.* London: William Heinemann,
1919.

Meisler, Stanley. "Daniel Libeskind: Architect at Ground Zero." *Smithsonian
Magazine,* March 2003. https://www.smithsonianmag.com/history/daniel
-libeskind-architect-at-ground-zero-77003660/.

Miranda, Lin Manuel. *Hamilton: An American Musical.* Atlantic Records, 2015,
MP3.

Murakami, Haruki. *Norwegian Wood.* New York: Vintage, 2000.

Nietzsche, Friedrich. *The Gay Science.* Translated by Thomas Common. Mineola,
NY: Dover, 2006.

———. *The Will to Power.* Translated by Walter Kaufmann and R. J. Hollingdale.
New York: Vintage Books.

9/11 Memorial & Museum. "The Meaning Behind Arrangement of the 9/11
Memorial Names." Accessed September 24, 2023. https://www.911memorial
.org/connect/blog/meaning-behind-arrangement-911-memorial-names.

Nooyi, Indra. *My Life in Full: Work, Family, and Our Future.* New York: Portfolio, 2021.

Nozick, Robert. *The Examined Life: Philosophical Meditations.* New York: Simon
& Schuster, 1990.

Nussbaum, Martha C. *Love's Knowledge: Essays on Philosophy and Literature.*
New York: Oxford University Press, 1990.

———. *Upheavals of Thought: The Intelligence of Emotions.* Cambridge, UK:
Cambridge University Press, 2001.

Oxner, Reese. "Disney Warns Viewers of Racism in Some Classic Movies with
Strengthened Label." NPR, October 16, 2020. https://www.npr.org/sections
/live-updates-protests-for-racial-justice/2020/10/16/924540535/disney-warns
-viewers-of-racism-in-some-classic-movies-with-strengthened-label.

Pfeifer, Joseph. "Chief Joseph Pfeifer of Battalion 1." Interview by Thomas J. McCourt, *New York Times*, July 5, 2002. https://www.nytimes.com/2002/07/05 /nyregion/nyregionspecial/chief-joseph-pfeifer-of-battalion-1.html.

Pierson, Brendan. "World Trade Center Developer Loses Final 9/11 Lawsuit Against Insurer." Reuters, August 2, 2018. https://www.reuters.com/article /us-usa-sept11-insurance/world-trade-center-developer-loses-final-9-11 -lawsuit-against-insurer-idUSKBN1KN2OL.

Rifkin, Glenn. "Clayton Christensen, Guru of 'Disruptive Innovation,' Dies at 67." *New York Times*, January 25, 2020. https://www.nytimes.com/2020/01/25 /business/clayton-christensen-dead.html.

Sagalyn, Lynne B. "We'll Never Forget 9/11. How Should We Remember Ground Zero?" *Washington Post*, September 9, 2016. https://www.washingtonpost .com/posteverything/wp/2016/09/09/well-never-forget-911-how-should-we -remember-ground-zero/.

Sokolovsky, Chad. *Prophecy Mechanic*. Modesto, CA: Quercus Review Press, 2017.

Solomon, Robert C., and Kathleen M. Higgins. *What Nietzsche Really Said*. New York: Pantheon, 2000.

Solomon, Sheldon, Jeff Greenberg, and Tom Pyszczynski. "The Cultural Animal: Twenty Years of Terror Management Theory and Research." In *Handbook of Experimental Existential Psychology*, edited by Jeff Greenberg, Sander L. Koole, and Tom Pyszczynski, 13–34. New York: Guilford Press, 2004.

Tolstoy, Leo. *"The Death of Ivan Ilich": An Electronic Study Edition of the Russian Text*. Edited and annotated by Gary R. Jahn. Minneapolis: University of Minnesota, M Libraries Publishing, 2020. First published 1886. https://open .lib.umn.edu/ivanilich/.

Wade-Benzoni, Kimberly A. "Too Tough to Die: September 11, Mortality Salience, and Intergenerational Behavior." *Journal of Management Inquiry* 11, no. 3 (September 2002): 235–239. https://doi.org/10.1177/105649260211300.

Whately, Francis, dir. *David Bowie: The Last Five Years*. Santa Monica, CA: HBO, 2017. https://www.hbo.com/movies/david-bowie-the-last-five-years.

Zak, Paul J. "How Stories Change the Brain." *Greater Good Magazine*, December 17, 2013. https://greatergood.berkeley.edu/article/item/how_stories_change _brain.

INDEX

Esme Michaelson

Nicole Fandel

Christopher Wong Michaelson is a philosopher with twenty-five years of experience advising business leaders pursuing meaning and providing work with a purpose. He is the Opus Distinguished Professor and academic director of the Melrose and the Toro Company Center for Principled Leadership at the University of St. Thomas and on the Business and Society faculty at New York University's Stern School of Business. Christopher lives in Minneapolis with his wife, three kids, and two dogs.

Jennifer Tosti-Kharas is the Camilla Latino Spinelli Endowed Term Chair and professor of management at Babson College, Wellesley, Massachusetts. She teaches, researches, and coaches others about what it means to craft a meaningful career and appreciate the risks and rewards of work as a calling. Jen lives outside Boston with her husband and two kids.

PublicAffairs is a publishing house founded in 1997. It is a tribute to the standards, values, and flair of three persons who have served as mentors to countless reporters, writers, editors, and book people of all kinds, including me.

I. F. STONE, proprietor of *I. F. Stone's Weekly*, combined a commitment to the First Amendment with entrepreneurial zeal and reporting skill and became one of the great independent journalists in American history. At the age of eighty, Izzy published *The Trial of Socrates*, which was a national bestseller. He wrote the book after he taught himself ancient Greek.

BENJAMIN C. BRADLEE was for nearly thirty years the charismatic editorial leader of *The Washington Post*. It was Ben who gave the *Post* the range and courage to pursue such historic issues as Watergate. He supported his reporters with a tenacity that made them fearless and it is no accident that so many became authors of influential, best-selling books.

ROBERT L. BERNSTEIN, the chief executive of Random House for more than a quarter century, guided one of the nation's premier publishing houses. Bob was personally responsible for many books of political dissent and argument that challenged tyranny around the globe. He is also the founder and longtime chair of Human Rights Watch, one of the most respected human rights organizations in the world.

.   .   .

For fifty years, the banner of Public Affairs Press was carried by its owner Morris B. Schnapper, who published Gandhi, Nasser, Toynbee, Truman, and about 1,500 other authors. In 1983, Schnapper was described by *The Washington Post* as "a redoubtable gadfly." His legacy will endure in the books to come.

Peter Osnos, Founder